MY DEAR
BESSIE

Also by Simon Garfield

Expensive Habits

The End of Innocence

The Wrestling

The Nation's Favourite

Mauve

The Last Journey of William Huskisson

Our Hidden Lives

We Are at War

Private Battles

The Error World

Mini

Exposure

Just My Type

On the Map

To the Letter

MY DEAR BESSIE

A LOVE STORY IN LETTERS

CHRIS BARKER & BESSIE MOORE

EDITED AND INTRODUCED BY

SIMON GARFIELD

CANONGATE

Edinburgh · London

Published in Great Britain in 2015 by Canongate Books Ltd, 14 High Street,
Edinburgh EH1 1TE

www.canongate.tv

1

British Library Cataloguing-in-Publication Data
A catalogue record for this book is available on
request from the British Library

ISBN 978 1 78211 567 0

Typeset in Minion Pro by Cluny Sheeler

Printed and bound in Great Britain by Clays Ltd, St Ives plc.

MIX
Paper from
responsible sources
FSC
www.fsc.org   FSC® C018072

Only on paper has humanity yet achieved glory, beauty, truth, knowledge, virtue, and abiding love.

George Bernard Shaw

Contents

Introduction

In the autumn of 1943, a 29-year-old former postal clerk from north London named Chris Barker found himself at a loose end on the Libyan coast. He had joined the army the year before, and was now serving in the Royal Corps of Signals near Tobruk. He saw little action: after morning parade and a few chores he usually settled down to a game of chess, or whist, or one of the regular films shipped in from England. His biggest worries were rats, fleas and flies; the war mostly seemed to be happening elsewhere.

Barker was self-educated, a bookish sort. He fancied himself as the best debater in his unit, and he wrote a lot of letters. He wrote to his family and former Post Office colleagues, and an old family friend called Deb. He wrote about the local food and customs, and the occasional trip away from camp with his brother Bert. On Sunday, 5 September 1943, he found a spare hour to write to a woman named Bessie Moore. Bessie had also been a Post Office counter clerk, and was now working in the Foreign Office as a Morse code interpreter. They had once attended a training course together at Abbey Wood in south-east London, a time she recalled with greater fondness and precision than he did. Before the war they had written to each other about politics and union matters, and about their ambitions and hopes for the future. But it had always been a platonic relationship; Bessie was stepping out with a man called Nick, and Chris's first letter to Bessie from Libya regarded them as an established couple. Bessie's reply, which took her several weeks to compose and almost two months to arrive, would change their lives forever.

We do not have this letter, but we may judge it to be unexpectedly enthusiastic. By their third exchange, it was clear to both of them they had ignited a fervour that would not easily be extinguished. In under a year, the couple were planning marriage. But there were complications, such as not actually seeing each other, or remembering quite what the other looked like. And then there were other obstacles: bombs, enemy capture, illness, comical misunderstandings, disapproval from friends, fear of the censor.

More than 500 of their letters survive, and this book distils the most alluring, compelling and heart-warming. It is a remarkable correspondence, not least because it captures an indefatigable love story. There is no holding back, and the modern reader is swept along in a gushing sea of yearning, lust, fear, regret and relentlessly candid emotion. Perhaps only those with steel hearts will fail to acknowledge an element of their own romantic past in this passionate tide. But there is so much more to enjoy, some of it banal, much of it humorous (that is, humorous to us, while evidently vital to them), all of it composed with a deft and elegant touch.

The vast majority of these letters are from Chris; most of Bessie's were burnt by Chris to save space in his kitbag and conceal their intimacy from prying eyes. But she is present on almost every page, Chris responding to her most recent observations as if they were talking in adjacent rooms. We follow their transactions with the eagerness of a soap opera fan; the main villain is the war itself, closely followed by those they berate for keeping them apart. The erratic nature of the postal service as Chris moves from North Africa to hotspots in Greece and Italy is another bugbear, though it is also a constant wonder that the letters got through at all. We fear for both of them; the greater their joy, the more we anticipate disaster.

Chris and Bessie met only twice between his first letter in September 1943 and his demobilisation in May 1946, and their postal romance describes a fitful and compacted arc. Older readers may recall the advertising campaign for Fry's chocolate bars, a treat Chris particularly enjoyed. In the adverts, five boys are each depicted with a different facial trait: Desperation, Pacification, Expectation, Acclamation, Realisation. We get a similar range in this correspondence, not always in that order, often within a single letter. We pass swiftly from overwhelming physical compulsion to domestic furnishings. But we detect no hint of irony from the writers: they just let rip. Many of their letters were several pages long, and contained fleeting and dutiful observations of little interest to us today. There is also much repetition, not least of their romantic yearnings. Occasionally, Chris embarks on extended philosophical discussions of trade unionism, family politics and the state of the world in general. In my attempt to present a progressive and engaging narrative, I have chosen to retain only the most relevant, substantial and engrossing details. Accordingly, many letters from Chris have not been included at all, while others have been trimmed to a few paragraphs.

Who were these two people? What occupied their thoughts before each other? Horace Christopher Barker (or Holl to his parents) was born on 12 January 1914, and the austerity of the period never left him. His father, a professional soldier, spent the Great War in India and Mesopotamia, and later became a postman (with a sideline in emptying public phone boxes of their coins). Chris was brought up first in Holloway, north London, and then four miles away in Tottenham. When he left Drayton Park school at the untimely age of fourteen his headmaster's leaving report noted the departure of 'a thoroughly reliable boy, honest and truthful, and a splendid worker. His conduct throughout was excellent: he was one of the school prefects and carried out his duties well. He was very intelligent.'

His father had lined up a job for him in the Post Office, confident of a secure, if predictable, lifelong career. Chris began as an indoor messenger boy in the money order department, fared well at the PO training school, and found a position as a counter clerk in the Eastern Division. His passions were journalism and trade unionism, and he combined them in his regular columns in several Post Office weeklies. He was a pedantic, reliable, headstrong man. Not the life of the party, perhaps, but a solid fellow to have in your corner. He was certainly no Casanova.

The Barker family moved to a semi-detached 'villa' in Bromley, Kent, shortly before the outbreak of war, and Chris lived there until 1942. His training as a teleprinter operator ensured his status in a reserved occupation before the demand for army reinforcements brought him first to a training camp in Yorkshire in 1942, and then to North Africa.

Bessie Irene Moore (known as Rene or Renee to her family and some friends) was born on 26 October 1913, two years after her brother Wilfred, and she spent her early years in Peckham Rye, south London. She had two other siblings, neither of whom survived infancy. Her father, also called Wilfred, was another 'lifer' at the Post Office. Bessie won a scholarship to her secondary school, passed her exams with credit, and became a postal and telegraph officer in the female-only offices in the South Eastern, Western and West Central districts. She shared Chris's view that there could be no more worthwhile employment, filled with human incident and variety, and dedicated to public service.

Bessie was twenty-five when she moved with her family to Blackheath in 1938. The Moores enjoyed a relatively prosperous lifestyle, taking regular holidays to the seaside and frequent trips to West End theatre. Bessie particularly admired the work of George Bernard Shaw and Kipling, and developed an interest in gardening and handicrafts. Shortly after the outbreak of war, her training in Morse led to a job at the Foreign Office deciphering intercepted German radio messages. She endured the Blitz and engaged in fire-watching duties, and volunteered for the Women's Auxiliary Air Force until her mother died in 1942 and she began looking after her father. When her relationship with her boyfriend Nick broke up in 1943 she believed she had wasted far too much energy in the pursuit of love.

~

Chris Barker in Libya, 1944

I first came across Chris and Bessie's letters in April 2013. I was completing my book *To the Letter*, a eulogy to the vanishing art of letter-writing, and I was becoming increasingly aware that what my book lacked was, unpredictably, letters. More specifically, it lacked letters written by people who weren't famous. I had been concentrating on Pliny the Younger, Jane Austen, Ted Hughes, Elvis Presley and the Queen Mother, and I had been talking to archivists about how historians will soon struggle to document our lives from texts and tweets. It became clear that what the book needed was a significant example of the ability of letters to transform ordinary lives.

And then I had a stroke of luck. I had mentioned my book to Fiona Courage, curator of the Mass Observation archive at the University of Sussex, of which I am a trustee. She mentioned the recent arrival of a comprehensive collection of papers of a man called Chris Barker, a pile of boxes that included newspaper articles, photos, documents and many letters – a musty, lifelong stash. I arranged to visit the archive immediately. After ten minutes in a room with the letters I was sure that his correspondence with Bessie Moore was just what I was looking for. Within an hour I was close to tears.

That these were valuable documents would have been evident to the first historian to encounter them. Almost all their letters were handwritten, many dashed off with evident hurry and distress. (The physicality of correspondence is another pleasure all but lost to us now, and one need only look at the manic array of stamps and inscriptions and directions on the outer wrappers to understand that these letters did not enjoy a smooth journey.) Shortly after my visit I was talking to the man responsible for placing the papers at the archive, asking to use some of them in my book. I expressed the distant hope that they may one day form a book of their own. Permission granted, I selected about 20,000 words from just over half a million, and interleaved them within my existing chapters.

When my book was published a few months later, readers responded to Chris and Bessie with enthusiasm; rather too many said they skipped through the main chapters to discover what happened to the couple next. Shortly afterwards, Chris and Bessie featured in a series of performance events called Letters Live, where superb readings from Benedict Cumberbatch, Louise Brealey, Lisa Dwan, Kerry Fox, Patrick Kennedy and David Nichols won them even more fans. And so, by what I can genuinely claim to be popular demand, here is a fuller account of their story.

What lessons may we learn from their exchanges? First, that the generous intimacy of letters casts a spell like no other. Grand histories have no time for the peevish minutiae of the infested billet or the unfortunate wartime shopping purchase, much less the silent devotion of lowly combatants. But beyond the grand sweep of adventure, it is these incidentals that hold us most: the Larkinesque disappointment of the film show; the jealous sideswipe at a former companion; the corduroy trousers ahead of their time; the cadging austerity that wormed its way into the soul; the way a postal delay brought on by a thunderclap over France could cause a person to fear the very worst.

Secondly, we know that Chris was a breast man. He had all the standard urges of a healthy male in his lustful prime, compounded by desert deprivation. The sexual highlight of the week was too often a man dressed as a woman in a touring variety show. Chris did not fail to express this hormonal bottling. In my edit – reducing more than half a million words to about 85,000 – the simplest task was trimming the references to Bessie's chest, and his desire to embrace it in a multitude of original ways. One imagines that even Bessie would have tired of this malarkey after a while, although perhaps not. It is clear from her letters that she needed constant reassurance that he was not going off her; moreover, her own frequent references to her anatomy seemed certain to arouse him further. (In the second half of their correspondence, having seemingly satisfied his urges, Chris shifts his lustful gaze towards the purchase of carpets.)

It is also clear that they wrote with far more passion than they could ever express in person. Chris repeatedly regrets being tongue-tied and ineffective during their two intermediate meetings. Their graphic intentions may have gone some way to alleviating the sheer damn dreariness of it all ('We put up a tent. We take it down,' Chris writes at the war's end with the weight of all the wasted years upon him).

I am certain that for years to come we will read these letters with a sense of wonder and delight. Something magical happens here, as well as something commonplace. The postal service to which Chris and Bessie dedicated their lives in turn rewarded them – and us. In the many years that followed their written romance, the couple lived to tell their tale. But they never told it like this.

What appeals to me in particular is the lack of heroics. Our correspondents are vulnerable, fearful, occasionally pitiful. They frequently berate themselves for their thoughts and actions. Yet it would be hard to imagine a more immediate expression of naive, rambling and utterly candid engagement. When the war is still, the couple create their own turmoil. When rockets fill the air, their own turmoil becomes an even greater reason for survival. I'm tempted to suggest that, while unannounced in the grand Churchillian speeches, it was for the likes of Chris and Bessie that we were fighting; not so much for the sunlit English pasture as the freedom to unite lovers upon it.

1

A Smashing Reply

5 September 1943

14232134 SIGNALMAN BARKER H.C., BASE DEPOT, ROYAL SIGNALS, MIDDLE EAST FORCES
[Tobruk, North Africa]

Dear Bessie,

Since Auld Acquaintance should not be forgot, and I have had a letter to Nick and yourself on my conscience for some time, I now commence some slight account of my movements since arrival here some five months ago, and one or two other comments which will edify, amuse or annoy you according to the Britishers' war-time diet or whatever you had for breakfast.

The 'security' advice of a Signals officer that in our travels we should keep our bowels open and our mouths shut seemed not to have been heard by the populace en route for our port of disembarkation. Wherever they were, they shouted 'hooray', waved Union Jacks and cryptically gave the 'V' sign.

The behaviour of the troops on board ship was bad. They shouted, shoved, swore and stole to their black hearts' content. I lost about a dozen items of kit, and was able to replace most of it from the odds left about on the disembarkation date by chaps who had first pinched for the fine fun of it. I cannot include my razor in this lot. That was removed from the ledge I had placed it on, as I turned to get a towel to wipe it.

Our disembarkation arrangements were perfect and after a not uncomfortable rail journey we were brought to the above address. I had expected to be parked on a pile of sand, and told it was 'home', but the depot is a very pleasant place, surrounded by pine and eucalyptus trees and spotted with frequently irrigated earth-gardens where grow wallflowers, daisies etc. The water comes from a tap, and one sits down to meals. There is a church hut, quiet and fly-free, an Army Educational Corps hut, where are excellent books, a good NAAFI* (so far as these autocratic institutions can be good) and a cinema.

A little further away is a tent, run by voluntary labour, where refreshments are served (not thrown at one) at reasonable prices, and there is a lounge, library, writing room, games room, and open air theatre, where a free film show takes place weekly, also a concert. There is a lecture one night, bridge and whist another, and a more 'highbrow' musical evening another night.

Directly I arrived, my brother applied for my posting to his unit, and after two months of Base life I started on the wearying but interesting journey to him. I met him, after a separation of 26 months, and had a fine time talking of home and all that had happened there – the rows and the rejoicing – and in the

* Navy, Army and Air Force Institutes; a social club and general store.

evening walked through the sandy vineyard to swim in the blue waters.

Since leaving the Post Office Counter School and joining the Army, a period of twelve years, I had little real rest. I was either actually on the counter or doing some Union work. If I did relax, it was not for long and I was conscious of being guilty. Since joining (or being joined to) HM Forces, I have had a great deal of leisure, and I have spent most of it reading and writing.

Oh, the Pyramids; yes, I have seen them, sat on them, and thought what a gigantic case for Trade Unionism they present. How many unwilling slaves died in the colossal toil involved in erecting these edifices? And how insignificant the erection compared with Nature's own hills and mountains?

I visited the Cairo Zoo, happily in the company of two young Egyptians who were being educated at the American mission. They made the day a success. The cruelty of having a polar bear (noble creature) in this climate, and the effort to console him with a 10 second cold water dip!

Excuse the writing, and confusion of this effort. But it's me, alright. I hope you are OK Nick. It's a long way from our Lantern Lecture on Sunny Spain at Kingsway Hall!

All the best, Bessie.
Chris

~

14 December 1943

Dear Bessie,

I received yesterday your surface letter of 20th October. I read it avidly as from an old pal, noting that though time has chattanooga'ed along, your style remains pretty much as it was in the days when we had that terrifically intense and wonderfully sincere correspondence about Socialism and the Rest Of It, unlike the present time, when, hornswoggling old hypocrite that I am, the Rest Of It seems infinitely more attractive. Thanks for the letter, old-timer. I am sending this by Air Mail because it will have enough dull stuff in it to sink a Merchant ship.

Yes, I remember our discussions over 'ACQUAINTANCE' and my views are still as much 'for' as yours remain 'against'. I have, perhaps, one hundred acquaintances (I write to fifty) yet I could number my friends on one hand. The dictionary:-

ACQUAINTANCE: a person known. FRIEND: one attached to another by affection and esteem.

You are known to me, and while I have affection for you it does not amount to an attachment.

I am sorry that Nick and you are 'no longer', as you put it, and that you should have wasted so much time because of his lack of courage. You must have had a rotten time of it, and I do sympathise with you – but are you writing to the right bloke? I'll say you are! Joan gave me my 'cards' a couple of months back, though I had seen them coming since April, when I got my first letters.

I can quite believe your estimate of the way the London-leave soldier improves the shining-hour. You can understand chaps who get three or four days leave before a campaign opens, painting the town red, but unfortunately quite a large number who are in comfortable Base jobs have their regular unpleasant habits. When I was at Base our evening passes bore the injunction 'Brothels Out of Bounds. Consorting with Prostitutes Forbidden.' Where we collected the passes there was a large painted sign, 'Don't Take a Chance, Ask the Medical Orderly for a –' doodah. The whole emphasis of Army Propaganda is 'Be Careful', even the wretched Padre at Thirsk, when he said a few words of farewell, said merely that most foreign women were diseased, and we should be careful.

At the Pyramids when I found a preventative on the place I had chosen to sit down on, I thought it was a nice combination of Ancient and Modern! Whoever told you Pyramids told the time was pulling your leg. No iron or steel was used, cranes or pulleys. Ropes and Levers only. Their erection was due to Superb Organisation, Flesh and Blood, Ho Heave Ho, and all the other paraphernalia of human effort.

I bumped back along the desert road, meeting my brother very easily and getting him successfully transferred into my Section. We share the same tent and this situation suits us fine. We discuss everything in common, and have a fine old time.

Much rain lately has made an ornamental lake of the wide flatness; but we have now got grass and some tiny flowers where before was merely sand. I have transplanted some of the flowers into a special patch we have made into a garden. Bert and I play chess most of our spare-time, on a set we made with wire and a broom-handle. There are some dogs about the camp, which is far from anywhere. No civilians. We have two pigs fattening for Xmas, poor blighters, though I believe the uxorious male has given the sow hope of temporary reprieve.

I hope you hear regularly from your brother and that your Dad and yourself are in good health.

Good wishes,
Chris

~

21 February 1944

Dear Bessie,

I received your letter of 1st January on 7.2.44, since when I have been busting to send you a smashing reply, yet feeling clumsy as a ballerina in Army boots, who knows that her faithful followers will applaud, however she pirouettes. I could hug you till you dropped! The unashamed flattery that you ladled out was very acceptable – I lapped it up gladly and can do with more! Yes, I could hug you – an action unconnected with the acute shortage of women in these parts, and mostly symbolic of my pleasure at your appreciation of qualities so very few others see, and which really I do not possess. I must confess that your outrageous enthusiasm banishes 'acquaintance' from my mind, and that I recognise the coming of a new-kind-of-atmosphere into our interchanges, and one which you will need to watch.

To be honest, rather than discreet: letters from home sometimes contain curious statements. 'Paddling' one of my own, I had told them of my first letter from you. Back came a weather forecast: 'Perhaps she will catch you on the rebound.' I, of course, have no such wish, yet I certainly haven't told anyone of your latest letter, and was glad I was able to conceal it from my brother. I find myself engaged on the secretive, denying dodge that has marked the opening stages of all my little affaires since the first Girl Probationer crossed my path. I can see that willy-nilly I am having a quiet philander, and I want to warn you it'll end in a noisy flounder unless you watch out. I haven't a 'aporth of 'rebound' in me. I warm to you as a friend and I hope that remains our mutual rendezvous, although I feel that the more I write you, the less content you will be.

I hope you will not think I regarded your letter as purely a back-pat for me. As I read yours I wha-rooped too, and gentle tintinnabulations commenced. You'll find this effort somewhat forced. I believe it is true that when you want to be natural, you aren't. If you understand me, you have made me a bit 'conscious'. I'm blowed if I am not trying to impress you.

You say your mind is a rambling rubbish box, and your youthful desires for improvement remain unfulfilled. Congratulations on getting the rubbish in a box, mine spreads in a heap. I don't remember having many youthful desires (except that I do recall Madeline Carroll featuring in one of them). I am glad you accept my view on others not being informed of the contents of our letters. It will be much more satisfactory, we shall know each other much better through an 'in confidence' understanding, which is implicit in our different relationship.

Your comments on Abbey Wood* etcetera rather puzzle me, and if you feel like enlightening me, please do so ('I remember also the day, when I found that you never understood why I cut my losses, you returned those letters, a very black day,' is what you say). I am more than hazy on the subject. What letters did I return? I like your observation that you can never dramatise for long, and 'humour wins the day', it is my own view, too.

You say it is odd that I can be so ignorant about women, but apart from the important omission of never having slept with one, I regard myself as capable of detecting a wile when I see one, and I do not think women are so very different from men in any important aspect. If I were really plonking down what I did know, I should have to admit that I am puzzled very often by the behaviour of many of my own sex, and not a little quizzical about my own at times. Certainly I am no quidnunc in the labyrinth of sex matters. How bored I should be if I was, my mysterious Bessie!

I am sorry you felt the least bit 'weepy' at my chess, garden, pigs. The things your tears are best reserved for are beetles this size, and fleas whose size is much less horribly impressive, but whose powers of annoyance are far greater. I exult in the possession of a sleeping sheet, which is very nice to have next to the skin compared with the rough Army blankets. At night, if the fleas are active and I cannot subdue them with my fevered curses, I take my sheet and my naked body into the open, and turn and shake the sheet in the very cold night air. Then I get back into bed and hold the ends of the sheet tight around my

---

* The Post Office training course in south-east London where Chris and Bessie had their first opportunity to get to know each other.

neck, to keep out my nuisance raiders. The last few months have been very pleasant as regards heat, and fleas have been few. I am not looking forward to the summer.

A Sergeant Major is usually a curt, barking, more-in-anger-than-in- sorrow, kind of chap. Yet the one we have here couldn't treat us better if he was our Father. He does more fatigues than anyone else in the Camp, asks you to do things, never orders. When he came here three months ago, we had one dirty old tent to eat our meals in, and that was all. Since then, we have added several more tents; plenty of forms and tables; a Rest Tent with a concrete floor; dozens of games, a regular weekly Whist Drive, a small library. Once we could only bathe in our tent, petrol tin fashion. Now, we use the showers in town, doing some forty miles in the process. If this is the Army – well, it's not bad.

Christmas Day was quite happily spent, as I haven't been away from home long enough to feel bad about separation. True that last night I dreamt of my Mother, and as she called me in my sleep, I awoke to hear my brother calling 'Holl!' (my family name), as, in a vague kind of way it was my turn to first brave the morning air and put on – what do you think? – the shaving water.

We have been doing very well lately for evening entertainments. On five successive evenings we had an Accordion Band and Concert Party, which was very good and clean; an RAF Concert Party, which dripped muck and innuendo; and an ENSA* show, 'Music Makers', who rendered popular classics, and gave a thoroughly good evening, though the audience thinned out when 'legs' did not show. We get a Film Show every Saturday; whatever

---

* Entertainments National Service Association; the troops soon renamed it Every Night Something Awful.

the weather, it is held in the open air, the audience (stalls) sitting on petrol tins, while those in the gallery sit on top of the vehicles, many of which come several miles for what is usually the only event of the week. I have sat in the pouring rain with a groundsheet over me. I have sat with a gale bowling me over literally while Barbara Stanwyck (in *The Great Man's Lady* – she was a brunette) bowled me over figuratively. We take our fun seriously, and when we can get it, though I always think of the Open Air Theatre at Regent's Park, seeing *Midsummer Night's Dream* on a brilliantly lit sward, with a pre-war searchlight dancing in the sky above us.

I did not go to the commercial cinemas in Cairo – I was a bit horrified by the prospect of being solicited as I sat in the 15 piastre seats (as not infrequently happens, I am told).

George Formby has done a lot of talking since his trip here, but not a word (publicly) about losing ten bottles of beer from the back of his charabanc. Some chaps I was with at the time did the pinching and subsequent drinking, so I know!

Have just been on my first 'charge' (crime), having been caught, with eight others including my brother, for dirty rifles. This is usually a serious offence, and is very easily framed. We were lucky and got 'admonished', which is like a 'minor offence' in the PO and is wiped out after three months. Being 'tried' was just like a Court of Law, without the wigs. I have been very fortunate in my Army misdemeanours which have been ingenious rather than numerous.

Our OC is not a bad chap as such, but is very 'La-de-dah'; he has a race-stick and the other day he was seated on it watching a football match when – it broke. Our side all wanted to stop the match and laugh.

Consider my earlier comments upon 'rebounds', but let me have you full and frank and enjoyable. Keep away from an anatomical examination of me. Tell me what you think. I'll revert to blustery Barkerisms at your request.

Best wishes, Friend (The Lord Forgive Me),
Chris.

~

27 February 1944

Dear Bessie,

Letters take such a long time, and I am so keen on remaining in good touch with you that I have decided to write you fairly regularly, irrespective of the replies received, until such time as I detect that you are disinterested, or it appears that our present happy association is not so happy.

So on to our pigs – yesterday came the day for the male (boar) to be sent away for slaughter. Half a dozen of us were detailed to hold various parts of the massive, dirty, unfortunate creature, while the man who knows all about pigs got a bucket firmly wedged over the poor thing's head and snout. I was originally deputed to take hold of the right ear, but in the opening melee found myself grasping the right leg, which I held on to firmly as it lumbered out of the sty, and heaved on heavily as, somehow, despite a terrific struggle and the most heartrending screams, we got it on the lorry, which was to be its hearse. In the afternoon it met its man-determined fate, and this morning as I came away from dinner, I saw its tongue, its heart, liver and a leg, hanging from the cookhouse roof. I had my doubts about eating it in the days when it was half the eighteen stone it weighed at death. But now I have none. I certainly can't help eat the poor old bloke. The sow lives on, she has a large and sore looking undercarriage, and will be a Mother in three weeks. I suppose we shall eat her progeny in due course.

I recently made application for 'The Africa Star,' which most chaps here are wearing. I have first heard that I am to get it. When you know that I arrived out on April 16th and the hostilities ceased May 12th, you can see how very easily medals are gained. It is the same very often with awards supposedly for gallantry.

My Dad, a thorough going old Imperialist, will be delighted that he can talk about two sons with the medal, and mentally they will be dangling with his – EIGHT altogether, though his nearest point to danger was really the Siege of Ladysmith (in a war maybe you would have condemned?). Since the war, my Dad has had medal ribbons fitted on most of his jackets and waistcoats, and goes shopping with them all a'showing! My Mother comes in bemoaning the fact that there is no suet to be had. Dad comes in with a valuable half-a-pound he extracted from a medal-conscious shopkeeper. I can tell you plenty about my Dad, who has many faults and the one redeeming virtue that he is all for his family, right or wrong.

I have just seen a Penguin, *Living in Cities*, very attractively setting forth some principles of post-war building. I always think how well off we suburban dwellers are compared with the people who live in places like Roseberry Avenue or Bethnal Green Road, and die there, too, quite happily since they never knew what they missed.

I saw a suggestion for a new house to have a built-in bookcase, or place for it, and thought this a rather good idea. I have often sighed for some shabby volume in the short time I have been away from home. I carry with me now only an Atlas, a dictionary, Thoreau's *Walden* (ever glanced at it – a philosophy), Selected Passages from R.L. Stevenson, and *The Shropshire Lad*, by Housman.

Do you remember when we did some electioneering? Was it at Putney? I would have enjoyed being at Acton lately, as I read in the local *Gazette* (sent to the other chap in our tent) that one of the candidates (later withdrew) was walking around with a steel helmet bearing slogans on it, and a big notice urgently advising electors to buy potatoes and store them under the bed. Did you vote in 1935 (I did) and with what result? Maybe we can get together for a bit of postwar canvassing?

Cheerio, friend.
Chris.

~

6 March 1944

Dear Bessie,

I hope I am not guilty of indecent haste if I commence another letter only a week after my last. I cannot claim that anything special has happened (in fact, thank Goodness it hasn't) but I am brimming over with many things to tell you, my confidante, and it will be a long (and I hope a pleasurable for both of us) time before I have really unloaded my cargo of news, ideas, tales, things that have occurred since I left the country on February 24th last year, and also some of the things that occurred before then.

I have just come away from the pictures, the mobile van, screen at the bottom of a slope and projector at the top, with the audience seated in the dip. Not bad tonight; two news reels only six months old and *Girl Trouble*, Don Ameche and Joan Bennett, fair entertainment as films go, quite a little smart talk which I rather enjoy.

This afternoon I was just going off to sleep when my Sergeant woke me and (despite my protests that I was on night duty tonight) told me I must report at 3 o'clock for the ABCA (Army Bureau of Current Affairs) Spelling Bee. I went along there and suggested it be abandoned in favour of a discussion on 'strikes in wartime', and we did discuss strikes, fairly interestingly. The strange thing about most of these affairs is that so very few people can open their mouths to any effect in public. I am always congratulated on my contribution and looked at with greater respect afterwards by my companions – this 'Gift of the Gab' as it is called, is a dangerous thing for the welfare of the people. I am very suspicious of good talkers, very attentive to the stutterer.

From the pictures, I had intended going straight to the other farce out here, *The Egyptian Mail*, our daily newspaper, and *The Egyptian Gazette*, its Evening (which we do not get) and Sunday consort. I am sending you a few copies in order that you can see what a hotch-potch of old news and English newspaper rubbish it is. It has frequent typographical errors, and is very unreliable. It puts the wrong headlines to news items, and is more amusing than informative. Once it said the Aga Khan had come fourth in a horse race, another time that Somerset had declared at cricket 1301–7.

I am not sorry you did not join the WAAFs [Women's Auxiliary Air Force], because most of the chaps seem to regard uniformed women as uniformly willing to be pawed about. One of the girls in my district used to push her breasts into my stomach (it seems that she was a little short! – anyhow, I used to feel it was like that) and hold my arm, every time she saw me. This was around 1937–39, not in the younger days, when I thought, like most youths, that I was handsome. Anyhow, this girl joined the WAAFs shortly after war was declared. And I don't think it was patriotism.

It is the usual practice to swop our free issue of 50 cigarettes weekly for eggs, 10 for 1 egg. We also get 2 boxes of matches; these also fetch an egg each. We do not get many Arabs round here, but in other parts you can get a live chicken for 40 cigarettes. They may be scraggy things, but I am told they eat well. Of course, all trading with the Arabs is strictly forbidden, but goes on just the same.

And now away. I am going to have a few busy thoughtful days, as tonight got the job of opposing the motion 'That woman's place is the home,' at the first of some debates I have helped to get going here. Am quite looking forward to it. It's like old times!

Good wishes always,
Chris

≈

25

13 March 1944

Dear Bessie,

It looks as though Air Mail is wunnerful quick these days, your Letter Card of 5.3.44 having fallen into my waiting hand only a couple of hours ago. You must use LCs more and hang the expense, for if your sea-mail is anything like this LC, I shall be writing you poetry in a few weeks.

It seems that my frankness has not been without its effect on you. For there you are (I was about to write 'here you are' till cruel geography poked me) ready, even eager, to go back seven or eight years to Abbey Wood, and here am I so ready to embrace the project, if not you. How far distance has lent enchantment to the view, and disappointment gilded the scene, only events will show. But I warn you now against any prospect of me doing 'the honourable thing', and beg you to note that I have not yet, in my pastime 'affairs', done anything dishonourable. If you are hopeful, willing, expectant, it is in opposition to the facts, for I confess myself unlikely to possess in the future much more capacity than to entertain (howbeit brightly) as a rascal rogue, roué or rake. So let there be no hugger-mugger about it. – A kind of 'Mistakes cannot afterwards be rectified' spirit must reign as you invite me to change your pound, and, I gleefully hand you £19 6s. and a dud tanner* you are only too pleased to accept. I hope you will understand the metaphor. Euphemisms are so bracing.

Keep on talking about yourself. I promise that I shall treat you gently. Whatever may be true about men concerning themselves

---

* Sixpence.

with things rather than people (about which I will write at length later) let you and I consider ourselves: – my Army Book 64 tells me I was born 12.1.14, and that at enlistment I was Church of England; 5 ft 9 ins., 143 lbs., Max. Chest 36 ins., Complexion: Fresh; Eyes: Blue. Hair: Brown! (It doesn't say I was going bald but it's the awful truth!)

I am glad my last letter sent your spirit rocketing sky-high. But please to remember the Fifth of November and what happens to the rockets when their celestial brilliance is ended. They descend to earth, flat as a pancake, so don't start understudying for the lead in another 'Punctured Romance'; although I am an old (30 years) hypocrite, and when you say you find me 'so satisfying', I cannot help but think of circumstances in which you really would do so. But this is all very naughty and Chris-like.

Now to exult as I read you again; to write you some more; and consider the promise that is YOU.

Chris

~

14 March 1944

Dear Bessie,

I had not expected that my Air Mail letter would travel so quickly, and am delighted that you should already have it, and have spent some time, probably, in reading it. At the moment, and for the present, there isn't a shadow of doubt that we are both in the same mutually approving mood, and that if we were within smiling distance of each other, we should soon be doing rather more than that. Of course, maybe the safety of our separate distances permits us to indulge in these happy advances. Perhaps we would beat hasty retreats into our shells if we knew that the seeds we are now sowing were due for early reaping. I might be on another planet for all the chance there is of hearing you say the good things you've written. But how much I enjoy you, how jolly fine it is to know that you really do understand what I write, when only a little while ago I was saying that I felt like Marconi would have done on the morrow of his invention, had all the world gone deaf.

If I had the chance, I might do a lot of things, or nothing. As it is I shall remain very polite and become as friendly as I dare without undertaking obligations I have no intention of fulfilling. I am safe from physical indiscretion for a long while, but I am also wanting you seriously to see that while we might have fun (certainly I could laugh heartily at the moment!) at a later date, it would not be so funny for you ultimately. I can't help being your hero – and I breathe heavily and exultingly at your clear, bare admittance; but please don't let me make you break your heart in 1946 or 47, when I scurry off with 'one, two, three, or more.' If I was a wise guy I would not write you and thus encourage your racing thoughts. I admit to a state of gleaming, dangerous excitement as I read again and again your written words. You fascinate and weaken me, and make me feel strong. Presumably you wrote the same in the old days (in an earlier letter I said I was hazy even about any letters), have I become so much more susceptible to flattery, or is the change due to the fact that I have been away from home fourteen months, and haven't seen a woman (other than about four on a stage) in the last six?

Don't be a man-worshipper, or an anything-worshipper if you would be happy. The main difference, emotionally, between men and women, is said to be that a woman is loyal to one man always, but that a man's attention wanders more than a little. This sex item is the biggest there is, apart from the instinct to survive, because no one is impervious to it and it controls us always.

I believe and I deplore that too many people with Left views think they must free-love, be vegetarians, atheists, walk on the wrong side of the road, and so on. I think I have mentioned that one chap of 18 who I met in hospital told me he had 'had' 35 girls, several on the first day of meeting. This 'loyalty' of the woman has been blown sky-high during this war – one of the chaps here asked his girl why she hadn't written for six weeks, and she replied she had been busy, didn't he know there was a war on?! You say that men have a 'much more powerful nervous force' – I'm not sure I know what this means, but I am quite sure that a chap in love (while he is in that happy state) feels it as deeply as his lady. Perhaps it doesn't last so long, but while it does it is pretty potent.

In your letter-card you say 'I regret to admit I am feminine,' and later on, 'forgive me for being all feminine' – yet, of course, you know that you are bristling femininity now, quite unregretful and not desiring to be forgiven. You know I am male and for the once attentive, therefore you don't want to be anything but female. You want your old hero to be your new lover.

What a pity that they have just given me my mosquito net for my second summer, and not a ticket for an air journey home. I am writing these particular words at midnight 13.3.44 – I could have breakfast with you on the 14th, if only one or two people would co-operate. It might be a little late, but what matter. Here am I, wondering when I last saw you and what you look like. I have an idea, I wish I could confirm by personal investigation. Do you still smoke? – a bad habit.

Expectant, willing, and compliant as you are, I seem to have discovered you anew. I find you very warm and appetising. I rejoice at our intimacy for the present. I simply wallow in your friendly sentiments which I feel as keenly as if a couple of seas and a continent did not separate us. You have smashed my perimeter defences, I am all of a hub-bub, and as I write my cheeks are red and I am hot. When I finish one letter to you, I want to start again on another, as today. I hope that I shall often have something to comment on, rather than initiate my own discussions. I know this strange unity of expression and understanding cannot last, for I feel just as though I was sitting at your feet. This is bound to peter out sooner or later. You say 'here's to the beginning of a beautiful friendship.'

You are a terrific love-maker by letter. I can but wonder what you are like at it in the soft, warm, yielding, panting flesh. Please pardon the rub-out, and the re-writing hereabouts. Truth is that with the morning I became timid and decided on deletion. Let me go back a few lines, say that I can but wonder, and warmly do.

I must avoid writing one whole letter slobbering, however pleasant it is for both of us, I must make a pretence of telling you all about our camp. 'Jeannie', for example, has had seven pups, two of which have been drowned in order to give her a better chance. She had them on Friday, and on Monday she was racing about after her bête noire – desert rats. The other mother, the sow, has hardly energy to move. At least eight are expected shortly. Our picture on Saturday (luckily I was on duty) was as childish as the previous two I have described earlier. *Stars Over Texas*. Stage Coach hold-ups, and pistol duels. We are getting more than disgusted.

Having interposed that sentence I can return to our new thrilling relationship, to be fully enjoyed while it lasts, and unlamented when it is done. I am 'all for you, dear' and the prospect of soaking in you, luxuriously for a while, of touching you where you will let me, from here, is absorbingly, naturally, before us.

Chris

~

15 March 1944

Dear Bessie,

I suppose that Spring out here has the same effect on a young man's fancy as it is popularly supposed to do at home, because I sent you a LC on the 13th, an a.m. Letter on the 14th, and here again, for the third day running, I am putting pen to paper to relieve my rushing thoughts, which are all about and of you. Unfortunately we only get one green envelope and one LC a week, but the latter is censored in the unit and therefore not suitable for my purpose. We only get one of this LC type monthly, and here I am spending two months' supply in three days. What does your Father think of your several letters, and do tell me that it is still you I am writing to, and not you, plus Iris, plus Cliffie, plus –?

For goodness sake disregard everything I have said that sounds the least endearing. This is a fever that I have which makes me hot and dispossesses my mental faculties whenever I think of you, which is more and more often. It is irrational, illogical, nonsensical. I am hopelessly lost in contemplation of YOU – and I last saw you – when? Yet I have heard from you – applauding, approving, invigorating. I feel a King. I think I made a mistake about you years ago and I rush to make amends – yet I cannot rush physically to you though I positively ooze appreciative emotions and impulses.

Tonight I have to speak for fifteen minutes in that 'Woman's Place is the Home' Debate. I should be deciding what I am to say, and how. But here I am, improvidently assuring you of my poor surgings. In a month or two, I may revert to brusque bonhomie. For the present I am entirely 'gone' at the thought of you being in the same world. You suggest in your LC that men are less emotional than women. I, at least, am as emotional as you. I revel in your sentiments, I return them in full. Whatever the reason, for whatever the period, at this moment, you have me. To be sensible, I should withhold all this, to avoid your inevitable later disappointment. But I simply cannot.

I was quite OK before I got your first letter. I was rational, objective. But now that you have my ear – I must give you my heart as well! No doubt it is wrong, certainly it is indiscreet, to blurt out such things when the future laughs that only present conditions make me like this. But I am like this. I am always consulting my diary to see how soon you will get my letters, wondering how soon I will get yours. I feel that you are doing exactly the same, and share my upset. I can't do anything without wanting to put my hand out to you, to touch you. I know you would encourage me. I find you wonderful, you delight me and thrill me and engross me. But as I said earlier, disregard these purely Spring emotions. I might mean it very much today, but it is tomorrow that matters in such affairs, and I am certain to revoke a dozen times in the long tomorrow. This is a real sane note to end on, as I sit here, hot-faced and desirous, ready for you as you are ready for me.

I am but a miserable sinner!
Chris

~

19 March 1944

Dear Bessie,

Here again to greet you, four letters in four days – and really wanting to write four each day. Stupid and silly, but since my thoughts are around you and I am pulsating still, I am going to follow Oscar Wilde's advice 'The only way to resist temptation is to succumb to it'. Really, you should reply to me that I am an ass, and that you have been kind enough to burn my words before I want to eat them. But I am sure that you won't, and that almost for certain you are down with the same ailment, wanting me the same as I want you.

I want to say I'm sorry for Abbey Wood and the opportunity I missed. I want you to say you're sorry I'm miles and time away from you, that you fully welcome me, and glory in my present affected state. I warn you of the transient nature of my emotions. I cannot say I love you, because tomorrow I shall be sorry for doing so.

Do not tell me anything you do not feel. And of what you feel, please tell me everything. Discard dignity and discretion and live knowingly. Tell me what you think, in your letter that is not liable to be censored like this one. You delight and thrill and excite me. I want to touch you, to feel you, to possess you.

Now to the impersonal part: The Debate took place OK. Everyone was there, forty in all. The proposer was a decent chap, a Scottish signalman. His seconder was a Major, mine was a Lieutenant, jolly good chap, also a Scot. I had heard that my opponent was a good speaker, and I had wondered if I would fail to shine. I need have had no doubts. He had written his speech word for word and read it from the paper, which he held in his hand. I've a bad memory, and at present, anyhow, I am more concerned with the possibilities of you. After the almost grim speech of my opponent, I just got up and sparkled. I made them laugh when I wanted them to. I just had them in my hand. I had to stop at fifteen minutes, but I could have gone on for fifty. Imagine how cockahoop I was – I was far and away the best speaker there. After all this – and we were overwhelmingly argumentatively superior – the vote ended 35 for 5 against. In other words, man's deep prejudice was undisturbed by argument.

This afternoon I visited our hospital, some fifteen miles off. At an exchange a couple of hundred miles away there was a chap with a very high-pitched voice, just like a nagging wife; I had not heard him for a couple of days, and on enquiring his whereabouts was told he had collided with a grenade. So I thought I would pay him a visit and cheer him up. He was very lucky, and only got badly sprinkled with shrapnel. No fingers or hands off. He is said to be 17 years old. He looks 15. I got a lift (there is a nice 'taxi' spirit on the road here) there in a truck which was taking [a man] to hospital with smallpox. I hope I don't get it!

Coming back to the camp, I found a tortoise, not more than three inches long. I put it in a grassy tin to show my brother; during the three hours it was confined it made ceaseless efforts to get out, and when my brother had seen it, I sent it on its travels again. Once, we despatched one after writing 'Barker' in indelible pencil, on its back! A horrible thought is that many of the beetles around hereabouts are the same size.

I trust you to receive me gently and forgivingly, not to expose me to the ridicule of the third party, and let me go quietly when the storm within me has subsided.

Chris

~

20 March 1944

Dear Bessie,

Life here is not bad if events elsewhere are borne in mind. I should like to watch the ducks in St. James' Park, but I daresay they themselves get a bit scared at the nightly display of human ingenuity, 1944 model.

In these parts I daresay we take (perhaps I should say, 'I take') a greater interest in 'human' things than we would do at home. A sow is due to have young – that means a daily visit to the sty. She has them. Before breakfast that day I take my first look at piggywigs four hours old. The camp dog, Jeannie, produces seven lovely little pups. It's a treat to see them snugly around her and a lark to speculate on their parentage. We once had a cat who had six kittens. The day they were born the presumed father did a bunk and hasn't been seen since. Of course, he might have gone up in smoke, following contact with one of the thousands of mines still littered around here.

I hope you are OK and fairly happy. If you ever get a chance to come abroad – don't.

All the best,
Yours sincerely,
Chris

◇

21 March 1944

Dear Bessie,

I was surprisedly delighted to get your LC of 12th, today. It's a blooming nuisance how other people take such a keen interest in 'affairs'. The only way of holding them at bay is to tell them nothing. 'Oh what a tangled web we weave, when first we practise to deceive' my Mother used to say to me. I've deceived a little since I first heard that. Accordingly, I enclose a letter you can leave in a bus without giving me heart failure. If you think my friend Ivy (of whom more later) would be interested, what more natural than that you should show it her? Please, please, let my admittance of you to my heart be a splendid secret for us both, to be enjoyed so long as it lasts, and remembered pleasurably if and when it ceases.

You will be replying to letters I haven't precise remembrance of. A pity, since I very much want your reactions. I want to know whether you are feeling in the same exalted state as me, and I hope you'll 'let me have it' anyhow. I have felt increasingly nervous about your reception of some of my words. I can only ask you to read them as though they were poetry and not regard me as altogether mad. I may be sorry that you will no longer think of me as the 'strong, silent' type. But if I gabble now it is because your approach has found me in a weak spot. I must tell you of the feelings that you have aroused, because for the once I am primitive and the respectability veneer is off. It is not easy to write when, at one point, a letter may be censored, and I hope you'll make allowances. I think you will have gathered by now that I am

37

like a raging torrent, and as you know there is no arguing with such things. I am impatient and intolerant of anything but you, and although I am bound to discuss nonentities and mediocrities, through it all I want you strongly.

Need I say I am waiting to get your next letter and the next, and the next? And that it is good to know you exist.

Chris

PS The other letter can be suitably produced if you get an enquiry – 'Heard from Chris Barker lately?' 'Yes, typical letter' the reply!

∼

26 March 1944

Dear Bessie,

This war will delay many marriages as it will cause others. I shall either marry quickly (and take the consequences) or court for about ten years, by which time you'd know your future wife as well as your own mother.

Did I mention I'd seen *Shadow of a Doubt* during the week? It was directed by Alfred Hitchcock, ought to have been good, and for photography and direction, certainly was. (Do you hate or approve Orson Wells – *Citizen Kane* whirled me round a hundred times, but I believe I bit it, and I liked its different-ness.)

My brother was out on a run. As I walked along in the rapidly fading light I saw a familiar slip on the ground, and picked up – an Egyptian pound-note! I hope it came from an officer but I fear that the wind whisked it from a fellow-other-ranker. I was delighted to find it ('Unto them that hath shall be given') as my brother is always finding odd coins, notes, valuables. We share luck, and I happily preened myself as I handed him his 10s. just now. The last time I found any large amount was when I was taken as a 9 year old, by my brother, to the AA Sports at Stamford Bridge (I got separated from him in the Underground – those new automatic closing doors were just coming in – remember the guard at the old trellis-pattern gates?). I found a purse, containing 19s. 11d. and a visiting card. My Mother returned it, and with such a horrible 'you ought to be thankful an honest person found it' air, that the poor young girl remitted a 5s. reward to me, almost by return post. I always felt the small fortune was a little tainted.

How do you get on in the Air Raids? I hope you continue to have good luck. If we were together I guarantee we could ignore them, just as I want to ignore everything now, so that I may touch you. And I want to do that badly.

Is your Dad in the PO? Mine retired a month after the war was declared. Pension £1 5s. weekly. Gets about £2 a week for two days' work in a bakehouse. His trade was baking before he came in the PO, and when he applied for a job in 1940 they asked him how long since he had been in the trade. He said '27 years'. They said 'OK – start tonight.' One good thing is that he is entitled to bread and cakes, and can bring home bunmen, studded with currants, for his grandson!

Tonight Churchill is speaking from London, and I hope to be amongst those who gather round the wireless to hear his latest estimate of the war's duration. We all take it very good-humouredly but the language is sometimes lurid.

I hope you are well. I am thinking of you.

Chris

At the back of my mind I have some idea of selling books at a later stage in my life. I would, I think, like to start a second-hand bookshop mainly. It's not for the money one might make, but only on the basis that books are good things whose circulation must assist reasonableness and progress. What do you think?

~

13 April 1944

Dear Bessie,

I think we are so near to each other that our reactions to similar occurrences are very much, if not exactly, the same. So that you know the excitement I felt when I saw your handwriting on the LC my brother handed me. There was one from Deb and another from Mum; and, of course, I had to read these first. And I could read yours only once, and then had to put it in my pocket, while my poor old head tried to cope with its contents as far as I could remember. You have come at me with such a terrific rush of warmth, and I am so very much in need of you.

Well, I washed and made my bed (it was six o'clock before I received your letter) and fidgeted around. Then I thought, 'I must read it again before I sleep' – so I pushed off to the latrine (where the humblest may be sure of privacy) and read your words again. The comic expression 'It shakes me' is true in a serious sense about this deeply thrilling state of well-being that you have caused or created.

How impossible to sleep with thought and wonder of you hot within me! As I toss and turn and wriggle and writhe I think of you, probably doing the same. Isn't it blooming awful? I know that if I think of you, I will not sleep; yet I keep on thinking of you, and get hotter and hotter. Phew! I could do with a couple of ice-blocks around me. Finally, to sleep. Up in the morning, my first thoughts, of your nearness and your distance from me.

Unfortunately there is no likelihood of my early return. I must be another year, I may be another three or four. Relax, my girl, or you'll be a physical wreck in no time. Regard me as what you will, but don't altogether forget circumstance, distance, environment.

Since tiffin I have played a game of softball; had a haircut from a chap brought in specially to lighten us; five games of chess; dinner, a game of netball – scoring a goal though my side lost 5–3 (a lucky goal), then pictures (*Three Stooges* and Andrew Sisters in *How's About It?*)

As I was saying, relax. Take it easier. In the film tonight there was a crack, that the state of being in love was the happiest way of being miserable. So be miserable happily, don't look over your shoulder too much; enjoy what is, so far as you can. I am a born worry-er myself, but feel I could be all that you wanted me to be. Probably more important, I know that you are what I want, not in any limited sense, but in all. I want to confide in you. I want to creep into you. I want to protect you.

You spoke of yourself being 'guilty of slobbering' – it's no crime, I'm proud of it! If your incoherent babblings mean what mine do, it's jolly good. Regard me as a promise rather than a threat, and pick holes in me where you can – so that I seem less regal! Remember we are both in this together, and that it has somehow occurred undesignedly, unrehearsed, because we had it in us. During the day I simply lap you up and cause trouble at night. 'Engulfed' describes my state, too, a rather floundering, uncertain one. I am sorry I cannot relieve your ache.

I wonder what you look like (don't have a special photograph taken). I know you haven't a bus-back face but I have never looked at you as now I would. I wonder how many times I have seen you, and how many we have been alone. Now my foolish pulse races at the thought that you even have a figure. I want, very much, to touch you, to feel you, to see you as you naturally are, to hear you. I want to sleep and awaken with you.

Let me know if you think I'm mad. When my signature dries I am going to kiss it. If you do the same, that will be a complete (unhygienic) circuit!

Yours,
Chris

~

2

More Than Is Good For Me

15 April 1944

Dear Bessie,

I received today your letter dated 1st March. It has taken such a long time to come and I have felt so disappointed and unsettled at its repeated failure to arrive during the last fortnight, that this may explain my dis-satisfaction as I reached the end. I am puzzled by some of the things you say. Perhaps I should amend dis-satisfaction to 'unsatisfaction'. I hope you understand the feeling.

I will attempt to reply to your paragraphs and tell you what I cannot fathom as I go along.

You ask 'Where shall we end, Chris?' Well, I dunno, but I'm sure it won't be very dreadful. It might be a great adventure for both of us. I have an idea, but I am not wearing my planning trousers.

Emphatically, I agree that most of us want to love and be loved. Tell me, please, what your reaction is to a marriage where one party is not imbued with one-hundred-per-cent enthusiasm for the other, but marries perhaps for companionship and the wish to avoid loneliness. Do you think she is playing the game?

If my brother asks me why I am getting letters from you, I shall tell him that we are engaged in an interesting correspondence about life. If he asks (and he won't – but your questioners might) if I am proposing to court you, I shall laughingly deny it, as you (I hope) will do the same.

So I may write as I feel – would that I could! These words would burn the paper and scorch you. (If you get ashes one day when you open the envelope, you'll know that's what has happened!) You'll recognise my tantrums as they occur. Trouble is that you'll forgive me before, during and after my stupidities. It will be wise for you to commence the development of (or acquire) a critical faculty regarding me, otherwise I am going to be one big unredeemed disappointment for you.

I cannot write you daily but I do think of you hourly. You set all my senses humming, and make me sweat. I want to feel you. I want to go with you to a quiet place and tell you with my body what I can only half say in words.

Yours,
Chris

16 April 1944

Dear Bessie,

There are a couple of points in your letter which I did not reply to, and will do so now. Dictionaries – although I am what people call 'a good speller' I found when I came away from all my reference books that I was very shaky on some things. So when I was in Cairo I bought a small dictionary. I add to my vocabulary as I can, otherwise I should speedily relapse into baby talk. I have always investigated and made a note of unfamiliar words, and I also enjoy learning the exact shade of meaning of all words. It's no good me telling you anything about quidnunc; you will look it up in a dictionary one day and remember it the better. Perhaps when I give my delightful new-found words an airing I ought to mark 'em with a star?

This afternoon, with great speed, I received your wonderful Letter Card of April 8th. How I long to be what you think I am, and bring you all you desire. You can tell me no more than you have already done, yet I need you to keep on telling me that I am essential to you, as you, my dear, are indispensable to me. I thrill to you. You write about my 'powers of self-expression' – I have none without you.

You will notice an improvement in my last two letters. It is becoming clearer to me that you are my life's work, and that I must see that I do hold onto you, and please, please, please, do hold me tight. 18–30 are different ages, but I am happier that you loved me first when you were nearer the former age. I know that

I am not the victim of a desperate, blind, unloving grasp. I shall keep on saying I want to feel you, and I want you to know that my desire is no less than yours, nor ever will be. My head is on your breasts, my hands are about you.

I love you.
Chris

~

18 April 1944

I WILL ALWAYS LOVE YOU

Dear Bessie,

I have just stuck down a Letter Card, and I must straightaway carry on writing to you, around the subject of yours of the 8th April.

Our association in the future depends on your ability to put up with me and my defects, not my ability to put up with yours. And that if we are spending much of our time regarding the other as a bed mate that is a very natural thing, since we are likely to be in that position before too long; I hope it doesn't mean we are very lustful, but if it does, it doesn't stop me wanting to tell you how I stiffen and ooze as I read your words and imagine you writing them. I am your servant and your master at once.

I will command you and be commanded by you. Your breasts are mine.

I do not feel very happy at the thought of the practical difficulties in the way of setting up house after the war. Every shark in the commercial world will be up and about.

Unfortunately I used to donate most of my money to various 'good causes' and I did not start to save until the end of the war in Spain. I think I had about £75 when our own war started; I did not increase this until I joined the Army. At the end of last year I had (my Mother told me) a mere (for my purpose) £227. I think that I am adding to this at about £2 10s. a week. I do not know what will be required. I don't think there's much doubt that we will be old enough. Incidentally, I think that engagement rings are jewellers' rackets, and that marriage is more properly transacted at an office than mumbo-jumbo'd at a church. I am sorry you don't already know my views on this. You will have to be told sometime.

Can you see that it is gradually dawning on me that you are too good to be missed? Do you observe that I am refusing to bow to my own change-ability? Will you tell me that we may be together really one day, and you will hit me if I start wanting to go?

I am in the permanent state of hoping for letters from you, but I must have flushed my delight an hour ago, when I was handed your LC dated 1st, but postmarked the 3rd. The last three letters had come to me via my brother, and I have been annoyed. He has got an 'idea', I feel sure. I had to eat tiffin and delay reading you until I went to work. But now I have done so four times so far. Oh, I do desire you! Oh, I am not really alive except in you, and through you.

Certainly let us mention marriage. Consider me as the one you will be with always from this day, if you want me and will chance it. You are right about it being 'heavenly' – but oh hell, angel, you are a long way away! Bessie, Bessie, Bessie, I want to be with you.

I love you.
Chris

~

18 April 1944 [Second letter]

Dear Bessie,

I think that I will now start to tell you something of myself and family from the Year Dot to the present day. I think this is necessary because I want to (it is very difficult to write – all I want to do is tell you I LOVE YOU) marry you very soon after I return to England, and I want us to do most of the talking through the medium of our letters. There is a lot more to tell you, and I hope to do so. Deb knows much of my history as a person; I want you to know as much as anyone, if only so that you shall never be party to a conversation and be at a loss about it. You won't remember everything, and I am not certain how I shall proceed. But I think it is desirable. Your time is much more precious than my own, but I hope that you, too, will give me an abridged 'something', so that when we do, wonderfully, finally meet, we shall know more about each other than could be obtained by a contemporary or current correspondence.

We have met only comparatively little in the past – and I expect I discussed the weather as much as possible! Some of the things I tell you will not be news, one of them you will need to spend a little time (at least) thinking about, and all of it I hope will be of real interest because it is about me. My ignorance of you can be judged by the fact that I don't know if the B.I.M. stands for Ivy, Irene or Itma, I don't know your birthday, or your birthplace. I want to know your food dislikes, if any; if and what you drink; whether you still smoke; how you housekeep or if someone else does it somehow. Please, please, please, tell me of and about yourself, so that I may breathe you in, and wallow in news of you. For by now you must have serious doubts of your ability to escape marrying me, and wondering what the Dickens you have done to deserve it. Please regard me as a serious challenge, your confidant now, your mate when you give the word, your 'lawfully-wedded husband' if you will.

I think I can make a start on my career now by telling you that when I was born, my Father was 34, a Postman, and getting about 25s. a week. The family was increased to six (I have two brothers and one sister), and had to move from rooms in one part of Holloway, N.7., to a four roomed house in another part. It came under a Slum Clearance scheme when I was 13, and we were rehoused in a 5 roomed house on the London County Council Estate at Tottenham, until I was 26, when we moved to our present place at Bromley, which my brother owns. I am the

49

baby of the family. My sister is 33, my second brother, ARCHIE, is 36, my eldest, HERBERT REDVERS (Bert, after a Boer War General!) is 38. Dad is 64, Mum, 62. My early memories are few. I remember digging big holes in our back yard and lining up for the pictures. I don't know how much you recall of the last war? I remember the great fun of making cocoa after we had come back, seeing the R33 (which I thought was a Zeppelin); wanting to be a 'Spethial Conthtable' when I grew up; my Dad, a strange, awkward, red faced man, coming home from India.

Things here (I'll leave The Story of My Life II till later) are about the same, except that today we have gone into Khaki Drill which is much nicer than Battle Dress, and can be washed anytime one wants. I am playing chess as usual and Bridge at night when possible. I'd like to creep away somewhere and do a bit of hard brooding about you, but I have to go through the motions of behaving normally, like you. Whatever I do I am conscious of the fact that you are in the same world, and it is a pretty great thought to be getting on with, rather overwhelming at times. I hope the time we are away from each other will not seem too painfully long, and that before 1999 we shall be able to TELL each other what now we can only think.

I love you.
Chris

~

25 April 1944

Dear Bessie,

This will be in pencil because it is the only writing material I have with me at present, as like an ass I forgot to bring my pen with me.

This afternoon a dozen of us had a truck to the sea, by a different route from that we normally walk. It was a terrible (and enjoyable) ride ⁓⁓⁓⁓⁓, but worth it, although I found it too cold to dally long in the water. Our way was through the usual shells, burnt-out vehicles, bits of guns, and odds and ends left by retreating armies. Needless to say none of us were very pleased to discover a bleached skull on the beach, only pausing to wonder whether it was one of 'theirs, or ours'.

A pity that today I got your LCs of 12th and 14th BEFORE TIFFIN. After I had read them I wanted ambrosia and nectar, not dehydrated potatoes and corned beef. Consequently I ate little. I have heard that it is pretty serious when your appetite is affected. This is my first experience and I'll not give it the upper hand.

The smaller your writing gets, the better I shall like it, please.

You say that I am sweeping you off your feet, 'such a terrific love' you don't really think it has happened to you before. My dear girl, it has not. I address you as your future husband.

I think of your breasts more than is good for me. I am sure you are not entirely disinterested in the fact that I have hairs on my chest. Then we start wondering other things. Where shall we live, do we want children; how about your age. You tell me you have £85 10s. in the POSB [Post Office Savings Bank] without knowing I am just writing you that I have £227.

Thank goodness you did not send me a cross. Really, I am scornful of such things. I have no patience with its religious intent, and I know very well that the gold-cross-laden women at home wear them as no more than lucky charms. They probably forget that Christ was crucified. I hope you didn't seriously think of sending me any such thing. I must risk hurting you, my love – I hope you aren't RC [Roman Catholic]. I'll say no more for the present.

Can you understand how I burn at the thought of you, and stretch my arms to enfold you?

I love you.
Chris

~

28 April 1944

Dear Bessie,

Tell me of your clothes. Tell me of your room, the furniture, so that I can better imagine you, more easily come to you when you are alone.

Throughout the years, I have remembered the Abbey Wood sun glinting through the trees that you and I were under. It is my one real physical memory of you – I know that you are not a toothless old hag. As I kick around here thoughts of your body excite me, thrill me, but I want you to understand that our minds are the things we have to keep together. If either of us cheat, it is no good.

You say you'd like to be vamping me 'right now'. I wish you were. Although I suppose I would soon be telling you that life was a serious business and we must 'behave'. I hope you realise that in marrying me you will be the wife of a man who believes in 'wearing the trousers', but not his wife's skirt as well. I do not want you to be terribly, terribly, terribly anxious to 'obey'. I believe you and I will get on well together and bring the other great joy, not of the physical kind only, but of the mind.

My autobiographical details seem to have been neglected. I suddenly dropped the idea under pressure of telling you that you are lovely.

But I will potter along for a bit now. I was never christened. My mother had a lot to do at the time, it was somehow overlooked! Now she is very keen that I be 'done' but I am quite pleased with my status. I believe that if a child dies without being christened he must be buried in unhallowed ground. That makes me very keen to rebel against the rubbish of that dictum.

I went to Drayton Park (Highbury) LCC School. I was probably a very ordinary pupil but good at English. I never won a scholarship despite parental ambitions. When I had done very badly at Arithmetic once I had to stand up before a class. The headmaster said that a chap with a noble forehead like mine should have done much better. I was elected Editor of a new venture School Magazine, but somehow never got out an issue. I left too soon. I remember, at an Armistice 'treat' when I was very young, putting a banana in my pocket to 'take it home to Mum'. When I got home the banana was just pulp. I had the usual fights, during playtime, and before and after school. I supported Cambridge, The Arsenal, and Surrey. (I got these from my eldest brother who has been a big influence on me throughout my life.) I only remember having one 'good hiding' from my Dad when I was about 11. I made a swing, tied one end to the mangle, and smashed it completely when it fell down under my weight.

I started in the PO as a Boy Messenger at the Money Order Department on Mch 8 1928. I enjoyed the experience. It was good to be earning money, and I spent most of my pocket money on second-hand books. I was elected Editor of the Messengers' Magazine too late to publish an issue, as I left in November 1930, when I started at the CTO [Counter and Telegraph Office]. The first girl I ever went out with was a Girl Probationer, whom I took to see *Sunny Side Up*, one of the first 'talkies'. I took out several other Girl Probationers, but I can't recall quarrelling with any of them. I was Secretary of the Cricket Club, but my highest score was 16, and that must have been unusual or I shouldn't remember it. I played little football. I must have been poor. I was 'Junior boy' for nine months, and had a terrible time being dragged all over the kitchen by my seniors, 'ducked' in the water, and generally leg-pulled with. One of my jobs then was to clear away the Controller's (O.J. LIDBURY, he has got on since then) tea tray. I remember still the pleasure of drinking the creamy milk he used to leave.

That is enough for this episode. We'll carry on later if you can stand it. Please try something similar on your own account, as I am very keen to learn about you, very anxious to get an insight into your history. Do you know French, Shorthand? Understand if you can, how much I want to know all there is to know about your past, so that I can better gather you. Just at this moment, I want to rummage around you, run my hands over you, your hair, your breasts, your arms, your loins, your legs.

I love you.
Chris

~

2 May 1944

Dear Bessie,

What more elevating thought, what more useful can this page serve, than to contain a list of the books I have read since I have been out here. I should very much like you to tell me what books you happen also to have read on the list.

> *Science in Everyday Life* – Haldane
> *While Rome Burns* – Woolcott
> *How Russia Prepared* – Mr Edelman Dachau
> *For Those Few Minutes* – Eric Gill
> *Carry On, Jeeves* – P.G. Wodehouse

Lord Jim – Conrad

De Valera – Penguin

Victoria the Great – Edith Sitwell

Literary Lapses – Steph. Leacock

A Life of Shakespeare – Hesketh Pearson

Black Mischief – E. Waugh

Mr Moto is So Sorry – J.P. Marquand

Sherston's Progress – Siegfried Sassoon

Confessions of a Capitalist – Sir E. Benson

I have read plenty of other stuff, not worthwhile recording as it was unexceptional. If you have not read them, I should like you to get [these] from the library (not buy) as I should like to know that you had read them.

I hope I used up the public part of this letter card in a useful fashion. I did not like using another of these LCs so soon after the last, but it is about the only way I can rush to tell you what a lovely silly thing you are.

I have to end this now in order to catch the post (it goes daily here of course), but I hope that you are getting to realise and appreciate that you and I are 'us' and 'we'. Maybe we are only just beginning to feel that vital identity of interest, that significant attachment to the other's person that will enlighten and enliven us in the days ahead. But everything has to have a beginning. Don't you worry about any end. Sigh for me, want, desire and need me, as I need you, my dear.

My love,
Chris

9 May 1944

Dear Bessie,

I sent you a LC in reply to your near-lament at the absence of mail. If you must have 'nagging worries' as you call them, please let them be around the prospects of my return by Christmas (oh, oh, oh, what a chance!), the chances of a house, the helluva job getting things will be. Please don't conceal your 'naggings', please do tell me everything about you (oh, Bessie, I love you!), please continue to trust me.

Yes, I agree that the body-beautiful is overrated, but that doesn't stop me wanting to see you in puris naturalibus (I bet you have to look that up. I did!), to drink in your glory, to put my hands on your non-flat bottom, (Bessie, I love you!), to forage around you, to rove over you, to subdue you, to possess you.

I've never had a Turkish bath. I should think that the sun out here has a similar cumulative effect. Will be glad to get your account of the process; will you go again?

Deb had told me you would be visiting her again, and seeing the American Communist. (I am afraid I have written Deb very little and somewhat forcedly since her refusal to reply to my arguments about my Mother-fixation.) My first reaction is – thank Goodness you haven't fallen in love with him! It would shake me considerably to think you were bound for Alabama or Tennessee. Please don't fall in love with anyone else, my dear. Please let me be the future recipient of your favours, and maybe, the future target for your rolling pin.

The other night we had a very amusing 12-a-side 'Spelling Bee', Signals versus RAF, won by the latter 64–38, as the RAF have a different if not better type of chap as a rule. I was very successful with the words I was asked and 'I don't want to swank' (an expression made famous by myself in the Junior Section days) and scored 7 of our points, the most of any. Like an ass, I spelt the flower CHRYSTANTHEUM. I must have been thinking of my second name; we were each asked 5 words, I gained the others through correct spelling of words RAF couldn't manage. My brother was poor (he never could spell) but others were worse.

Do you get a glimmering of my delight in you, my need for you, my love of you? I wonder.

Chris

~

17 May 1944

Dear Bessie,

A lot of good things have happened to me lately. Today, after what has seemed a long, long, time I have received two LCs from you, thus terminating any doubts that I had that you had been bombed, or run off with an American, which seems the modern equivalent of the 'fate worse than death' lark.

Good Thing No. 2 is the news that I should be commencing leave on the 22nd, and should get seven clear days in Alexandria, bathing (which is nothing new but nevertheless delightful), eating excellent food and ices, drinking all the milk and minerals my stomach desires, and looking, once again, at houses and paved streets, young children and trees.

The third Good Thing is that this week I am doing an easy job, not telephone operating, which enables me to write in peace (I wrote five letters today and have ten more to do, such has been my inertia of late) and sleep at night (tonight is the first time I have had five consecutive nights in bed since November.

Now to your letters and our love: Where did you go for leave, and with whom? (I imagine, Iris.) Tell me all about it at your leisure please. Please prepare for about a fortnight without letters while I am away. I shall try to write if there are facilities, but remember I am chaperoned.

Did you understand that my fellow sitter in the photo, the 'chap named Barker', was my brother? He is a fine chap, sorry you cut him to pieces.

Congratulations, before I inconsiderately forget, on the really good efforts you are making at small writing, I hope you'll maintain the standard.

So your Dad knows . . . It couldn't be avoided. It was inevitable, and perhaps desirable. But do keep on holding him to practical silence. If your brother Wilfred tells any of his pals, the secret (for what it is worth) will be out within a month. You had better tell him, but urge him to treat it as a whisper. I think it is better to keep our state shielded for the present, but no doubt we shall have to talk later. But I want to tell you something first, and I can only do so in my own time. If you feel I should write your Dad, let me know and I'll do as you say. I always remember 'God gave us our relations, but he left us to choose our friends'.

I feel very relieved that you are not RC, and that the cross had no real significance, and that at least we shall not fight over religion, the cause of so much fighting. I am an agnostic, but I have 'C of E' on my identity discs (usually I do not wear them, but I shall do so next week in case I get slugged).

One day I shall actually see you. One day we shall really be together. Then we shall really begin to live, and our education will have begun. I hope you really have got an appetite (the other chap in our tent never eats a dinner, only a sweet) but anyhow I'll give you one. You'll never get an easier bloke to cook for if you live to be a 100.

I don't remember calling you a 'flapper' but I expect I thought it was justified. My dictionary tells me it means 'A young girl, not yet out'. It sounds as though I was right, don't you think? Anyway, we are now both flapping wildly at each other in a pretty successful endeavour to persuade the other that this is 'it'. One day I shall come to you. I shall take you and you will be glad. Together, we will rejoice.

I love you.
Chris

A photo strip sent to Bessie in 1944

20 May 1944

My dear and lovely Bessie,

Today there came your LC of May 10th, to tell me that Iris (but oh no, not Lil Hale!) was now aware of our altered state. It doesn't worry me at all, and I fully understand the difficulty of concealment. Probably I should have told you to tell Iris, as there is no doubt that she would have divined something. However, I don't think it will be long before I get a letter from someone commenting on the new alliance. You can think the position 'safe', but nothing travels faster than a shared secret. But please do not accelerate the publicity if you can help. If you can't help it, well, I haven't it in me to rage at you. I just would prefer you to keep it dark.

One thing that I really do want you to guard against is 'sharing' me with anyone, whoever it may be. For goodness' sake don't quote any 'funny bits' I may rise to in my letters. Please do not refer directly to anything I say, recognise that this emotion I feel is for you, not for anyone else. So don't quote me. If you think a thing I have said is worth repeating, do so as though it was you who had thought of it. I do not want that to read the least bit unpleasantly, what I intend expressing is my desire to come to you direct and fully, and stay with you, not dispersed. On other occasions you will find I am a jealous and selfish lover who demands the un-demandable. I shall snarl at appropriate intervals to suitably impress you. I am not afraid of the interpretation you will give to any act or thought of mine, but I do not want an audience of two nor desire the help of anyone else. Do not expect others to share your view of my virtues, please do not try.

You say if you lose me you will have lost all. Nonsense. First, I am not 'all'. Second, you are not going to lose me through any act of mine. I am going to hold onto you as tightly as I can – a sort of death-grip!

No, I should not wish you to go out to work, though I should resist you becoming a home-tied, house-proud drudge. I don't know about children. I am glad you don't sink to the bottom upon entering the water. I can't swim very well, you know, but I can keep afloat and I have confidence. We shall swim together one day. I'll 'find you lazy' you say. You'll have to improve, if you are, but I don't suppose you are. If you are, I'll shake you. (Aren't I horrible?)

You must understand how I ache for you, want my light-brown arms to enfold your white body, my hands to forage around, my body to give you its message, my whole being to dominate you yet be subject to you. I want you to receive me. I want to pierce you and be part of you. I want to tell you that I love you.

Chris

~

25 May 1944

Dear Bessie,

I am writing this in 'Alex'. The first leave I have had in 16 months. You can understand that I am a little elated to be my own master –

be it only for a little while. We only have one military function to perform, i.e. salute every officer we pass. I salute them with great gusto, believing the while that my act is another nail in Hitler's Coffin!

27 May. I am now in the new, clean, bug-free billet, and am enjoying the change from the desert. Have had many fine ices, ice drinks, and meals hastily cooked and nicely served. It is nice to drink tea from china cups and see the whole of the face when one shaves.

The clothes of the people here ('Europeans') would make you go green with envy. Very fine cloth, well made. I have yet to see a pair of trousers under £5, prices are very high. There are many clubs here, and some are really fine, in leafy, green, quiet surrounds. Have had some swims, but the facilities are not so good as I had expected, as the sea wall prevents bathing too near the central part of the town. Have been on a 'sight-seeing' tour with the YMCA, this morning, but it was not very good, some of the alleged Roman wall-scrawlings looked to me very much like 1944 daubings.

Have had a number of photographs taken and I think some are like me. We must have a lot done, as my Mother wails that my eldest brother is looking so old, and we have to keep on having photos done till we get one which says the reverse. Will send you copies later. There are many luscious 'come-hither' types around here. I must tell you the whole yarn later on. I have bought a 'Swan', but as you can see by the bad writing, the nib is not very suitable.

Strawberries are 2s. a lb. here, potatoes 6d. a lb. I am looking forward to getting your letters upon my return. For me that is the only 'snag' of this leave. I hope you fully realise just how I feel. My apologies for this very poor effort. My brother is a foot away!

My love.
Chris

~

11 June 1944

My dear and lovely Bessie,

How can I start to reply to the seven letters that awaited me when I arrived here, the two that came the day after, and the one I received yesterday? Shall I reply to them chronologically, or in order of importance?

These letters of yours are just like an English river running through green fields, clear, refreshing, bright, confident. You come rippling down at me, surround me with your beauty and your meaning, and just as I am thinking 'that was wonderful', you come to me again to say that you still are.

So will you accept my humble thanks (you make me feel humble) for these many evidences of your feelings, and allow me to commend you on all the fine, small writing you did. Don't try to make it any smaller or you'll ruin your eyes.

The story of my return from Alexandria is a sorry one. I will leave all the other leave details till I have replied to your other letters, but I must tell you this. We did not last out the third week, but on the Wednesday had to en-train. I awoke in the barracks with a bad headache (I never have headaches usually) which persisted throughout the train journey which lasted the usual 24 hours. My brother had to cart all my kit about, while I carried only the rifles. Arrived here I saw the Medical Corporal, went to bed, had tablets, slept a little. Following day saw the MO [Medical Officer] who gave me a good general examination and said there was nothing wrong with me. He excused me duty. More tablets and bed. The following day I only had a pretty bad ache around my eyes, again excused duty. Today I am somewhat cloudy in the eye-region, but expect to be bunged on the switchboard any minute.

By the way I have a typewriter, Underwood (cost me £14 14s. in 1938). Would you like to have it, if so I'll try and think out a scheme. I could get £25 for it any day I think, but it is more useful than money and is just lying about useless at home.

I am glad you like the second-hand bookshop idea.

I am sorry about your gumboils. I should leave your private (acquisitive) Dentist and pay at least one visit to the Dental Hospital at Leicester Square, which is concerned with saving teeth, not making money through extractions and dentures. Don't have your teeth out before you need do, and without seeing the Dental Hospital. They are good people. I shall make some lighter remarks in a later letter. The enclosed photos (most grim) show some of my teeth fairly well. I lost two on my right, upper, through private dentists. You do want me to tell you, here, that I love you though you be molar-less? I do!

I give you my glad sympathy at your efforts to abate the smoke nuisance. You are a good girl, Bessie. We are now getting 50 Players/Gold Flake weekly out here. Pity I cannot send mine to you.

I must again say I don't want you to think of me as a superior. Of course I kid myself I have a sharper perception of some (maybe unimportant) things than most others. But you are better than me at French, Algebra, Arithmetic, and I am confused (and remaining so) about Morse and Electricity and Magnetism.

I love you.
Chris

~

12 June 1944

Dearest,

It is a little bit pathetic for you to tell me I am 'such a lover', when all I have been able to do is put on paper a few sentences conveying what I mean, but not, surely, the force with which I mean it. You have been wonderful in gathering my intentions, you will be wonderful administering to my needs. Please never forget that I have needs, and that you are my greatest.

It is not much good me trying to tell you that I shall not flirt with hundreds of others. Events will show you.

But for goodness' sake, go steady on the near-occult. Do not trust your ordinary brain to deal with extra-super ordinary things. I became interested in Spiritualism years ago, but after I had read a book (I think it was *Valley of the Mists* by Conan Doyle) that made my head whirl with thought and possible happenings, in no spirit of mock-humility, I decided it was a subject which I had better leave alone. My brain was, I thought, too ordinary.

You ask me if I want you to be a modern woman par excellence, and you 'rather hope I am the least bit old-fashioned'. Well, I am sufficiently old-fashioned not to want you to work after marriage. I want your main job to be looking after me. But, as I have said earlier, I do not want you to go house-mad. I want you to take an interest in other things, and if necessary, join up with people like yourself who may be similarly interested. I have seen (theoretically!) a woman stop being useful to the world upon marriage. I want you to develop, say, something that the circumstances of your working life have prevented you following. I can therefore be, not the bloke who bangs the Harem gate shut, but the one who gives you the chance to do something (quite accidentally); obviously I am marrying you because I am selfish, not because I think a little leisure may make you another Van Gogh.

Don't rush to the photographer, there's a good girl. I shall be very glad to have the snap of 'The Author at Age 20' – as, my love, one day I shall be very happy to have you.

You amuse me when you say you don't think managing money is my strong point. (I haven't got any strong points except those you make.) I expect you will find me a horrible old skinflint, but I hope you'll agree to have pocket-money, as I shall have it, and that should enable you to be at least independent in little things. In any case, you will be doing the housekeeping, and I shall assist only at your invitation.

If anyone in the Ministry of Labour asks you what your war-work is, you can show them my dark-frowned photo, and you can tell them your trouble with me is only just starting.

I've never really asked you, have I – Will you marry me, Bessie (for better or for worse)? There are no good reasons, but the only excuse I can offer is that I will love you always, my fashion. Reply by ordinary LC won't you?

Thank you, Bessie, for telling me you want to be at my mercy. One day let us hope you will be, and then we shall really meet. You make me feel a little drunk when you place yourself at my command. I so much want to caress you, to lie with you and commune. You do not wonder at my wish to rummage when it is your lovely body that I seek? Do not mistake the depth and the age of my desire to enter you. I want to kiss your breasts till they flame, I want to squeeze them till my roving hands move on to your buttock and hips. I want to mould your loins with my hands and kiss you again and again. I want you to receive my homage, my love, and then I want to come into lovely you myself.

Chris

∼

14 June 1944

My dear Bessie,

Yes, I got those corduroy trousers a few months after the war started, and long before everyone adopted them. When I got them home, my Mother said, 'You silly young ass, only artists wear them!' She was approximately correct. They are grand trousers, though, and wonderful material. I am glad about your non-puritan thoughts based on their contents. I already feel accustomed to your bedroom, and I hope you will increasingly know within you that I am thinking of you there. I don't altogether swallow the explanation for the sag in the spring bed, but we will try and make it worse, shall we?

Do not let the emphasis on the physical make you think for a moment that I under-rate your mentality and intelligence. So prepare for me as though I was an ordinary person, not the Agha Khan.

Yes, my Mother will be a bit of a nuisance to her prospective daughter-in-law. Not because she is mine, but because in-laws are nuisances. But I shall be able to help you where necessary and when the time comes. My attitude in similar circs. would be 'Blow the lot of them'. I am not over-fond of relations myself.

You say 'I am so much in your hands'. Would that you were, my dear. I am afraid of losing you. I am so glad the Yank turned out a bit of a wet blanket. I shall try hard to keep you. Forgive me for my constant thought of your flesh. Your body is always before me, and I find my own crying for union, companionship. These gifts which you wonderfully bestow on me are the greatest I could ask.

I can now commence to tell you about my leave. It could have been so much better had you been there: as it was, my brother's pretty constant attendance was a great nuisance. I could have wept sometimes. I had all sorts of great hopes about buying something in Alex., but in the event, I had to admit defeat. Cloth was tremendously dear, and its despatch under the eagle eye of Herbert, impossible. So I am afraid that all you will get in a couple of months' time will be a kind of leather shopping bag, with zip fastener. You've probably got half-a-dozen, or maybe you wouldn't be seen dead with one. But perhaps it isn't a shopping bag. You must tell me what it is when you get it! Anyhow, it's leather and should be OK for soling your shoes. Next time, please tell me what you'd like, and (if I can get rid of Bert for a little while) I'll try hard to be perspicacious. What is your shoe size please?

Please have a thought of me.
My love.
Chris

~

16 June 1944

Dear Bessie,

I am now starting my account of the visit to Alexandria.

In Alex. you can get what you want if you like to pay for it. Two chaps in our party had nights out which cost them £3 apiece each time. They assured me it was well worth it. Almost anywhere you go, little boys, old men, or the women themselves will say 'Want a woman?' 'Want a —?' 'Hello dearie.' I must say that I shudder somewhat at the thought. A boy about 6 in one street invites you to buy a preventative, with as much loud enthusiasm and as little discretion as the chap who sells newspapers at Oxford Circus. *Lady Chatterley's Lover, The Well of Loneliness* and other items are on sale everywhere, but although they are advertised as unexpurgated, judging by the disappointment of a chap in the train who had bought one, they are pretty much like tracts.

Street entertainers are more numerous and original than our own, there are never any singers or bands only. Monkeys and dogs jump through hoops at their masters' behest. One man has a couple of long batons, which burn at the end. He pretends to swallow them, but only puts them in his mouth, where they go out. A 'good' one is, he swallows paraffin (I mean puts it in his mouth), then expels it into the air, putting a match to it. Done quickly, it seems that he is breathing fire . . . Then he lays back on a great nail-studded board, while his mates dance on him, after which dancing barefoot on a bag of glass is child's play. All this to the accompaniment of drum-banging and other noises.

One of my nicest afternoons was watching cricket, on matting-wicket surrounded by a fair amount of pleasant looking grass. We had tea as we watched. I had a macaroon.

On the last night I was able to leave the barracks, and spend an hour with 'Mohamed Hassan Ali' at one of the Clubs. He gave an 'Hour of Magic', and picked on me to be his stooge. For half-an-hour, at first rather embarrassed, I was his assistant, up on the stage. I threw dice, burned £1 notes, tore up playing cards, tied knots in rope, tried to extricate hoops, picked eggs from my pockets. The queerest thing of the lot was when he said to me, 'Say, come out McTavish' and told me to put my hand down my shirt. From my sweaty breasts came a dear little chick. He told me three more names, and I extricated three more. A bit of hard luck for the chicks, but Egyptians are very cruel to animals, and not much less vicious to their fellows.

With you as my companion, anything would be wonderful. This would have been wonderful too.

Love,
Chris

Chris in Alexandria, 1944

3

Into the Blouse

17 June 1944

My lovely Bessie,

What do you think about us starting to number our letters? It is a good check-up, a missing number is easily spotted. I shall not commence it unless you wish it. I don't want you to think this is pedantry, but I think we will find it useful. Don't say 'Yes' if you think it is just a silly idea of mine. We number our letters home. Have reached No. 56 this year so far.

I am sorry that the actual start of the Second Front should be such a real stab for your consciousness, and then again, I am not. I want you to be aware of the terrible things that are happening, yet I want to shelter you from their consequences or prevent you looking too closely. Look at my Mother's jumbled-up homeliness: '. . . your usual two letters haven't arrived this week. I suppose this invasion is causing the delay, the day before and all night there seems planes about, woke your Dad up, they are going over in hundreds today as well. I hope you were able to get some good shows in and pictures, I shall not go this week, don't seem right somehow not knowing that poor old Charlie may be lying dead somewhere, it is a worry . . .' (and later she again mentions Charlie (my brother-in-law, a sailor), and her thankfulness that we are not involved).

This war, at close quarters, is very bad, but the historians will record it as just another war. Perspective is invaluable. Seek it, be thankful you are not making all the sacrifices, and do all you can for those who are.

I love you.
Chris

~

29 June 1944

Dear Bessie,

I thank you for the 'Yes, yes, yes' acceptance, the honour that you have done me, and the confidence you have reposed in me. I promise to do all that I can, at all times, to forward our union, to work for your happiness and to care for your interests. I shall try hard not to be wilful, unheedful, thoughtless, I shall try to be considerate, kind and helpful, and where I fail I shall ask and expect your forgiveness. I think we can be very happy, and I hope we shall always try.

I hope the flying bombs have been a good way from you. My mother is usually very good, but she doesn't write very happily at present. I think it is the 'uncanny' part of the thing which is worrying her although that is actually its weak point. All we can hope is that their range is very limited and that progress in France will steal their launching bases.

Don't ever think this feeling between us is ordinary. Always regard it as something big, real, living.

I love you.
Chris

~

2 July 1944

Dear Bessie,

I am hoping to get at least one letter card from you tomorrow, but will say a few words now. Actually, there is a lot I have to tell you. First there is the autobarkergraphical tale to be told in outline, and then I wanted to tell you about events since I left England in some detail.

My Dad really grew up without any idea of home life. Until he met my Mother he hadn't any sympathy or kindness shown him. His father was a drunken wretch, his mother died at his birth, having had (it is said) nineteen previous children. He spent some of his time in the workhouse, ran away a number of times, had a really hard life which 'made a man of him', but also prevented him acquiring some of the gentler habits which 'Home' does induce.

When I think of 'us', I look forward to our Home atmosphere, which doesn't depend on the material things or whether one has Hot and Cold in the bathroom. It depends upon our love, flowing between us, uniting us.

3 July 1944. A smack in the eye for me today, nothing from you. I am wondering about these pilotless planes. I hope you go in the shelter, and do not try and be 'brave' by going to bed.

4 July 1944. No mail today. I do hope you are OK. I know you must be seriously disturbed at least. It doesn't matter about me getting letters, but it does matter about your safety. I trust you will remain safe.

I have never seen a break of seven days between your letters before, although I am beginning to know the terror of these new bombs and the greater job you must have in finding conditions enabling you to write.

I am very sorry for you, I am very proud of you. If bombs constitute your life nowadays, well give me bombs in your LCs as you give them in your conversation to Iris Page. And then, don't start worrying about my 'morale', don't keep on writing because you think I must have letters. Write my name etc on the outside of the LC, and tell me you love me, inside, and I shall find that eminently satisfactory. Send me a scratch telling me you are safe, don't trouble yourself with sounding the aitches.*

* The 'letter cards' were folded in a particular way so as to contain both a public area visible to all and a private internal space. Chris and Bessie's intimate exchanges were necessarily contained within the latter.

I do not regard you as lazy, and that is what counts. If you are lazy, I shall shake you up as far as I can. (My brother's wife left London a week before war was declared. Bert and I went to his second floor flat to clear up for him, and close the place down. An ordinary sized bath had been left by her, half full with all the (used) crockery they had – weeks of undone 'washing-up'. I took (I don't remember exactly) over 20 milk bottles down to the front doorstep.) I could not countenance the skimping of household tasks, and I don't suppose even you would try to frighten me with assertions that you'll never do them.

I love you.
Chris

~

9 July 1944

Dear Bessie,

There are more fleas about here than previously, probably because the weather is a little hotter, but by no means as bad as it was this time last year. We have a pinky sort of powder which really smells nasty, and is not liked by fleas, etc. I had been losing a good bit of sleep through these aggravating midgets, three and four a night deciding to bore into me, so that I determined to really shake them. I smothered my three blankets with the powder and put a lot inside the sleeping sheet. I had been in bed for about ten minutes when I started burning like anything in my tender parts. Phew! I had to get out of bed and start rubbing furiously with soap and water. I finally got the burning to stop, and tied a clean handkerchief round that part.

I do not think I will say a lot in reply to your comments; I had better say that now the body acts during sleep, and that I have no wish to consciously assist. I am appreciative of your soothing words and your calm assessments. I do not know whether you do fully understand what a massive weight this particular ignorance has been, but you appear to do so. Sometimes I feel I must burst. I want very badly to burst into you. Perhaps it is a pity that I am not meek and mild in my feelings, because as it is I feel I want to crush you and press myself into you until we are both breathless. 'Breathless' – am I not already breathless at the thought of your beauty, that awaits me, that you have told me is mine. The wonder of you, the miracle of this our understanding, is a really breathtaking affair.

Pleased you liked the Alex. stuff. I did not intend you to think that most of the chaps on leave or stationed there got their fun in not-so-pleasant ways. The great majority are good chaps. Understand that I am a humbug, but I shall try hard not to humbug you, I shall try to present myself to you as I am because I do not need to pretend to have the brain of an Einstein or the body of a Fred Astaire, to capture you. Here I am, be-spectacled, bald headed, often bemused – and Hey Presto! there are you, nevertheless all for me. It gives me a grand feeling. I think you will understand that my physical thoughts about you are not very restrained, that they are rather violent and terrific. I like to think you do not mind.

I love you.
Chris

~

12 July 1944

Dear Bessie,

I heard on the news that the flying bombs left London alone last night. I hope you made the most of it, and got a good night's rest for once in a while. Do you go in the shelter at night and what kind of a shelter have you got? What happens in the daytime, do you just carry on working? There are so many people to whom this war has brought disaster and distress. One of the chaps in my Section has just learned that one of his brothers has been killed in France. He has another brother there also.

There is something like the cry of a child for its mother in the way my inside cries for you, and then again there is not, there is the just as strong instinct of mating, for in our roundabout fashion, that is what we have come to the threshold of – mating.

You would be glad of the 'drying winds' out here. They are terrific. I, too, look forward to the day when you'll be ironing my shirts. I don't know how 'heavy' I am on clothes. Darned socks, the trouser bottom where it touches the shoe, and frayed cuffs are the only repairs I can think of offhand. You should see my darns nowadays! Great big lumps of wool, but they never seem to hurt me, so they must be OK.

I was delighted to get some idea of your dresses, though it will take me some time to assimilate them. Sometimes will you tell me what you are wearing when you are writing to me? My thoughts raced at your mention of your coral pink blouse (sports). My hands want to insinuate themselves into the blouse, so that they may hold your breasts, hold them tight, tell you all you want to know. And now, could you enlighten me regarding the difference between a '(sports)' blouse and a mere ordinary blouse?!

I love you.
Chris

~

14 July 1944

You Dear Creature,

Thank you for making today happier for me. It was great to get a new letter, and to discern, feel, bathe in, your gracefulness.

You say you are absorbed by me. I believe you. I have no doubt of it, and I love you for it. I wish I could be with you, to hold you tight and crush you till you cried. I wish I could kiss you fiercely, then tenderly: tenderly, then fiercely.

Bessie, my love, can you send me some little thing, personal to you, that has been very close to you, for me to finger and kiss, sometimes? A little piece of cloth, that has touched you. You could send me a few square inches in your next surface letter. If you think I am an ass, you must tell me so, but I am so desperately in need of you. I want you so much. I think of your breasts, your breasts, your breasts, and my great urge is to hold them and assure you of my love.

Since writing the earlier pages I have had some sleep, and then been forced by chaps not playing at the last minute, to turn out for our cricket team against a South African eleven. I have very little idea of actually playing, though I like the game for exercise. Our side scored 13 (which was terrible, including half a dozen 0's, of which mine was one). And they declared at 112 for 7, giving us another whack. This time we scored 44, and to my delight, I scored – 1! We had cake and tea, a bumpy ride there and back, and I felt all virtuous for blooming-well turning out at some inconvenience and 'saving the honour of the side'.

I wish I could be with you to bathe in the wonder and magic and splendour of you. 'Wonder, magic, splendour'; if it should happen that you read this on a nasty morning after an alarming 'bomb' night, you may look askance at these words. But I want you to accept them as illustrating how I regard you, the source of things good.

I love you.
Chris

~

17 July 1944

My dear Bessie,

I received today your No. 5, and my impression after reading it was that you were unhappy, and I had caused it, a thing I never want to do. Please, my darling, do not get depressed or downcast, sad and sorrowful on account of anything I may say. I do not mean to question you or your conduct.

I assure you that, however discouraged I may be by the world scene, I am not miserable about you and I, and that nothing you have said in any way detracts from my appreciation and love of you; for you to even metaphorically have a 'suicidal feeling' is very silly, and right against the facts.

You say that when I am 'fed up' with you, you feel cold and stiff and useless. Whenever has a letter of mine told you I am fed up? My whole effort has been to impress you with my hunger for you. And I believe that I have succeeded, I do not really feel that you are seriously thinking I am not perfectly satisfied with you. Whatever emotions I have had about any other person in the past are quite dwarfed by this that I have for you. Do not talk of me leaving you when my one big desire is to come to you, to come to you as your lover, your mate, and take your everything.

I am glad you mention about avoiding people. We certainly must slobber alone. What a wonderful day when we are really together, in the flesh, looking at each other. What wonderful days when I am holding you, mating with you. Of course you are silly for thinking I might leave you. And I don't believe you think it.

You know that you have me now for good. This morning I was looking at some of your 'old' letters (they are new and alive to me always now) and saw you say 'You know that with me you have come home', and I thought how splendidly true that was. You are my home. My life rests within and through you.

You say you yearn to please me. Well, you can do that by not worrying your head about me and my desert needs. I am much more concerned about bombs on you than anything like getting you to send me anything, even if I needed it! Penguins you can look out for, please: A99 *A Book of English Essays*. A98 *An Anthology of War Poetry*. Don't wear yourself stiff getting them. Give up the chase, if, as is probable, they are now out of print. Remember that I'd prefer one letter from you to the whole of the Bodleian.

I love you.
Chris

≈

25 July 1944

Dear Bessie,

I have today posted you a registered parcel. I suppose it will take a couple of months to reach you, so that you should, by the end of September, be the proud possessor of *Bartlett's Familiar*

Quotations. You may have heard of the volume previously, but I rather think you would not have one already. It is a classic; I bought my first *Bartlett's*, published in 1884, second hand for four pence. It was very fine. The latest edition has all the 'modern' quotes; I had a good deal of trouble getting those I got in England. The publishers gave me the last copy they had. The book cost a guinea when I bought it first, but has since been raised to £1 10s. When I saw one for £2 in Alex. on leave I thought 'I must get it for Bessie'. (The 10s. extra is because of agreed prices for sale of English books in Egypt.) I had hoped to hold on to the volume for another month, to ensure its arrival near your birthday. But that is not possible, and I hope you will regard it as my first birthday gift to you, with all my love and affection, my regard and esteem. I hope that we may spend many happy hours looking into its pages together.

I do not really remember the things that made you sad in my 6/7 letter and which were dispelled by my No. 1 letter which arrived in the evening. My only feeling is that your imagination works overtime on things which might make you miserable and unbelieving and undertime on things that might make you happier. If ever something arises about which I feel very strongly that you are acting unwisely, I shall tell you unmistakeably.

The 'bursting' feeling that you mention I have in varying degrees, and there are times when I feel desperate for you, for your flesh, for your body, for your breasts. Always I long to feel you, but I have my 'peaks' of wishing for you.

Glad you like the numbering system.

I am sorry about your bomb troubles. Please tell me all about them, as they occur to you. I shall not comment on them as I do not want to start repeating horrors 'at' you. I suppose your bad 'sleeps' are inevitable. I wish I could come to you in your sleep and drive your nasty shadows away.

We shall never know if, really, we have met 'a bit late'. Perhaps it is a fluke that we have come together. I am hoping that we are going to make the best of it. There are years and years and years ahead of us. Probably we shall be able to recollect our present correspondence only as a small part of our happiness.

Although I may be able to wangle it somehow, I shall perhaps be forced very soon to destroy some of your letters, the great majority, actually, as it is space which I must consider. I am sorry about this. Please, forgive me, but probably I should have had to do it sometime, anyhow. I shall not forget any of the things you have told me. I shall remember every embrace, every endearment, every caress.

I love you.
Chris

⁓

28 July 1944

Dear Bessie,

I very much hope that you will have a wonderful time in Sheffield, as the surrounding countryside is very fine and you only need good weather to ensure a good break. In any case it will seem grand to have real sleep, in a bed. I hope that you will dream of me . . .

I shall be pleased to receive the photo in due course, although I shall not be surprised to hear that you have had a lot of trouble getting it done. Phew! What a lot of room paper takes up. Today I hope to get a chance to burn your letters.

I am glad you thought No. 2 was a smasher – oh lucky mortal to be able to keep your letters. I am so sorry I must dispose of yours. I think I may ask you to send me a letter, which is only composed of the nicest sentiments and the most truly expressive phrases, so that I may always keep it with me, never have to dump it and can always pull it out and let me see what you think. Perhaps when I get settled, I will do the same for you, oh my Darling. I am so pleased that you are not feeling meek and mild. I am often just like a roaring lion. I want to roar, and bore into you. I want to feel you all over, touch you lovingly in secret places. For me, you are beauty, glory and delight. Please, my dear one, accept that as a profound meaningful declaration on my part, of deep desire for you, of real everlasting intention to be with you in all ways, and whatever may happen.

I love you.
Chris

$\sim$

3 August 1944

My Dear Bessie,

Unless I am very careful I shall be slobbering throughout the whole of this letter.

Honestly, I cannot be casual about what you are saying to me. You are stirring me till I gasp. Although I bravely but sorrowfully burnt almost all your other letters, I feel now that I must keep these latest ones, and so, because I cannot trust you to my kitbag, or that artful little corner in my gas respirator where rests my odd other letters, I needs must have a big pocket bulging in front of me, containing what you have sent.

About our after the war programme, I don't know. We shall settle our troubles better when we know what they are likely to be! It may be a week, a month, but I know that it cannot be much longer. Fortunately our furniture does give something of a start, and we shall have a fair amount of money between us. I expect your Dad will let you have your bed (although I suppose it is part of your other possessions) and no doubt my Mother would let me have mine.

I am wholly in your power. And I know that you are wholly in mine! This cloth (perhaps a small handkerchief) – will you place it on your breasts (no, rub it on them) and then send it? Please. It will take a long time to come, but I shall know when it does, and I shall treasure it and envy it its luck.

I can understand your rows with your Dad. I haven't been on the best of terms with my brother since you enchanted me. He seems to be in the way, obtrudes.

Thank you for telling me the costume you were wearing. I would give a lot to see you in it, though I suspect you would not be in it long. I must take you somewhere, a long way from anyone, away to our own spot, as soon as the time comes.

I love you.
Chris

~

4 August 1944

My dear and lovely Bessie,

You can imagine how I felt today to get your photographs, on top of these LCs I have lately received! How lovely you are! How really nice! How much to be admired! Dear, dear, dearest Elizabeth, what are you doing to me, what are we doing to each other? How did I not see you, why was I blind, what can I do? I do not want to use ordinary words and usual language to tell you how dear you are to me, how I ache and wait for you. You are worthy of so much more than I can ever hope to give, yet your love inspires me, and makes me think I might succeed with you. I shall return later the photographs taken at Great Yarmouth and Rannoch Moor. Both may be a little bit precious to you, and the FOUR (it's grand to have so many) others will be wonderful for me to drink in.

Already I have had a dozen quick furtive looks. I am looking forward to the time when I can take my first long look at them, when I am by myself, when I can imagine the better that you are with me. Now, when you look at my photographs, you can wonder if I am looking at yours at the same time. There will be many times when that happens, for I shall look often. Look at you holding your skirt, look at you showing your bare feet, look at you by the boat, and be delighted at the curve of your breasts revealed by the jumper. Look at you with the other girl ('I'll soon polish 'er 'orf' – Sweeney Todd), at your little velvet trousers, your bare knees. Whew! You have done something now!

I LOVE YOU.
Chris

∼

12 August 1944

[Italy]

My dear and lovely Bessie,

This will be a short and hurried letter to convey to you the news that I have recently had a short and safe sea journey, and am having a most interesting time, as well as looking forward to the times ahead. You can imagine my relief when I discovered I was not bound for India, and my pleasure to be again on the same continent as you. The sand that fell on the stone floor here when I made my bed here last night is the last I may ever sleep on again. I have no great complaint about Libya, but it is good to get away from the eternal camel, sand, khamsins,* and to see again trees, houses, streets, civilians and other near-England sights. As I have only been here a day, you will not expect much news of the place. Apart from varied uniforms, there is little sign that there is a war on, and no sign of lack of food. Many of the young children present a similar appearance to those in Egypt, but the adults are well dressed and look true to type. The women are attractive, languorous, and their clothes are of many types and materials. (I gave my issue of preventatives to one of our chaps whose appetite is larger than my own.) There is a good NAAFI, and a YMCA. At the latter I bought 2 cakes (with a penny each) and a cup of tea for – 6d. (10 lire). There are some fine, but very dear, silks and satins on sale. Strangely, not many ice cream shops, although I had a wonderfully cold limonata today for 6d.

There are plenty of nice tomatoes about, almonds, pears, etc. I was unfortunately unable to travel with my brother, but will shortly be joining up with him again, to recommence our journeyings together and swap recent experiences. The best thing about the sea journey was its shortness. The conditions below decks, in the space provided for the Other Ranks, were slightly worse than those I endured for seven weeks, eighteen months ago. You could not imagine those conditions, and I am not going to attempt to describe them herein. Later I will send you a letter

---

* A khamsin is a hot, dry, sandy wind.

I shall submit to censorship. I am sure every ordinary soldier abroad lost a stone in weight during the journey. The behaviour of the chaps was very much better than previously, and the food was greatly improved. I slept on decks both for comfort and as a safety measure. The main thing about any wartime sea journey, however, is one's safe arrival, and I thank the chaps in the Navy for mine.

Now I want you to understand that from now on my warnings of a few months back, about imagining that my lack of words means lack of fundamental interest in you, really do hold good. At my desert station I had plenty of opportunity for writing. Now, I am on the edge of a new life, the brink of adventure, the fringe of something I have never experienced before. I do not know where I may go or how long I shall be there. I cannot say to myself, 'Ah, I'll write Bessie tomorrow' – for I shall not know where I shall be tomorrow. I want you always to bear my new circumstances in mind, and never to think I am for a moment leaving off thinking about you with my head, and writing you letters in my heart.

Censorship will naturally be more frequent, and I shall find myself rather discouraged in illustrating the strength of my desires regarding you. I am very sorry that this is so, and I hope you will not fail to appreciate the new position. I shall always write you as often and as much as circumstances allow. I shall think of you, you will be a part of me, now and in the future as you have been in this recent wonderful past. I shall dream of you in whatever awaits me as I have dreamt of you amidst the sand, and, lately, on the sea. Do not worry about my safety, do not worry about the sureness of my love for you, or the glory you mean to me; you, you, you, alone.

I love you.
Chris

～

23 August 1944

Dear Bessie,

I can quite easily understand the appeal of My Lady Nicotine in present circumstances, and had awaited some such little 'confession' as you are good enough to offer. You can be a human chimney if you want to be one. I know you will be able to reduce it when conditions make human beings of us all, again. I wish I could let you have my free issue, which in this Command is a weekly 60 cigarettes (Park Drive last week, Craven A this), 2 boxes of [matches] – and one bar of chocolate. I wouldn't worry too much about saving money. We shall be fairly well off compared with many. I forget how much I am saving each week. Either £2 10s. or £2 15s., I know.

I do not carry your letters about with me now. It was only on the boat. I could not risk you being 'dispersed over a wide area'. In any move, you – your letters – travel with me. I am sorry I had to burn so much of you – later I will tell you of the few letters I saved.

So your Dad is now retired. A little job would be useful for the reason you give. You are bound to get on each other's nerves. Don't think I shall regard you as a horrid cat if you do flare up. I'll control you alright! Glad you are still getting the *Statesman*, thought you might have lapsed it.

I want to hold you now and always.
I love you.
Chris

~

27 August 1944

Dearest,

I have now moved from the dusty camp, and after another journey by cattle truck, the details of which are too Army-ish to describe, have arrived at a site, perhaps the most pleasant I shall ever be in, whether in the Army or out of it. Just as I am overpowered by you and not very eloquent in telling you, so this place is so full of natural beauty that it defies the efforts of an ordinary man to describe it. We are in a valley known locally as 'Happy Valley'. On three sides there are the hills, covered with trees of infinite variety and much beauty – and on the other side – the sea; ten minutes' walk from the camp, from which it is always visible. (I am sitting on the beach in the cove writing this, at the moment, having just been in the warm sea.) This place might be anywhere in England for the forest aspect of the hills, anywhere along the coast for the peaceful quiet of this cove. When you find a place like this in England you hope that no one else will 'discover' it. Out here there is no fear of anyone else coming, as there are only half-a-dozen farm houses to be seen situated on the slopes of the valley.

We climbed a pear tree and ate what we picked. We ate blackberries, thick upon the bushes. There were lemons on the trees, oranges, pomegranates, limes, walnuts (not yet ripe), almonds, figs, prickly pears (from cactus), elderberry bushes: locusts. Events in the war send me hoping ahead to my hope of early return to home; to you, to your arms, your lips, your bosom.

We met an old man who took us to a couple of fig and pear trees, shook them and told us to help ourselves.

Love
Chris

~

3 September 1944

My dear Bessie,

No mail came yesterday, but I am, as usual, quite hopeful that some will arrive today. The news about the Allied men in France is very good, and I hope it leads to the end of the flying bombs. I suppose there is a good chance of them setting up their sites elsewhere, but they cannot again be such a menace.

My decision to burn your letters was the sort of decision one has to make when a move is made. You should witness the heart-searching that goes on, when chaps consider whether they shall or shall not discard books, papers, letters, tables, beds, chairs, lamps, tin cans, buckets, and private kit and excess kit. Slowly, then rapidly as the necessity for doing so sinks in, a pile of odds and ends grows on the floor. It is tossed outside, and if there are chaps staying behind they come along and take what they want. In our little move yesterday I gained a German aluminium 'Trinkwasser' container. It holds about 2½ gallons of water, and is very light. I have had a private ambition in this direction ever since I first saw one. This one has been used to hold paraffin, but I am washing it out frequently and it will be OK to drink from shortly. Just as the new dress or new suit makes you a little happier in peacetime, so last night, I was a little happy when I went to bed.

Today, Sunday, fifth anniversary of the war, is a strange day here. Thunder and lightning and rain. The rain is nice to be in, but if it keeps on for any length of time, we shall be in some trouble. Tent life after rain is no joke anywhere. There is much that is very enjoyable in the kind of unit that I am in (almost non-combatant in most cases), and after the war when one comes back to streets, trams, houses, every day except Sunday when perhaps a 'hike' may be undertaken, most of us will notice the difference. Do you get one 'rest day' a week, or less frequently than that? Do you get only one Sunday off each seven days, and how do you feel about working on a Sunday? Even in the Army there is always a little difference about Sunday; 'Reveille' and Breakfast are usually half an hour later, and probably one only works in the morning.

Throughout all this movement, shifting, this war, I think of you and want you. I can sigh for you. I can cry for you, and know that you can hear me.

I love you.
Chris

~

5 September 1944

I am now having a daily massage for my hips. I omitted it yesterday because the previous day I had had diarrhoea (a result of some grand black grapes) and had to report sick with it. I suggested to the masseur that it would be unwise to do his stuff that morning. I had a day's excused duty, and am on 'light duties' today and tomorrow, though I am quite OK now. While I was there I saw a chap who was going to hospital with malaria. Yesterday his temperature had been 106! Terrific, isn't it?

I expect you are delighted with the news from the fighting fronts. I hope you are, to yourself, quietly understanding that the people to whom honour and praise is most fittingly given are the dead and the wounded whose efforts have made the successes possible. The non-appearance of the Flying Bomb for several days is a fine bit of news for all of us out here who are from London. I hope there will be no more.

6 September. Hard luck, I have heard the news since writing the above and learned that you had some Flying Bombs, but I hope there will not be much chance of the Germans launching any more.

I went for a walk in the valley last night, and was delighted to add three more fruits to the list I sent you earlier: apples, damsons, plums. I sampled them all, the plums were jolly fine, although we only saw one tree bearing them. They were grand. When I think of our plum tree at home, the blossom of which is carefully counted by my parents to discover whether we shall have 13 or 14 plums this year, and look at this tree, it makes me wish for a little of the Italian climate over England. I do not want you to buy it, but I should be pleased if, at your convenience and when you are looking in a bookshop on your own behalf, you would have a look for some kind of popular book on Geology.

I love you.
Chris

~

13 September 1944

Dearest,

I received this evening your LCs: 22, 23, 24, 26 and 27. I was very, very, very pleased to get all these letters after so long a break.

I was a little sorry to discern that you are still uncertain about our future, still doubtful of the depth of me. But I want you (I have warned you) to remember the varying circumstances of my writings, and always take for granted that I LOVE YOU, that I know what that implies, that I know what I am saying, and am determined to keep on saying it so long as you will let me. (Please read that last five lines again [from 'always take for granted . . .'], slowly.) I have been leaving the public page blank lately because sometimes I feel it would be a bit of an anti-climax to use it and always I have to bear in mind that there are 'nosey' people who can see what I am saying if they care to look (chaps playing cards on same table as this).

It doesn't depend on what you look like or whether you can cook or have ever read *King Solomon's Mines*. I love you in my bones.

If my letters stop, will you again wonder about my constancy? If you get only a few words on a LC, or a Field Service Card, will you again be a'doubting and a'worrying? – Please don't. I want my lips to meet yours in understanding, I want to caress you, to kiss your breasts, to put my hot hands full upon your breasts, to squeeze till you cry out. I want to put my face in your bosom, my hands to your loins, then to kiss, then to salute, to meet you there.

I love you.
Chris

22 September 1944

Dearest,

The White Paper on demobilisation, published this morning, is all that is being talked about by our chaps. I think that it might be worse. I have written to Sir E.T. Campbell, my MP, urging him to represent that (1) no scheme shall be allowed to detract from the need for bringing home quickly all men who have spent any length of time overseas, (2) that for such service, one year shall be added to the age, for each two months spent abroad. I don't hope for much from Campbell, but I think it right to let him know the view of most chaps here. He is a Conservative, a supposed poet, responsible for these lines:

> 'It is Hitler, the Hun, we are up against,
> For all that he does is sinister,
> And the best way to put an end to him,
> Is to assist Churchill, our great Prime Minister.'

Don't, for goodness' sake, spend more than a couple of shillings on Geology. I should be disgusted if you did, as I shall have the run of the libraries when I get home.

You say my sex (as though I care tuppence about them) have been dirty dogs to women in the past. I am under the impression that men have been 'dirty dogs' to men, and 'dirty dogs' to women, and that women have been 'dirty dogs' to men and 'dirty dogs' to women. But I think most women are (unfortunately) fairly content to be regarded as nice pieces of furniture. Honestly, right now, wouldn't it suit you? And aren't you prepared for me to treat you as a piece of furniture at some time or other, despite my high flown equality reasonings? If you are not, then you will probably be shocked. Hope your plums will delight you – next year. Sorry, too, about these flying bombs. I wish they'd finish so that I could have a little more peace of mind.

I love you.
Chris

~

23 September 1944

I have now finished skimming through the great file of printed papers that Deb sent me. One of the reviews in *The New Statesman* was about three recently published works on Geology.

In my last LC I asked whether you did not expect sometime that I should treat you as a piece of furniture. Really, I think I am bound to do so, though I shall probably try hard not to do anything you don't want. But you can be sure I will occasionally forget and on those occasions expect your forgiveness, which is a sauce, but natural. You see, I want so completely to dominate and possess you. If I were less certain of you I should find my thoughts less riotously arranged, but I know that you await me and have waited long, and I want to fling myself upon you and devour you.

I do not think I mentioned that while in town the other day I went to the ENSA pictures. – *Frontier Badmen* – the only one I remember in it was Diana Barrymore. It was all about cattle selling and more or less rustling. Set in 1869, the gunmen all had automatic pistols that appeared to fire on and on and on. We shared a box (free, by the way) with a couple of Americans, and I felt like an argument about the superiority of US films, but there is a certain barrier between us, and nothing happened. We are like their poor relations.

Here, because there are no real washing facilities, I get my laundry done by a woman about here. The other day she invited me into her living room (there are no passages, one foot over the front door and you are on top of the big double bed). I went in, rather awkwardly, and looked about me – shrine, stone floor of course, pots and pans, but not dirty. On the wall a photo of a male child, aged 2, I should say, nude and front view. Funny way of going on, to us, but I suppose that everything is due to be judged by different standards. I gather that no one out here eats tomato skin. They are thrown away. The main meal seems to be a hunk of browny bread, with tomato pips and juice on the top.

I hope you are well.
I love you.
Chris

Geology For Everyman – the late Sir A. Seward (Cambridge, 10/6)
Teach Yourself Geology – A. Raistrick (English Universities Press, 3s.)
Geology in the Service of Man (W.G. Fearnsides and O.M.B. Bulman)
   Pelican 9d.

26 September 1944

My Dearest, Dearest One,

I am pleased that *Bartlett's Quotations* arrived. Was it badly knocked about? You do not seem to be as delighted with it as I imagined. Have you seen the Index at the back, you can put your finger on anything with its aid. It had a lot of Shaw, so you should be able to remind yourself of much. Have you looked up Kipling? Read A.P. Herbert 'When love is dead'. There is hours of sampling to be done, if you will. I don't expect to use quotations with you in those far-off happy days when we shall be TOGETHER. I shall be original if at all possible.

I have just bought one of the long handled straw brooms to use in these parts (60 lire). Had to get a receipt and took the Interpreter along. The lady who sold the broom could not write, but her 13 year old daughter could, and signed her name: Maschia Maria Bruno. Excuse my occasional failure to start the letter off properly. Oh for a place where I can write you fully and privately.

You ask me about the chaps who have been abroad, whether they are depressed as much as a newspaper article says. My comments on this if in full would require to be censored. I have no desire to talk of 'blooming old newspapers' as though they were benevolent Uncles. Apart from *Reynolds* and a rare exception elsewhere, they are owned by people who would chain my body and cloud my mind for ever. The regulations do not permit denunciations, so how can I say much? 'I want to go home' is everyone's chorus out here, although the reasons are not always the same. YOU are my main one.

I love you.
Chris

~

4

Nuts

28 September 1944

Dearest,

In the last six months (and it is not much more than that since we turned to each other in gladness and relief, for comfort and security), we have seen much of what is in the other's mind. I see you more clearly. I love you more dearly. From having a hazy idea, I have a clearer outline. I have learnt to respect you, I think a little more, because, although there are things to be straightened, there is so much evidence of our mental suitability, and that, whether it is my mind or not that is the clearer, we are nearer each other than we thought. I do not want to think of you as a fool, and I have had no reason to do so during this period. My every glance at your letters tells me of your intelligence. I want you to believe that. I want you to know that I think it. I want to tell you that I am proud of you.

You know that, before I left the desert, I had to destroy most of your letters. I kept a very few, I felt that I must because you had said so much to me in them. I kept your surface mail of the 1st January – 'I plonked up the blackout, slightly lopsidedly and with hat over one ear' – 'I am wallowing . . . in the past, and having a wonderful time'. You asked me what I had that 'other blokes hadn't got'. I knew I had nothing, but I knew that you had always thought I had. I can't understand why my reply took 12 days to write, but it did. Yet I really think that 7th February, the day I got your letter, was the day I started wanting you, since when I have grown to want you much more. Remember a letter where you said you were alive between the legs, that you were damp, that I had made you so? I kept that. Because I glory in your dampness, because you make me damp. Because I am interested in your body and between your legs. Remember writing of 'all guards down', of being attuned to me, of sharing my upsets, of your lower regions aching with desire for me? I kept that.

I stare at your photographs: I don't know how I got on without them. But the day will come, the years will go by, and I shall be at your side, to do your will.

I love you.
Chris.

∿

1 October 1944

My Dearest Elizabeth,

It has been raining hard for nearly twenty-four hours, and things are pretty damp around here. This does not affect me very much at present (my main concern is the dampness of the latrine seat!) as we are in a big house and the rain does not get in, but of course most of us react to weather very quickly, and it is miserable to have leaden skies where once was blue, and to see everyone wet and miserable and bedraggled. I didn't have any mail yesterday from you (though three from home with the good old newsy items about my brother's romance, the wireless breaking down, and so on) and none came for anyone today, so my one hope of cheering up through the general depression has gone. I am having a very easy time just lately and doing some tidying-up and writing around. This afternoon – goodness me Sunday afternoon, but it is no different from others – I have been reading extracts from Dickens in a book *The Younger Characters of Dickens* and it is good to be reminded of Oliver Twist, Squeers and Mrs Squeers, Old Fagin and the rest. The chap who remains in the office with me asked what I was reading. I told him, and he said 'Piffle – I like a good cowboy yarn.' I need hardly say that his views on other subjects are those of an obedient stooge of the kind produced by reading the *Mail* and the *Sketch*, and that unwittingly he does just what they want him to do. His history is bad, his geography is worse.

I hope you are liking better *Bartlett's Familiar Quotations*, for, honestly, I think it is a magnificent collection. My own little book in which I enter noteworthy things, I have called 'Barker's Unfamiliar Quotations'. I have entered the one of Goethe's (how do you pronounce his name?), 'All your ideals –' which you sent me.

We shall not have an easy time immediately I return, because restraint will be necessary. I am hoping you will be able to do something in the way of house-finding before I return, but I know it is difficult. I also hope that when the flying bombs are finally settled you will feel like looking for little things of use in the home. You'll need potato peelers, egg whisks, all sorts of things which if you can get beforehand will save us a lot of trouble and delay. When we first meet perhaps I shall be a little rough, but with your help I cannot fail to improve. I will be what you want me to be. I want your beauty for myself – I want you, I want you, I want you.

I love you.
Chris

~

2 October 1944

My dear Bessie,

We have so much in common, so much need of each other, so much to say, so much to do, yet all these things are nothing to anyone but us, and we must wait our turn in the long queue of

107

human beings waiting their chance of happiness. There has been a recent order showing that the War Office is not unappreciative of an angle on the subject. Men who have been separated from their wives for three years may apply for compassionate leave if their wives are over 35 and, being childless, are desirous of having a child. This would suit us fine. The only barriers are (1) we are not married, (2) we have not been separated three years, (3) you are not over 35.

I have been hearing more of the customs of these folk in this village, and it is probably the same all over this part. There is no 'courting' before marriage. The young man writes his prospective wife's parents. They consent to him coming to tea. They are never left alone, and the first time he holds her hand is when they are man and wife. Some marriages may be arranged in Heaven, but none are around these parts! None of the girls dare be seen talking to men (let alone soldiers), lest they be the subject of gossip. Our chaps are not very happy about feminine availability, although some have had happy moments, though a little expensive.

I met a chap here, eighteen months younger than me, who went to the same school. We had a good talk about teachers and remembered pupils. I have also had a talk with a chap who lives in Leeds. Married a couple of years before the war, one child, been away from England two years. His wife gave birth to a child (by a married man with two children) in June. She asked for his forgiveness, but not unexpectedly, it has not been forthcoming. I have heard many similar cases, or variations on the same theme. It is nice to think we live in a world of constancy and adherence to vows, but we certainly don't. I rather except from this the quarrels of engaged people, and so on, because they have not achieved moral and legal responsibilities to the extent of the married. Some of our chaps moan about the Yanks at home, but there is plenty of evidence that many Englishmen do not act honourably.

I hope to goodness that I shan't go to the SE Asia Command after this European side is over.* Anyone who goes there from here will be very unhappy, although India is only 4 years now, which means I only have another 2 years and 4 months to do to qualify. Does 2 years and 4 months sound very long to you, my darling? Somehow, there are times when it seems not bad, and others when it is too long to contemplate. 850 days! Sometimes it seems only yesterday I wrote my first letter to you. Sometimes it seems that I have been writing you and wanting you all my life.

I love you.
Chris

~

3 October 1944

I usually smile a bit when I write 'private and family matters' on the back of this Letter Card, when addressed to you. All that I say

---

* Several of Chris's letters from this period contemplate his possible future placements once victory in Europe was achieved, which now seemed likely. He was clearly under no illusions that the defeat of the Germans would mean an immediate return.

is so very private! And I so wish we were in the same family, and your name the same as mine.

When you ask, in No. 34, received today, for 'ladles of applause' for your voluntary banishment of my Lady Nicotine, you do not ask in vain. Of course, I am impressed with the stand you are making, of course I admire the way you are denying yourself the queer satisfaction of the leaf, and of course I know that quite directly you feel you are doing it for me, and I, your servant, am pleased with you, proud of you, glad about you. If your appetite for food has improved since you kept in check your appetite for tobacco, I am pleased. I think that food, in the long run, does you more good.

With some of the things you say, I can almost hear you breathing, warm and close by my side. The occasion when you touched me (actually you 'grabbed' my arm) was during a Week End School held, I believe, Sept 1937. (It was the first we ever held, it was my idea to hold it, and I did most of the work behind the scenes, as I usually have done, although I have also been a possessor of the stage on most occasions.) We got there Saturday afternoon, a lecture I believe, and then all went for a ramble in the evening, some to a nearby pub. Somehow we became detached from the dozen or so other ramblers. It was a lovely evening (I mentioned in an earlier letter how the sun was glinting through the trees). Then you said 'May I hold your arm?' and held it for just that space of time I required to shake it off. I believe I quickened my step and rejoined the rest. I remember it well; a kind of significantly well, if you understand me. I wonder if you do? I have not suddenly remembered it because I want you now, I have remembered it through the years, throughout my little adventures. Probably because I made a mistake, because I should have let you hold my arm, because I should have gone on from there, with you. We might have done so much, we might even have done a little on that sun-glinting evening. But we haven't, we didn't, and here we are without more than hopes and expectations (they're great alright), with no real accomplishment.

I love you.
Chris

~

6 October 1944

My dearest one,

I am feeling a little tired tonight, so if this letter sprawls ungainly over the page, and I get irritable, please forgive me. I have done the last of four parcels for my brother – and – what do you think, sewn up another tin, this time containing a tin of green oranges (about a dozen) for you. I am a little dizzy now with what is on the way to you, but here is my diary record:

    Sep 18 – NUTS
    26 – NUTS
    27 -NUTS
    Oct 5 – NUTS (and 2 lemons)
    6 – ORANGES (1 lemon).

I hope they all arrive safely, and that the fruit is in good condition. I feel that you must get some, and if you don't I shall be extremely displeased with someone. I picked the oranges and lemons off the trees myself!

There are two things that have been in my mind to say since receiving the wonderful letters 33, 34, 35. One was to say that I do not like the word 'nipple', either. I hesitated quite a bit before using it, but decided I would have to, to say what I meant. You will see by now that I later on said 'tips' in another letter. I'm sorry; I hope you found the alternative acceptable. The other thing was the power you imparted into 'vital vibrant spot'. My dearest, I received everything, all the whole of what you intended. I was very close, I was very near, I was very stirred.

Your list of favourite poets interested me, but I was mistaken in my previous choice. I will have another try as I get the opportunity.

How is your tobacco taboo proceeding? I hope you are holding out and bearing up, my brave and courageous lady.

I wonder when I shall get your handkerchief, to smell, to feel, to hold against me. I want it a lot, something from you, something of you. Blow me, Bessie, I could do with you, near me, beside me, with me. Some day I shall come to you and speak to you, of what you are to me, of what you mean; I shall thank you for all that you have done. I shall ask you to take the big chance and marry me. I shall ask you to live with me. I shall ask for your sympathy.

I love you.
Chris

~

9 October 1944

Dearest,

As anticipated I was able to get into the nearby town today, and am writing now in one of the two excellent NAAFIs which it possesses. I shall be able to write this without interruption because I am my own boss for a precious brief period, and can do as I please.

When I first reached a side street, several little boys asked me if I wanted a girl: I thought it better not to try to explain to them that you are the only one I WANT. The stalls yielded no fresh treasures. I think it would be a good idea if you were to let me have your sizes (other than shoes, unless the 5½ slipper is a larger size than the ordinary walking shoe) and also tell me how many yards of material you need to make a blouse, dress, skirt.

Another thing I thought was, perhaps now that winter was upon you, your thoughts were turning to knitting socks for me. (Pardon the presumption if you hadn't toyed with the idea.) Well, please don't, and don't be unhappy at not being able to spread your activities on my behalf to my feet. I left England with 13 pairs of socks. Over a year ago, when we thought we were moving somewhere, I had to get rid of 10 pairs, the Army number being 3. The number is adequate, and others are an embarrassment at times when, in order to lighten the load, our kit bags are taken from us. Of course, I'd like you here to darn them (though I fancy they would remain undarned if you were here!) but that is not possible.

Various blokes have 'heard it on the wireless', but I haven't seen in the newspapers, a statement by Churchill that you may be able to confirm, that before being sent to the Far East, chaps out here would get home leave. It seems too fair to be true, but I wondered if it was. If so, and I came home under that scheme, we could get married if you then feel as I do, we could get married, we could live together and sleep together and be together. I used to feel that embarkation leave marriages (of little more than juveniles) was a mistake, but perhaps we are not juveniles and in any case if I was anywhere near you I could not keep from you, and I don't think I should try it.

What a joy in the meetings of everyday. To be able to see you whenever I wanted! To be able to go about together, to wash up together, to go to the pictures – and come home.

I love you.
Chris

$\sim$

10 October 1944

My dearest, dearest Bessie,

I must write this very quickly to be sure of its despatch.

Yesterday, after my town visit, I returned to the village fairly miserable, rather dejected, and hoped for mail. It was

10 o'clock at night, and there was mail. Your 37, and your pen and handkerchief. I tell you that I was struck powerfully with the wonder and delight of you. The pen (I am using it now, this is the first time. It is going well), an indication of you, the handkerchief – oh, my dearest, nearly a revelation of you. I was hot and weary. I unfolded it, took off my spectacles and buried my face in your sweetness. It was cool, fragrant, hope giving. I cannot tell you of the happiness and quiet sense of being at home that I felt as I kept my face to it, as I smelt YOU; it was an experience. A wonderful, wonderful lightening of my burden. When I finally took my face away I felt that I had had a little secret while with you.

I love you.
Chris

~

12 October 1944

My Dearest,

I had just sealed down No. 65 when your 39 was handed to me (38 missing). It was the one where you had been disturbed in the bath, an alarming affair which I can appreciate but little, even though I have had 'alerts' when in the bath at home. Such a little more clothes on and we feel so much safer. Of course, I had no comets overhead to frighten me. What a time you are having, and I do hope you will be completely safe throughout your upsets. I am glad you are not a bath fiend. The average working person hasn't the time to bath daily. I always think drying is a nuisance. If the water has been hot, the bathroom is very moist, and the towel does not really dry you, it just stops you being so wet. I can imagine you sitting in the bath and reading my letters, but surely looking at photographs and bathing is a hazardous combined operation?

I think that I had better take the opportunity of saying now that I hope your birthday passes happily, and that it will be the last one you celebrate as Miss Moore, Mrs Barker. I am sorry there isn't any chance of being with you in person, to celebrate the fact of you, and I feel that you are not likely to get a letter from me on that day. But do remember I shall be thinking 'It is the 26th. It is HER birthday.'

I like Richmond. I have been there often, and know it fairly well, but not in the winter when your 'low lying, near river' criticisms are no doubt well merited. Sevenoaks is about 45 minutes by train from Charing Cross, probably a little too far for us. But I like SE. Don't go anywhere special, please, just keep your eyes open and think where you would feel yourself most happy. Although we keep assuring each other that we shall be 'poor but happy', I think our financial position will be fairly sound (after Orpington, as I have heard the porter at London Bridge call out so often, the stations are CHELMSFORD, KNOCKHOLT, DUNTON GREEN, and SEVENOAKS).

I don't think you are likely to be a ball and chain to me. You are likely to be the grease on the banisters down which I slide. You have never shocked me, you never will. You always thrill me and make me glad and proud about the possession of you. Elizabeth, I love you. Let there be no regrets ever.

Chris

~

26 October 1944

My Dear Bessie,

I think I may now tell you what I can about this ship, which is travelling through the sea as I write this, with me looking out to sea. It is the best of the three ships I have been on. We have bunks, and I am in the middle of a tier of three, mattresses are provided, also two blankets, and the whole atmosphere below decks is much cooler than other ships, although a great deal of this is due to the weather, which here is no warmer than an English June day. Our meals are eaten in another part of the ship (not under our bed space as in my two previous ships) and they are excellently cooked and tastily served, although rather small. Instead of two sweating mess underlings attending you, the meals are served direct from the galley, cafeteria fashion; you only need your own mug and knife, fork and spoon, as your plate consists of a metal moulded tray, with six declivities of varying size: the bread goes in one, the sweet in another, the pickles in another, the cheese in another. The tray is a kind of stainless steel, shines brightly, and is rather nice. Probably you know the stunt, maybe your own British Restaurant ('Plonk – Plonk – Splash' as you once said) uses it.

It is a pity that I am now a few miles further off you than when I was in Italy, but so long as I am on the same continent, I am fairly happy. I have wanted for some time to go to places where Allied Armies had not tramped too much. I prefer to help blaze a trail (in this unit!) than follow after several millions have used it. I should be able to write fairly interestingly of this new country, but you will not expect anything 'startling', since anything in that direction is forbidden.

One thing, please do not seem to think that I think you are unintelligent or dumb. I think you are intelligent and no fool. That is not to say that I think you have got the right slant on the social life, insofar as you know the working people are being 'done', but you cannot really see much good in doing anything about it. I think you'll come to see the use of action as time passes, but in the meantime, please don't write as though I think you are silly. I think you are at least up to my own standard, and you'd probably agree if you knew how low it was.

I have just had a couple of hours on deck, 'under starry sky' as the poets would say, watching the phosphorescence on the water. Grand sight as the ship speeds through the dark waters. Would I have liked you with me on the deck? Would I! I am leaving the rest of this page until I land, to let you know the latest position that I can. Sorry this writing is so small, but expect you'll tire your eyes with great joy! Elizabeth, I love you.

Chris

~

26 October 1944 [Second letter]

My Dearest,

Today is your birthday, and I am thinking of you. I got up at six o'clock and my first thought was of you. I commence this at 7.30, on a very fine, Spring-like morning. The limited view from the window as I sit at my desk discloses trees, mostly pine, and in the distance, mountains. I am glad that we defeated distance in telling of our love.

I wrote the above before 9 a.m. this morning. Now p.m., and two good things have happened. (1) I have received 42, 43, 44 and 45. (2) We are now allowed to mention that we are in Greece, and, too, that we have seen the Parthenon, Acropolis etc, and visited Athens. It's mighty fine of the Censor!

I have just returned from a visit to the nearby town, and am just starting a night duty as I write this. I have done a great deal of walking and feel a little tired and not too capable of telling you all that has happened since we have been in Greece. Tomorrow

I should be able to write you the first of a properly connected account of the welcome we have had, and what it feels like to be a 'Liberator'.

SOCKS. – I am pleasantly appalled at your hard work on my behalf. Honestly the Army issue of three pairs is adequate, and it is all I have had for over a year, since I threw half-a-dozen pairs in a well in a Tripoli garden. But (aren't I good?) I won't throw yours away. I shall welcome them, wear them, and think of you. But, please, desist, my lady, desist. Please don't worry about sending me anything. I will tell you anything I need, without fail. Please don't send me your favourite book – but tell me what it is, so that I may know just that little more about you. Thank you for letting me have your measurements – your bust, your hips, your waist – lead me to them! is what I think, and I am sure you will lead me.

I love you.
Chris

~

27 October 1944

My Dear Bessie,

Athens is a city on holiday, a people celebrating after years of suffering, a great communal smile; laughter, happiness, joy,

120

jubilation everywhere. It would do jaded Londoners good to see what I, treading on the heels of the Germans, have seen. It would do them good to have the Athenian welcome as I have had it.

Imagine travelling with half a dozen other chaps in a truck, running through banner-bedecked festooned streets hung with bright coloured declarations of welcome and praise for England, being cheered and applauded, loud and long, by single individuals or groups of people, as we rushed along. Imagine everyone sitting outside a cafe getting to their feet and clapping. Imagine that happening at a hundred cafes. Turn a city into a stage, make the British Army the players and hear us warm to the genuine joyous proud applause of the appreciative audience. Imagine every house flying flags, sometimes only the Greek, but generally our own, the US, and the Red Flag. Imagine every wall painted with well meant slogans and salutations, many in English (some pidgin English!) and many in Greek: 'Welcome Our Liberators' – 'Greetings Allies' – 'Wellcome to our Dear Allies' – 'Good Luck to our Greit Allies' – 'Hip Hooray for the British Army' – 'Welcome Heroic English' – 'We salute our Heroic Liberators'. Imagine having flowers thrown into the truck.

Imagine walking along a street, receiving the full smile and the frank staring admiration of every passer-by. That is our luck as we make our way through the beautiful avenues and squares, the first non-goosesteppers since 1941. Whatever commercialism may do tomorrow, today the soldier is receiving his reward, on behalf of those in the British Isles who have not been beaten by German ingenuity. We may like to make our own reservations about the value of certain British policies and politicians, but in their naive trusting way these folks think of us all as a wonderful collection of people. It is a great feeling.

Have been to the Parthenon and Acropolis as well as seen the Parthenon floodlit. Currency here has been ruined by the Germans. 500 drachma to the £1 in peacetime. Now, 6 cigarettes cost 2,000,000,000 (two thousand million) drachma. I have several billions worthless notes which I will send you later. All for now. Hope you are well and happy.

I love you.
Chris

~

29 October 1944

Dearest,

I am glad you find my letters worth reading. There is nothing 'too good to be true' about this, our love. I know you have faith in me. I want you always to have the deep secure feeling that I love you and desire you.

It looks as though getting a place will be a harder job than either 'getting married' or 'living together'. I am afraid we shall be hard put to it to find accommodation. Have you thought that we might have to stop apart until we did get somewhere? It makes me sweat! Do not get too many mental pictures of me 'toddling round the house'. It is not good for you. I have already told you I have made a note of your measurements in my pay book. In Italy, as you say, there was a shortage, but it does not seem to apply here, though the prices are un-understandable at present, and we have to reorganise the currency for the Greeks. Until that happens, purchases are foolish and actually prohibited. But there are literally miles of all kinds of cloths and many other things which I will consider one day when the currency is stabilised. A little girl in Athens told me it cost her 10,000,000,000 (ten thousand million) drachma to pay for a seat at the pictures.

I cannot advise you on personal hygiene, and I am not going to presume to discuss the anatomical problems or marital difficulties. First of all, I am not competent to do so, secondly I should find it difficult to do so by letter. You will be silly not to see a doctor if you think he would assist. I should do so myself in similar circumstances.

I am a bit puzzled, too, about where we are to live. I hope to goodness that we escape Clerkenwell, or some such place, but it's a possibility. You'll be partner, assistant, follower, in turn, and I shall be very happy to perform for you as occasion demands. I have learnt much from you, and I am very ready to spend the rest of my time learning more. Remember, everything is mutual, and what we give we take back from the other, in some wonderful, satisfying fashion.

I can, when all is said, say no more than I LOVE YOU.

Chris

~

3 November 1944

Yesterday, I received a LC No. 47, and *Geology for Beginners*. Thank you for both. I am afraid that Geology will be a closed book to me for a little while yet, but my glance through the book confirms your intelligent choice of it, and when the hubbub has died down I hope to spend some useful hours learning from it. The scenery in this 'verdant suburb' is wonderful. Pine is the predominating tree, but there are many others. The earth is golden brown but the mountains look grey, black, red, white, most exciting, inviting us to visit them soon. I omitted to tell you of my move into the present billet, a very high class hotel in peacetime. Room 95, 4th floor, holds me (and my brother) at present. We have beds, mattresses, wardrobe, washbasin, table, two chairs, mirrors, bath (only cold water) across the corridor, lavatory a few doors away. The climb up is a little irksome, but I suppose Heaven itself would need some getting into. The floors are tiled, very easy to sweep and wash. It is easily the best billet I have ever been in. All the chaps are in the same position, two to a room. You would have needed plenty of money to stop here in peacetime and I am not worried by the fact that only a few days before I commenced to use it, my mattress was nightly the cause of a German having a good night's sleep.

Of course I shall wear the socks – and with pleasure and thanks. But no more or your eyes will be playing you games.

Ignore the news of early war's end, then if it does, you'll get a pleasant surprise. Japan, I believe, is immensely powerful.

I love you.
Chris

~

7 November 1944

Dear Bessie,

I hope you are not too horribly downcast and depressed at the form of my present letters. I hope you understand the newness and difference of things and that you will realise that in a little while I shall be settled down and more demonstrably attentive. Tonight, though, I am feeling a proper old crock, as I caught a cold yesterday and have a sore throat, running nose, etc., for almost the first time since I left England. You know what a hot-lipped, running-nosed, fuzzy-wuzzy-ed feeling one gets in England. I have it tonight, and oh my goodness, how I would like you to be my nurse!

I believe that coffee and cocoa are still not rationed in England. Could you, do you think, send me a quantity of both? We visit three families regularly and two others irregularly. I think I would like about two lbs of coffee and a pound of cocoa sent to me to present to them, I can split it amongst them. If you can get a firm to send it (there was a place by the Monument) it may be better. Register it, if possible, please. You may think this a funny request, but do you know these people have not had cocoa, tea or coffee for nearly four years. We have been able to take a few spoonfuls to a couple of them – they think it 'delicious'.

I love you.
Chris

~

12 November 1944

My Dearest,

The British Authorities have now announced stabilisation of the currency here, at 600 to the £1. Any of the old drachma issued by the Germans can be exchanged, at the fair price of 39 billion drachma to the £1. (39,000,000,000,000.) Soon we shall be able to buy fairly easily and know that the people are aware of the value of money.

All that I want to do now is to come and comfort you, to tell you the flying bombs and V2 rockets need not frighten you, that together we shall always be safe. I want to tell you that nothing can stop our union and our joining, our loving and our living together. I think I am more pleased now about your willingness to be a piece of furniture. You know that it is not that I shall ever treat you as such, it is that I want your complete trust, that you repose your full confidence in me to do as I will.

I hope to let you have some coherent account of Greece later. But for the moment, I am still in the overwhelmed state. The scenery is grand, everything is green and fresh, even to the little girls who spy you coming, rush to you with a little posy, and then run quickly away to watch you walk away with them.

No, I have not told my brother, or anyone, about my relationship with you. He must be most well informed concerning the number of letters that pass between us, and probably he wonders. But I shall not tell anyone. I suppose you had to tell Lil Hale.

Only little girls have wanted to kiss me. I do not get in the way of older females. In the nearby town there are many prostitutes. My Greek is much less limited than it was, although I do not swear that my pronunciations are always perfect.

I love you.
Chris

~

16 November 1944

My Dearest,

I am impatient to receive your second handkerchief. That is what

I must tell you before I go on to ordinary, trivial things. I want to smell it; I want to squeeze it in my hand; I want to press my lips to it. And I want you to know that I am doing it, proudly, gratefully, happily and in love of you. I have today sent some sultanas, and so on. But – what is the good of me mentioning anything but this great feeling I have for you now, will have for always.

I love you.
Chris

~

30 November 1944

Dear Bessie,

What a triumph for you with the pancakes! I wish I could have shared it, there and then. Did you have the lemon with them or are they long ago consumed?

Thanks for your good work with the cocoa and coffee. I am sure it will be appreciated by the Greeks, and you know that I appreciate it, appreciate you.

I am not a football fan, I am sorry to say. I have a far better idea of what constitutes 'off side' than you have, but I do not think I could pass as an expert before your Dad and Wilfred. The only knowledge of teams I have is of The Arsenal – my local team when I was a boy, and I could talk for a long time about Jock

Rutherford's bald head. You can tell me all about football. I shall not tell you much!

I hope you are feeling well and not too unhappy. These rockets must be shaking everyone, but I hope you will be as brave as usual, and that they will not interfere with your sleep too much.

Remember that you are mine, that I want, that I love you.
Chris

~

5 December 1944

Dearest,

I do not like you to say you feel I am going to lecture you. I do want you to think of me as one who is fully entitled to discuss all that you do, in the same way that I am very happy to discuss my thoughts and actions with you. If you place any restrictions or reservations upon our interchanges you are saying we are two, not one. And it has pleased me to think that we were one. We cannot explain your actions by flying-rocket bombs or a cold you may have. I think you had better read all my letters, all over again! Anyhow, I sent you yesterday a green envelope, returning your handkerchief. I hope you will accept this as symbolic of my needs, intentions and desires.

I am sorry the elastic has no present purpose with you, perhaps it would be handy for someone at your office who has a baby nephew, like we have. My sister says it is very good and we have just sent her about 10 yards of it.

Regarding your cookery programme. I have no doubt you'll be alright. I reckon I'd be alright myself after the slight Army training in independence that I have had. It could be a fair idea to buy a cookery book if you feel you need one, and I should get a second-hand one for preference. But you should certainly be doing some cooking now. I know that if I was back home I should want to 'have a go' at things, although probably only while the novelty lasted.

Tell me you believe. Do not worry about present happenings. I am perfectly safe, and like yourself, perfectly superfluous to the situation.

I love you.
Chris

~

The socialist-led anti-Nazi resistance movement EAM, and its military wing ELAS, had won control of most of Greece, apart from the large cities. This led to civil war between EAM and the right-wing, royalist EDES party. Churchill was alarmed at the prospect of communist rule, and with the return of George Papandreou and the British forces, confrontation with EAM seemed inevitable. After

15 communist protesters were shot dead, fighting broke out between ELAS and the British on 3 December. Chris Barker would soon be involved.

5

Untapped Resources

27 WOOLACOMBE RD

LONDON SE3

6 December 1944

Dearest,

So very worried about what is happening in Greece. On the news tonight, it spoke of it spreading and seems to have become a battle, my worst suspicions of what the British Army went to Greece for are fulfilled. I don't know how this is affecting you and whether the ordinary people are involved. Of course you won't be able to tell me much, I can only just hope for your safety. Your safety – oh Darling! The trouble seems to be centred in Athens, and you spoke of visiting it, so I presume you aren't billeted there. We should have them to settle their own troubles. We will regain the name of perfidious Albion again before this war is through.

Darling, I have no complaints about your letters, I am too happy that it is my body that you want, that occupies your thoughts. If you didn't write and tell me these things, I should suspect you of being interested in somebody else's body; you keep concentrating on mine, my breasts, my vital vibrant spot, my hands and my desires. You are mine, mine, mine, and don't you forget it, don't you ever forget it. I don't understand what the greater significance of a Greek engagement is, but ours has the greatest significance for me, no Greek one could be greater, you are mine, MINE, <u>MINE</u> – to have and to hold until death do us part. You are my husband to be, my glory, my heaven, my hell, we will ride this life together, if you were here now I'd bust your braces, you tantalising lover, Greek engagements! Greater significance! POOH!!!!

Well, I am glad you have 4 blankets to keep you warm, if I was there you wouldn't want any, you'd be hot enough. Here am I, a blooming iceberg of a maiden waiting to be roused into a fire, not just melted but changed into a fire, and there are you, miles and miles away, needing an extra blanket.

During this last month I have reached rock bottom, I now feel something like a convalescent – no longer need a nurse, Christopher, I need the whole vital man in you, your strength, your energy, when, when, when will you make me a whole woman, when will I be done with this frustration, when? Stunted growth, that's what I am suffering from! My body is stunted, my affections are stunted, even my blooming mind suffers from this incompleteness. I want to be your mistress, to be used to the uttermost, I want to fuss you, look after you, I want to be your companion in arms – away with depressions, fed-upness, waiting. Angel, I want to feel human, I am so sick of being a cold, haughty virgin. Crikey, talk about untapped resources. Why did I have to find the man of my life in the middle of a blooming desert, who then goes on a Cook's tour and then gets himself into a hot spot of trouble. Oh Christopher, I do hope you'll be alright.

'My apprenticeship' – books, books, books, I am sick of those too; I want to live, live with you, oh! Why couldn't you have come home instead of going to Greece, why can't I come out to Greece, so that I could stand in the way of any stray bullets.

Write poetry to me Chris? You have already written poetry to me, music as well, I doubt whether you could surpass it, it isn't easy to express these things in words, but you have done it, you have moved me, right down, down to the foundations, you have accomplished what I shouldn't have thought was possible, you have opened a vision of a new world, a new experience for me, I cannot help but be so very very grateful to you. With that in front of me, I can overcome my black moods and rise up again and know that this life is worth the living. Oh Christopher I do adore you so.

Pancakes, yes we had your lemons with them, that was why I made them. I rather think your lemons helped to get rid of my cold, maybe your letters as well. All those things help, you know, the lemons on the practical side, and the letters on the mental side.

Thank you for the sultanas which are on the way, I do feel considered, my thoughtful lover, such a nice sensation. You don't know what a relief it is to have a pair of slippers, I have been wearing my shoes in the house, it was wretched not having anything to slip my feet in, you know, for when you get out of bed, after a bath, for evenings.

Football – well, I shan't be able to tell you anything either, I don't exactly dote on sports, activities of the mind have always appealed to me more, thank goodness I shan't have to watch you perform on the playing fields, you seem to have plenty of outlets for your energy without that.

I had to giggle about my 'bravery' in bombed London. I live here, work here, and there isn't anything else to do but live here and work here, and like most things up to a point, you get used to it. It's one's low resources that one has to be brave about, all one's usual aches and pains get you down easily, any extra effort tires you out, but as we are all in the same boat, that isn't so bad as it sounds, it's communal you know, makes a difference, besides the battle fronts sound so much worse, I concentrate on that when I feel pathetic. I shall be concentrating on Greece, can't help it, the situation sounds so much worse, the news tonight says civil war.

Darling I love you, love you, so very much.
Bessie

≈

A portrait Bessie sent to Chris in Libya in 1944

8 December 1944

My Darling,

The stop-press of tonight's evening paper says it is quieter in Athens today, that ELAS have contacted the government today, I hope this is true. It is horribly difficult for us to get at the truth, Churchill calls them rebels trying to enforce a communist dictatorship, but the *New Statesman* says they represent the people. Whatever has happened, it has caused a shock in this country, but not enough to do any good, Greece will still be ruled from here by Churchill and co. When is Churchill genuine and when is he a humbug – is it necessary for us to enforce order? Feel very unhappy about it, fighting the Greeks sounds too awful, wicked. I hope all is well with you and our Greek friends. You said you were going to give me the family trees of the families you visit.

The weather sounds lovely there, whereas here, well – ! It tried to snow today, horribly cold. I don't know whether I told you that I bought a pair of lined boots (getting all prepared for the worst). I wore them yesterday and it wasn't necessary, and didn't today when it was. What is a girl to do in this climate, had cold feet all day. Very breezy these luxury flats – we have such a palatial entrance hall and carpeted stairs, but inside the flat, it's bare boards, the lavatory is always going wrong, and the water in the bowl won't run away – luxury?

Feel very worried about all those depressing letter cards that you are receiving, or are about to receive, my conscience besmites me, I didn't oughta have done it, I didn't. I wonder what your receiving mood is like, I do hope it's full of beans despite all the present trouble.

Our Xmas cake has been taken out of my hands. Iris's sister Doris is going to make it, she is rather an expert. I had thought my last effort was rather good, I took Iris up a piece and she said so, and she is quite a good critic because she likes cake. Beyond this our interest in Xmas is nil. I am working Xmas day. Xmas is a family time, children's time, I expect you will enjoy yourself in Greece with your friends' families, anyway I hope you will be able to.

Am just listening to the 9 o'clock news and it's most disheartening, it says it's spreading not slackening. Oh Dear Christopher! I really can't think of anything else, Darling, I do really want to be cheerful, but it's so blooming difficult. Xmas! And you out there. I love you, I love you, I love you, and my heart is aching, it is so lonely and desolate without you. My mind keeps going into such flights of fancy on how to get to you, from stowing away on a ship, to applying to the war office, so blooming silly, but it does get so bad sometimes.

I went to see *The Circle*, John Gielgud's production, a play by Somerset Maugham, didn't think much of it, so was glad you couldn't come. Lil Hale wasn't very impressed either and she is rather keen on Gielgud's acting. To me he seemed such a milk and water specimen, no fire, no life in him, just a beautiful voice, too too cultured. I think I have got a bit choosy over the theatre. Have seen some really fine plays during the war. My standard has got a bit high.

I have been horribly chatty in this LC, that's the result of worrying. I have kinda got you on my mind in a different way, the situation in Greece is getting in my hair, despite all efforts to remain calm. Keep calm is my motto, very tiring you know. But I do wish I knew how things were with you. Keep well, keep safe.

I Love You.
Bessie

~

9 December 1944

My Dearest Angel,

I expect the news of Greece has by now nicely alarmed you, and that you are not without concern for me. I hope you will take this as a token of my continued safety and welfare. I am enduring no hardship or privation, and am subject to very little inconvenience. Later on I shall doubtless be able to tell you something about the present happenings, but for the present you must put 2 and 2 together and – if you are wise – not be too sure that the answer is 4. I listen to the wireless news from London with great interest, and find much food for thought in this whole proceeding. A flickering oil lamp illuminates this page as I write now, for it is night, but when I wrote before, there was a smoke pall over the city and I could hear the 'PUFF-BOOM, BOOM-PUFF' of the guns. I should very much like to tell you what I think and know, but this is not possible with me a soldier. Perhaps you will feel aggrieved and misled that I did not tell you this was liable to take place. I could not have done so without breaking the regulations, and in any case, I did not think it would be so soon.

If one approaches things with the idea of learning from them, I cannot say I am sorry to be here. But this is one occasion when it would be far better for you to be elsewhere. But do not think you are out of my thoughts. You can never be that. I decided this afternoon that I had better burn all your letters that I had (my last was 57) and I did so. I dislike burning your letters, but they are so much mine that I always feel it is best.

I was sorry to hear on the wireless (invaluable link with the outside world always) that London had had a brisk time with rockets last night. I hope you are safe and will always remain so. I do not feel very hopeful about an early end now, to Hitler and his works (mostly his works) but I have felt a little happier about the chances of escaping Burma etc, because if they do send ME and CMF [Middle East and Central Mediterranean Force] men home before going to other theatres I should be able to talk a bit when I get to England. By that time, I shall be as bald as makes no difference! I am not too much interested in the thought of getting home, then being sent out again. What I am interested in is getting home, getting out of the Army, marrying you, settling down to a happy, domesticated existence. I want to be with you and stay with you always. I want the warmth and the strength and the beauty of you, and to you I want to bring all my ability to make you and keep you happy. Please do not worry over very few letters.

I love you.
Chris

~

10 December 1944

I had not planned to write to you again so soon, or to hear from you again, but your letter (No. 58) was dropped today, and eagerly I gulped the manna that was in it, quickly I must respond to your apparent need of me.

It is no good me trying to 'kid' you that I know very well how Londoners must feel under the swift threats of the rockets. You do know that I went through the blitz in 1940, but this is quite a small thing, a tangible thing, against present horrors. I believe that Zola worked in a coalmine for 6 months to get the atmosphere for his novel *Germinal*. I should have to hear at least one rocket before it really came home to me that there were such things. Similarly you'd need to live in the desert to understand the actuality of miles and miles of sand. In other words, imagination cannot take us all the way . . . yours, try as it may, cannot conjure up my present situation. You just, rather naturally, suppose the worst.

I do hope that you will not get too, too, too downhearted about your present mode of living. You must always remember that it is the world, and not you, that is wrong and at fault. So when you feel desperately tired and unhappy about bombs, the weather, your colds and other ills, don't take them as personal deficiencies, remember you are not responsible for them. Try and do as I have told you in the past, what I do, now that I am in the Army. Think about things as little as possible, and remember that no amount of worrying can alter them. The grim happenings here would perhaps have more worried me had I been a civilian in London.

But for us – US, more than anyone – life will be grand in the days to come if we will it so, if we trust. I shall come back to England, an England that I knew and in my fashion loved. (Have you ever been chestnuting at Sunningdale in October or blackberrying at Caterham in September?) And I shall brighten up your scene, I hope, and make you see things in a new and better light, so that we both realise we had not lived till we met, till we loved.

You are a little, I think, unduly anxious about my possible conduct away from you. In the desert there was no temptation and the chaps behaved well. Here, the married men vie with the single men in their enthusiasm for the new life. I can assure you that I have nothing but contempt for those who break pledges, either to their wives or their sweethearts. You are my sweetheart, I am pledged to you. I love you. There is no need for you to worry further. Probably I spend too much time contemplating you, but it is always you that I do contemplate. It is your warm beauty that I want to lie upon, to rub against; between your legs that I want to come. I want to touch you between your legs, I want to feel your hands upon my privates.

Tomorrow it will be lovely, for I will be with you.

I want you. I love you.

Chris

~

11 December 1944

My Dearest Angel,

The shame in my heart for the burning of those letters is burning a hundredfold, I have been in such a state over what is happening in Greece that I had been too worried to dwell upon that. But it has come back in a rush, your words 'I will love you though you never believe I love you', 'I will love you whatever blows you deal me'. Oh gosh! That got me badly, very badly, went much deeper than any censure. Wretched creature that I am, may I try to explain just a little what causes me to hurt you so senselessly, not consciously Chris, no no, not consciously, only the usual fashion of the bull in the china shop with the inside of a fawn.

Dearest Christopher, it is not easy to surrender myself so completely as I am doing, at my age, a much more tender age to be in love than at 20. What I feel for you, Dear One, is love, this is not settling down, getting married, and having children, it's something so much more, so much bigger. You have caused an upheaval within, an upheaval that contains so much sweetness, ecstasy and pain, something that I didn't think I was going to

143

know, something that I thought did not exist because I had not known it. It is new to me, you are new to me, I trust myself to you so gingerly, a little afraid of, not you Christopher, but of the unforeseeable. So that I am on the defensive, I let everything go with a rush and then put up a guard to ward off – goodness knows what. I guess it's the uncertainty of life in London that enhances it, I want to rest with you in peace, but you are so far away.

I just have not known anyone like you before, or perhaps it is no one before has made me want to give so badly, give so badly, so that the giving makes me feel afraid. Darling this is all so hopelessly womanish, I really don't know whether you can understand the paradox. I do understand your need, because it is my own, but can't you see how tremulous, how inadequate it makes me feel, because the opposite feelings go together, one doesn't exist without the other. It's like touching the stars and touching rock bottom. Darling, understand what after all I do not understand myself.

Rockets? Yes it could be, but it goes much deeper than that. The misery inside me through having to live without your presence, the misery inside me through the spectacle of the world engaged in destroying one another for five years. I suppose it's linked up with the rockets, but one doesn't think much about them until they drop, they don't occupy much of one's thoughts and imagination, not like the pangs of the world. You and Greece are hopelessly mixed up in my mind, torn all ways. I want the fighting to stop because of you, and yet I wish they could win.

I received the green envelope with the photo, and felt very touched by both your letter and the message on the back of the picture. You Darling man with the Dear bald head. You know it isn't quite bald yet Ducks, give it time, it will probably last ages like that, afterwards you can train one hair across the top. I'll look after it and encourage it, and you need never be quite bald.

Will be very glad to have a closer snap of you, always needing to look at you! Would be glad to see photos of the places you've seen also.

I shall keep the returned hanky as a hope of the future, our union, our union Christopher, it's a gasping thought isn't it.

Goodnight Darling.
I Love You.
Bessie

～

12 December 1944

Dearest,

I am particularly happy to get your letters just now, and I hope they'll come along in double quick time. You mention that you have the 'jitters' about the situation here. I wish I was as free as you are to comment. You'll understand that I am not. But do not worry about me in the slightest. I am quite alright, and sad though it may seem, finding things very interesting.

I may be very wrong, but I do believe that blazing lights and chocolate, ad lib, feature in most people's post-war imaginations. We should have something more than éclairs, but we should have éclairs, as well. We should enjoy the lights, too. You, more than me, because I have had lights (of Durban, Cairo, Alexandria, Naples, Athens, and many more) for two years. I cannot visualise meeting you when I return and not immediately living with you.

Everything here is very safe, and please don't think I am in any danger.

I hope that the rockets are not worrying you too much. In the hope that you will get this before Christmas, I will say I trust the weather will be as you want it, and that you have a nice time. Soon we shall have a Christmas together – all our days together. It is a grand thought to have. And wonderfully we share it.

I love you.
Chris

~

14 December 1944

Darling,

Oh Christopher. My dear sweet man, I feel so wretched at having hurt you so, feel all the pain of those unwritten words. You didn't have to write them Chris, I can feel them. I too have thought a great deal on 'why did I do it', honestly searching myself for the reason for that impulsive action. I have really trusted you so much, committed myself on paper to a point of outrage, in a way that isn't too easy, but you called to the depths of me and I had to answer, I just had to give you all I could in the only way possible, and I did it because all of me responded to you with a force that I wasn't aware of possessing. That is why I keep telling you of the newness, the wonder of this our meeting, our coming together. You are as precious to me as life itself, for it goes on and on. You move me now as in the beginning, in some ways more, because somehow it seems to have developed, somehow more solid or something, I don't quite know what, but I feel it.

This has taken such a long time to write, and yet somehow doesn't say what it should. I long for the words of the poets, for they don't keep repeating themselves. I feel under the stress of all this, I ought to be as creative as the poets, and put it all in such a new way, to convince you that there is no need for you to feel unhappy about my doubts anymore, not anymore, Christopher, my so precious Lord. Immediate evidence to hand, I did think of the returned handkerchief in the same symbolic way as you, angel, didn't I? I will hold it, keep it, crush it, and wish you could be as close, wish that I need only feel affectionate and could stretch out my hand to you and you would answer with your caresses over my asking body, wish that you could flood me with your warmth. Oh for the time when I might awaken during the night, hear you breathing beside me, feel the warmth from your body, and snuggle down in sheer happiness and comfort in the knowledge of your presence. Oh delight of tomorrow, when will you come?

The elastic-hum, what do you mean??? says she, coyly. If you were home I'd welcome it, yes I very much suspect I would, before and after wedded bliss, seems to me it would have wear and tear. (I hope.) It's beautifully strong elastic, should stand up to it well, perhaps we should hoard a supply.

My cooking activities will have to remain rare owing to circumstances. Dad has his dinner midday from Mrs Baker which absorbs our meat ration. Cake making is rare because we drink our sugar ration, even the cooking of snacks isn't very often because Dad is a bad shopper, and I can't shop often enough to catch the odds and ends that are to be had on occasions. My diet is a most uninteresting repetition, so that I have become disinterested. I had thought of buying a cookery book, but hadn't bothered because they are all war time recipes. I hadn't thought of a second-hand one, though I suspect with the book shortage, second-hand books have done a roaring trade, though maybe second-hand cookery books may not have been touched. I'll have a look round Charing Cross Rd at the first opportunity. Oh dear I would like to start putting us on the map, to start building our home. I want time, lighting, and no rockets. Perhaps in the spring, I wonder?

This you and I is breathtakingly wonderful, I can rest content in the future prospect. Oh so much more than content, but dash it all Chris, can you really expect happiness in me now? You are my horizon, that wonderful faraway horizon – I cannot be content, I cannot rest easy whilst it is like this. I strain at the leash towards the future, our future, I want you, I want you, I want you, now, now, now. You can tell me to be happy, to be content, to stop going up and down, but I cannot help it, you fill my imagination, but

I want you here, in my arms, the flesh and blood. You are right it is bad, bad, bad to be away from each other. I don't want to differ, I want to bend with you, see things your way, my way is so uncertain. This brings me to Orson Welles, was *Citizen Kane* just a flash in the pan? Time will tell with his next efforts for his *Journey into Fear* was not mad, it was just plain silly, kids' stuff, it made me laugh, and it wasn't meant to. Anyway perhaps we can see his next effort together, and I can change my mind or agree to differ. See things together!!!!

Don't get any stockings, please Chris, you'll probably take awful colours, the wrong size, and probably be swindled as well. If you feel anxious to get me something try hair grips, kirby grips if possible, you know the short metal grips girls use nowadays instead of slides, also a comb would be useful, very hard to get at the moment. Prices here are haywire, fantastic. Will prices remain in this haphazard state? I think not, for it is always shortage that causes it. When things are being manufactured again prices are bound to drop, it is foolish to buy now. As for the stockings, if I get in a really embarrassed state over them, I shall ask you, don't worry I shall ask. I am still in a repairable condition, which I think will last till the summer, anyway we get some more coupons in February and we have high hopes of them being more than previous years. After all this I see you want me to think up a list, hum, well it just isn't worth it, unless it's cheap.

Wish these rockets would pack up. I hope the information of your safety is true. Shall feel much happier if an agreement can be reached.

I Love You.
Bessie

~

16 December 1944

Dearest,

Yes, the news of Greece has nicely alarmed me, which is putting it very, very mildly, I am afraid. I am not much good at this soldier's wife idea. I try, but I feel I ought to do better, goodness knows what my temper will be like after a week of impatient patience. I have been stormily arguing about Greece at the office, and been thoroughly rude to one of the bosses, ended up by calling him a fascist. He came up the next day and asked if I felt better. He is the why-bother-with-politics type (it only makes you miserable), and I guess he represents the mass weight of public opinion, and I guess I am no improvement, for I do nothing.

Nearly all the press are supporting the Greek people apart from the *Telegraph* and Beaverbrook, all progressive sections are downright in their condemnation of the Churchill policy, but the whole mass I am sure are still behind him and he knows it. Perhaps the idea of the war being extended ad infinitum may move public opinion, but I suspect it is food that will tell. Oh dear, the best of man is in his imagination not in his actions. I suppose Churchill really does believe he is doing right, he must do, or he wouldn't go through with it. On reading this through it looks rather messy, but I feel rather like that. One wonders so much whether the war has been waged for nothing. Aldous Huxley insists that violence breeds violence and we get nowhere, in fact slip back. Perhaps he's right.

I fully appreciate your position as a soldier, that you could not say anything and cannot now. All I can do is hope that you will be alright, and worry my way through this time as best I can. I am thinking of you, hoping for you, with all that is in me, I too think of that 'settling down' time for us, though I don't think of it in those terms. For me it is 'beginning to live'. You want tranquillity now, quite natural, but when you have that, when you have a home of your own, when you have me for love, comfort and peace, always there, always behind you, you'll want to fight the good fight with even greater strength. Whatever you'll want to do, I shall fit in, and try and answer your demands, whatever they are. You'll make me happy by just being there, in our home, Dearest One.

Keep safe Darling.
I Love You.
Bessie

Bessie (second from left) with friends on the beach, 1930s

18 December 1944

Dearest,

I'm very tickled to find I have not sent you the season's greetings, either by LC or airgraph. Greece has put everything out of my head including Xmas. Don't feel very Xmas conscious anyway. I had hopes of some sort of an agreement, but they have gone to pot today, newspaper headlines say British troops in gloves-off offensive. There is still a lot of agitation here to make the government change its attitude, but not enough I guess. I really feel it's because people are fed up with war, not being informed about what it means to Greece, the average person feels that Greece is being unnecessarily troublesome. I don't suppose you'll get my little packet by Xmas now. Wished I sent an airgraph, I bought it ages ago and kept it for a suitable date, alack, alack. I hope you won't feel neglected by me of all people. I wonder what is happening to you, what you are doing, how you feel about all this. I received the hanky with one strand of hair, one strand of hair!!! I kissed it and nearly lost it, but only for one agitated second, it is safe now in my bag to carry around, to occasionally touch, as one day I shall touch so much more. You have been so close to me, so close.

I received No. 9 today, which I presume is No. 95 written 10/12. Though I was schooling myself to wait a week, I still kept my eye on the mat; you can't imagine my feelings at receiving the unexpected, and what a lovely unexpected, you Dear Dear Man. I never appeal in vain, when I so need you just that little bit more than usual, you come back at me with such a rush of warmth and understanding, somehow you leave me speechless, to be able to say just the very things I want to hear, and so beautifully. You really are a poet, it moves me to the vision of beauty – us in tomorrow. Christopher, you Darling, my heart is bursting. You have soothed me, caressed me, in such a lovely way, I gasp and gasp at the wonder of you, that you should have sensed so much.

You do not know how much these words meant to me: 'An England that I knew, and in my fashion loved'. I needed those words from you, more than anybody.

I shouldn't really feel anxious about your possible conduct while you are away, because we love so much, we do really care. I know it's just as unthinkable for you as it is for me, my heart is in Greece and nothing else can touch it, but I know of so many people whose lives have gone awry it's a bit horrifying, and I think you might feel tempted in a lonely moment. I don't mean cheap temptations. No, as I write that, I don't believe it, because like me you don't allow the situation to arise, there can't be temptation when all your heart and mind and body is straining to somebody so far away. No I won't worry further. We are one, we really do care, in each other we can rise above the second rate, you make me feel that. You do brighten the scene, indeed you do, we will, will it so, in those future days, grand days – we trust. Oh we do trust, Chris.

To go out together – knowing that we shall go home together, knowing that we shall pass the night together – to go out together knowing that – I think of that so often, really just belonging – that makes my inside sing, to be together so that I can answer your demands, make my own, just put my arm around you at any time, sometimes in public, would that embarrass you? I know it's rather a possessive thought, but I do feel rather proud that you are mine. I could be rather blatant over that in front of your friends. Am I being too awful, but I can't help that proud elated feeling. To put it baldly, you are a wonderful catch. I want everybody to know you are mine. How do you feel, Christopher, do you feel caught? Joy oh Joy. Nobody else matters really, it's just one of the joys on the side.

I have got to get down to dashing off some letters, and contacting a few people. I have solved one by telephone today, I hope to solve a couple more by telephone, another by a visit, and the rest will have to be letters. Have given up present giving with my pals by mutual consent, thank goodness. In the end it becomes a racket, much too wearing to keep up, most of 'em can't afford it, so found it kinder to cut it out. It's most awkward this business of being unable to give people anything without they must return it, most natural I suppose, but difficult with present financial straits. Funny how people get the urge at Xmas time for a holocaust of present giving. You should see the crowds in town, all trying to buy what isn't there. Perhaps it's just a day out for them. Dear oh dear what a game.

I wonder how you will spend Xmas, I guess I should feel different if you were here.

Oh! Darling, I Love You.
Bessie

~

On the day this letter was written, Chris Barker was stationed in Athens' Hotel Cecil. He awoke to shouts from ELAS (the Greek People's Liberation Army), of 'Surrender comrades, we are your friends.' He wrote in his notebook: 'At 11.30, ELAS started serious attack: shells, Bren, rifle, mortar. The last was quite frightening . . . Mortars started firing and got very close . . . Panic in the passage. "Close the door!" The Bren gunner still outside . . . got more ammo, then with Bert and Jack sat on the first floor landing. Ordered downstairs, then upstairs again. Bofors or dynamite through end passage. Much glass falling under shelling . . . Then, suddenly, "Cease Fire!" Joyously, all over the building the cry was taken up . . .

'Came downstairs, laid down our warm weapons and was greeted by long-haired partisans, with "Hail, Comrades!" during the dark hour, before dawn.

'Led away in small parties while above us the Spits (Spitfires) looked wonderingly on . . . Walk about 4 miles to a mansion. Lady partisans. Lovely, interested and approving. Water and 2 ozs of bread. Then about 15 mile march through the woods and forest glades. Led away to a mountain fastness blindfolded.'

~

6

Not Bournemouth

21 January 1945

Dearest,

Not having heard from Deb that your folks have heard anything, I am hanging on to the old old theory that no news is good news. The papers and wireless say that the exchange of prisoners of war has commenced, am hoping that this affects you, gosh I hope so badly. Churchill said in his speech that prisoners would be coming home and that the truth would come out, just supposing this also affects you. Is that too much to hope – to come home, to see you after all this worry, if it only could be true? I hope you aren't hurt or ill, that you have been warm and at least had enough to eat, feel sure you haven't been overfed, for they haven't enough for themselves.

Oh Darling, perhaps it won't be too long before I hear, I wonder how long the exchange will take. They do fiddle so, over these sort of things.

What thoughts have you been having during all this long time? About Greece, I mean. I would so like to know, for it is such a muddle, politicians lie so glibly about such important things; doesn't make post war years look very hopeful.

Just another missive, Christopher Darling. Keep safe.
I Love You.
Bessie.

∼

24 January 1945

My dear Bessie,

Technically this is my second day of Freedom though I have only just got off the truck which has carried Bert and myself through the cold Greek mountains over tracks that once were roads, and now, with the thaw, are becoming quagmires. The most satisfactory journey of my life. Now, the warm hands of the British Army are about us and we are as comfortable as possible.

The great worry of my non-arriving letters probably cannot be effaced from your 'system'. I must have added many grey hairs to those you have already. But now you can stop worrying, and get drunk tonight with easy conscience. (I have happily gulped two rum issues since I was released.)

Will write you very fully later. Use the usual address, and be sure I shall write as often as I am able. Our future moves are a matter of conjecture. Most of the optimists think we will be coming home. If you think we should there is nothing to stop you writing to the Prime Minister, suggesting our return to allay relatives' anxiety.

Forgive this note. I hope you are well and undisturbed by aerial terrors.
I love you.
Chris

~

26 January 1945

Dearest,

I have studied all the newspapers, but there isn't any references to prisoners in Greece. The *New Statesman* is still banging away on behalf of the EAM, and Sir Walter Citrine* is talking a lot of muddled unfathomable stuff about atrocities, so still don't know whether the censor is having all his own way. Surely there will be something in the press when prisoners are exchanged. A few small exchanges have been made, but nothing about the 600 prisoners that the RAF have been dropping supplies to. Unless I have missed something in a corner – don't think so. Oh!

Darling, what a day when I get a letter from you – telling me that you are alright, and maybe coming home. I wonder so much,

---

* Citrine was General Secretary of the Trades Union Congress.

wonder if one day I shall come home and find you – in person, on the mat – just dreams, of course. I went out with Deb, Lil and Iris, to a theatre last night. It was a good play with Alfred Lunt and Lynn Fontanne, so that made me forget for a bit, but somehow I can't manage to keep my mind on any conversation. I am no stimulating companion these days, more of a wet blanket I fear, though I do my best. Where oh where are you Christopher my Darling? Days have become weeks and still no news. I can't settle down to read, not even in the train, so I am knitting up into vests the spurned coupon-free cotton-cum-wool, instead of writing loving letters to you. Am I bottled up –

I Love You.
Bessie

~

28 January 1945

Dearest,

The return to writing in ink (and with your pen) is an indication that things are a little more normal. We had a short sea trip from Volos to Athens where we are at present. I have only had a truck ride through the town at the moment. It seems very little damaged.

Athens is only a temporary resting place for us. What happens depends on decisions already taken on what may be altered in the light of opinion. All the RAF personnel have been informed (in a printed Order which I have seen) that '– as soon as possible you are being returned to Italy and thence to England.' It would be quite unfair for unequal treatment to be meted out to different Branches of the service who have suffered precisely the same, and I know that those at home will represent this view as forcibly as possible. RAF people concerned are ground men only. If all goes well we shall get home with the RAF, if present indications are any judge, and if nothing is done, we shall not.

It is a little difficult for me to write very well when within me there is the jumping thought that soon – very soon – I may be actually telling you these things. But I will make some attempt and know you will not mind any deficiencies.

I spent some bad hours lying with my brother in a shallow trench outside the hotel, while all sorts of fire was shot in our direction. Mortars were the worst, and when we returned to the hotel an hour before the surrender, we counted ourselves lucky to be alive. We were attacked for a day and a half. Well, when the 'Ceasefire' was given we laid down our warm weapons and came out with our hands raised (just like the pictures!) past a bearded partisan who pleasantly said 'Hail Comrade.' We lost everything. I had £7 or so on me, and my two most desired (I think) possessions – my Overseas Record of Events and my 'Unfamiliar Quotations'. I still have them, and am delighted accordingly. I have just received your mail, 6 letters and four packets (2 coffee, 2 socks), a bit of luck as had they arrived before 'the day' they would have been lost. More about your dear letters later. I know how you must have suffered. But now it is alright. (The socks seem wonderfully well knitted. The photo was great.)

We spent the first ten days marching. About 120 miles, through rain, snow, hail, at times; always very cold, always hungry. Our overcoats were taken, and we had no blankets. Jack Crofts, Bert, and I had terrible nights. No sleep, very cold. It was best during the day when we could get some warmth through keeping on the move. The three of us regard ourselves as fortunate in our experiences. Many chaps had very bad times, boots stolen (you can imagine how this affected one, stockinged feet in the snow), underclothes taken, trousers and blouse removed and very thin, ragged clothes given in exchange. You should be wary of believing all that you hear. Many chaps with small minds are anxious to be thought heroes or martyrs or something, and we had enough press correspondents to interview them all. Everyone has a 'story'. Nevertheless, I must tell you that very few people take the same view of the ELAS as myself. As a matter of fact, most of my prisoner colleagues would like to shoot the whole of the Greek population.

I will try to write you a nice connected letter in the course of the next few days. Until I do that, please excuse the absence of mail. Every scrap of personal kit, and 'buckshee' letter cards, went in the fiasco. But your letters must be very very small writing, for I cannot have enough of you, and I want you to tell me all about how you feel now. It's a startling, thrilling, bumping thought to think we may be feeling each other shortly. There would be no doubt at all about early leave if I was in the RAF. Very quietly write your Member and Mrs Churchill urging equal treatment for all concerned.

I have read your letters and been moved by your concern and the power of your love. Please have no worries concerning my condition. I am not as fit as I was, but my rheumatics are my only complaint and I shall soon control that.

I hope you have been spared the worst of the rocket bombs, which (now that we see the newspapers again) were so active recently, and that your general health is as good as mine. I think of you. I think of you. I think of you. I will write as much as I am able, but bear with me as I have much to do.

I love you.
Chris

~

29 January 1945

My Dearest One,

I have just heard the news that all the Army men captured by ELAS are to return to their homes. Because of the shipping situation we may not commence to go before the end of February, but can probably count on being in England sometime in March. It may be sooner. I have only just left our Major giving the signal as received from General Alexander. It has made me very warm inside. It is terrific, wonderful, shattering. I don't know what to say, and I cannot think. The delay is nothing, the decision is everything.

I must spend the first days at home, I must see Deb and her Mother. I must consider giving a party somewhere. Above all, I must be with you. I must warm you, surround you, love you and be kind to you. Tell me anything that is in your mind, write tons and tons and tons, and plan our time. I would prefer not to get married, but want you to agree on the point. In the battle, I was afraid. For you. For my Mother. For myself. Wait we must, my love and my darling. Let us meet, let us <u>be</u>, let us <u>know</u>, but do not let us, <u>now</u>, make any mistakes. I am anxious, very anxious, that you should not misunderstand what I have said. Say what you think, but please agree, and remember I was afraid, and I am still afraid.

How good for us to see each other before I am completely bald! I have some fine little wisps of hair on the top of my head.

It is not much good me trying to write about recent experiences now that I know that I shall be able to tell you everything myself within such a short time. I will tell you odds and ends in later LCs. What I have my eye on now is the first letter from you saying that you know I am alright, and the next, saying you know I am coming to you, right to you, to your wonder and your beauty, to your breasts. Plan a week somewhere (not Boscombe or Bournemouth) and think of being together.

What a bit of luck I got taken POW. In my imagination I am with you now. When I was captive I used to try and contact you and think hard 'Bessie, my dearest, I am alright. Do not worry.' I never felt that I got through, somehow. But now it is over, and you know that I am alright and going to be with you soon, to join and enjoy. Do not get very excited outwardly. I am conscious of the inner tumult, the clamour, but I am not too much outwardly joyful. Moderation is my advice. Watch the buses as you cross the street.

The time that will elapse before my departure will be spent mostly in Italy, where we shall be going, probably in about ten days' time. There is much that I can bring, should you desire it. Can you let me know what I might try to bring?

We are free of duties and yesterday I went to our friends in Athens, taking some of your coffee and cocoa, which they were very pleased to have. Thank you for sending it. We were embraced very excitedly, kissing and so on, continental fashion. We both had tales to tell.

Later in the evening, having taken a letter into the Hotel Grand Bretagne earlier, I saw (with some colleagues) the TUC delegation – I thought it a good chance to present a fair account and (you may guess) impress the return of Army personnel on them. They were going to see to it upon return if necessary. Fortunately it is now not necessary. It was good to meet one's 'own people' so far from home, and I felt happy to have thought of the idea and carried it out.

If you feel like I do just at the moment, you feel, my darling, jolly good. The immediate future holds fine promise.

I love you.
Chris

~

31 January 1945

I am commencing to write this on board the ship which is to take me to Italy, from which country it will be posted. We have moved quickly, and I do not know how soon we shall actually be leaving Italy for home. We are intended as a great propaganda effort, and this may speed up things. I am keen to be another month, to allow me to collect things – and to avoid this very bad weather which you are having at present! Isn't it wonderful to think that, although I am not due home until August 1947, I am actually on the way to you now?

I hope that you will not start buying any clothes (if you have the coupons left), because you think you 'must look nice' for me. I shall be sorry if you do. Just carry on as near as possible to normal. My return at the present time allows us to make public our mutual attachment. Deb's letter told me of your phone call to her. To her, and to my family, I shall say something like this – 'Bessie and I have been writing frequently to each other for a long time, we have a close relationship and a mutual understanding.' I shall tell my family I hope to spend a week away with you somewhere during my leave. My counsel to you is to tell as few people as possible (you can ring Deb a few days after she gets her letter, which I shall post with this) and not go into the depths of anything. Be brief, don't say what we plan or hope for. To someone like Miss Ferguson you can politely reply to her observations that you thought it was *your* business, rather than hers. Try to avoid preening yourself and saying much. This is my advice, not anything but that. I hope you understand. I do not ever want it to be anything but our affair.

Do not permit any intrusion. I do not know how long leave I shall get. I could get as little as fourteen days, and I may get as much as a month. I hope you will be able to get a week's leave without any trouble, and because of the position, you must more or less decide where we are to go.

I had better stop in London for the first week. I have suggested to Deb and Jessie that they, Iris, and a very few others be my guests one evening in a convivial atmosphere. I shall have to be pleasant to people like Miss Greggains and Miss Rowe and many acquaintances. I wish the war was over and that I was coming home to you for good. Won't it be wonderful being together, meeting, getting on the train, eating together, sitting together, being together?

I am wondering how I shall tell you I am in England. Probably it is still quicker to send a telegram than a letter, and I hope to send you one announcing that I am on the same island. I will send another when I am actually soon to get on the London bound train, and you can ring LEE GREEN 0509 when you think I have arrived there. Tell me how I get to Woolacombe Road, or to your Park Lane house (the number would be sufficient, I shall remember where it is) and I will meet you there, or some other place you may say, as soon as I can. You must bear in mind that I shall be with my brother until we get home. Also, that, having been away from home for so long, my parents will want to see (and have a good case for seeing) a lot of me. I hope that everything will work itself out without any unhappiness to anyone. I shall be in great demand from two or three points and it will be difficult to manage without offence.

My brother and I had hoped to visit the scene of our capture at Kifissia, not so much to see our late billet as to see whether some personal stuff we secreted in the building earlier when surrender looked likely, was still there. Unfortunately, we hadn't the time and must say goodbye to the chance, although we have left some instructions with some other signals chaps we know.

It is a strange thing, but I cannot seem to get going and write very freely. All I am thinking about is 'I am going home. I am going to see her.' And I expect you are feeling the same. I may be home in as little as a fortnight. I may be longer – but I cannot be much longer. It is no longer speculation, or hope, possibility. It is a fact, a real thing, an impending event, like Shrove Tuesday, Xmas Day, or the Lord Mayor's Banquet. You have to be abroad, you have to be hermetically sealed off from your intimates, from your home, to realise what a gift this going-home is. The Army doesn't worry much about chaps when they have to stop overseas for so long. It is a military machine, not able to spend overmuch time on personal matters.

The few letters of yours that I had on me, I burnt the day previous to our surrender, so no one but myself has read your words. In the first ten days of our captivity I did not think any soft thoughts about you, all I did was concentrate on trying to tell you I was alright. But when we had a few supplies dropped by aircraft (at great risk to themselves in the misty, snow-bound Greek mountain villages) and we started hoping we might get sent home upon our release, I was always wondering about you, about us. We are on the threshold now, not guessing at a distant date. I am sorry about Abbey Wood, but so glad about you now. I want to touch your body, to know you. It is a pity that the winter weather will not be kind to us out of doors. But it will be nice sitting next to you in the pictures, no matter what may be on the screen. It will be grand to know that we have each other's support and sympathy. It will be wonderful to go away where no one knows us and be by ourselves.

I wish I was coming home for good, I wish I was coming home to a peaceful England, with the war over. But, at least, I am coming home, am coming home to you, to your lips, to your breasts, to hold you tight, and make you happy.

As I expect this letter will arrive home before I do, I am enclosing two photographs, taken at Volos before we had paid 2s. 8d. to a Greek barber for haircut and shave. You will probably recognise me through the hair, although it was a bit of fun deceiving chaps who did not know you without it.

I, in my turn, was very pleased to get your photo and agree that it was lucky the girl on the right of the snap was obliterated and not you. You might have felt the reverse, but you look young and happy and as though you are smiling for me. Which is a nice thought for me to have. I want to bring your handkerchief back to you. To be away from everyone, everything, to not have to worry about the world, the war, but just to have my face in your bosom, to do what I have said.

The socks <u>are</u> well knitted. But I am not wearing them yet (if you don't mind) because I want to save them a while. How you knitted away, for me, for me, for me.

I can say no more, no less, than that I love you.

Chris

~

Chris (left) and Bert after their release at Volos in January 1945

1 February 1945

My Darling,

This is so wonderful, oh! Gosh! Christopher, I have just received your telegram – how can I tell you how beautiful the world is, contact again with you, contact with life. Oh darling of my heart, I did not realise what a benumbed state I had been reduced to. It took about a quarter of an hour to sink in. I did not whoop or prance but my knees went weak, my tummy turned over, since when I have been grinning happily to myself with a beautiful inward pleasure. FREE, FIT and WELL, such wonderful words, the relief from these last weeks of possible sickness, you Blessed darling. I just haven't any words, no words Christopher, just all bubbles and tremblings.

I had been cheering up because as there was no news I felt you just must be a prisoner. But you know how your mind keeps worrying away in circles at all sorts of awful possibilities, well that's what mine had been doing, and now golly – how I love you! You Dear Delicious Christopher. Ouch. I want to hug you to bits, eat you, come to my arms you bundle of charms. Hurry up mail, I want to hear your voice again, hear you, loving me, wanting me as always. I have not been able to look at your photos or read your letters, much too painful, but I have now, I have now.

You have been with me in all these bad days. I used to talk to you, inside myself, and I always made you answer that you were alright, and I used to hope that it was the right answer. Am I a silly dope? But I have a few more white hairs. You are there, you are alive. You are in this world with me, we are together, we, we, we, US. Deep breath here! I suspect Deb will hear from your folks and will be phoning me, and I shall have to register surprise, ain't it gorgeous!

Darling, I suppose there isn't any chance of you coming home. I thought there might be a possibility, for Churchill said something about the prisoners coming home – don't know whether that could mean all of you, or just the sick and wounded. Coo – just supposing. I am getting ambitious, it's such a lovely idea to play around with. Meanwhile I can manage for a bit, with the knowledge of your safety. Dearie me, things are looking up, though this business of Germany fighting to the last ditch sounds rather appalling. Some silly blighter, an MP too, was asking for indiscriminate bombing of Germany. I should have thought what was happening now was grim enough to satisfy even the most bloodthirsty.

I feel in that excited state that anything can happen any moment, something is in the air, with all this news from everywhere. I really should say that it's me that is in the air, bounce, bounce, bounce. I am going to the pictures with Iris tomorrow – golly, I shall have to treat her. It's so wonderful, you are wonderful, the world is wonderful, everything is wonderful. Please come home, home, home. Please do, darling. Such dreams of our being – Oh My Love.

I Love You.
Bessie

~

3 February 1945

Dearest,

'How do I feel?' – such a large question, sweetheart, oh! Such a large question! So difficult for me to tell you. When I received your telegram, I sat down and wrote immediately but nothing would really come, I was like a sleepwalker suddenly awakened, didn't know where I was, felt all soft and pappy, tremulous and bubbly inside. And today with your letter, oh Christopher, all this warmth melting inside me, that I somehow want to wrap around you, to make up for all your sufferings of the past weeks, it seems a lifetime. I knew you wouldn't be warm enough, or have enough to eat, but I didn't think it would be quite so bad. Oh Chris, I wish I could have a damn good howl, but I can't, I am all het up and tense, wondering whether you might come home. I try not to think of it, try not to bank on it, try to be rational, to stop dreaming that it could come true. Each night before I sleep, I fervently say to myself, come home Chris, come home, somehow trying to pull you home. During the early period I literally died, but as time went on and there was no news I gained hope.

I will write those letters tonight, about coming home, surely it means everybody not just the RAF. It must, must mean everybody, they must not treat you so, such a terrible injustice. Surely they won't overlook you. I feel like going to 10 Downing Street.

Rockets – well my sweet pet, I honestly haven't given them a thought for many weeks. The last bad period I remember was last November when Wilfred was on leave. I can't recall what has been the position since then. They have been falling, but I am very hazy about the quantity. I woke up to rockets when Iris came back from leave about a week ago. She had been to her sister's in Sheffield and came back feeling a bit scared at having to face up to them again. Her agitation made me realise what a coma I'd been in – even rockets had left me cold. I suppose our imaginations can only cope with big fears, one at a time. I suppose I shall become rocket conscious again.

My health is OK now, I had a very bad flu cold about 2 or 3 weeks ago, and had a week off, for which I blame you by the way, talk about depression!!! Poor Iris thought I was going into a decline. Iris and Lil have been watching me like a couple of anxious mothers with their first born.

I must try and get off a letter to Wilfred sometime, and tell him the news, for he has been very interested in your stay in Greece from the beginning, wanting to hear the soldier's viewpoint. It seems odd talking about you and Greece calmly, can't get used to the idea. I liked how you wrote of the ELAS; the bulk of the press are still banging away, trying to bring pressure to bear on the government. Of course, I will bear with you, I understand that you have much to do.

I Love You.
Bessie

~

5 February 1945

Dearest,

I am not sure how we can manage our first meeting. We must talk and talk when first we meet. I have been trying hard to think of a restaurant which would allow us to talk and *look* at each other in some privacy. You must think for me, as I have been unsuccessful.

I want to do so many things at once, but I can see that first I must talk. I am not sleeping at all well now, for the thought of you is upon me, and I cannot lose it.

Did I tell you that your four photos were amongst those lost at Kifissia? If you have the negatives perhaps we could have another print done. The photo I have of you is a real delight to me, although I wish I had more opportunity to get it out and glance at you. And I keep on thinking and feeling right inside me, 'Soon, I shall not be just glancing at her photograph.' Soon I shall be really looking at you, really meeting you, really knowing you.

Here, the mimosa, carnation and narcissus bloom. But you are in England, and I am coming to you, to claim you and to call you lovely.

I love you.
Chris

~

6 February 1945

Darling, Darling, Darling,

This is what I have been waiting for, your freedom left me dumb and choked up, but now, oh now, I feel released. Oh Christopher, my dear, dear man, it is so, so wonderful. You are coming home.

Golly, I shall have to be careful, all this excitement is almost too much for my body. You must be careful too, Darling, all this on top of what you have been through, it is difficult to keep it down, you can't help the excited twinges in your midriff can you? Do keep well, Angel – I shall have to say that to myself as well. You are coming home, I shall see you, talk to you, be with you, touch you, hold your arm, hold you against my heart, my body. I must pinch myself, is it true? Yes, your LC says so, and I now have such a funny photo of you, with a beard, but you look a little grim, as if you need loving, as if you need tenderness.

Marriage my sweet, yes I agree, what you wish, I wish. I want you to be happy in this darling, want to make you happy. I make a plea to whatever gods there be to make me greater than myself, so that I can make you as happy as humanly possible, to help you over the bad days, and swing along with you in the good days. Whilst you are afraid, you will not be happy. We must get rid of those fears. I want you to come to me, quite unafraid. We will wait. Anyway it is rather nice to go a-courting, don't you think? Also confidentially, I too am a little scared – everything in letters appears larger than life size. Like the photograph, it didn't show the white hairs beneath the black, the decaying teeth, the darkening skin. I think of my nasty characteristics, my ordinariness. Yes, I too feel a little afraid. About what happens on arrival, of course you'll have to spend the first part at home, I suspect I can get my leave when needed; we only have to sign for the actual summer period, otherwise they are very accommodating.

Oh dear, dear, dearie me, plan a week somewhere, bonk, up comes my heart, a week somewhere, by the sea, WITH YOU.

Where shall we go? Of course I'd choose north Devon – sea, country and air, but March raises the question of weather. Might we go to a largish town? I prefer villages normally, but with you I guess I'll do what you want. Also I feel that you'll need looking after, don't think you should walk around in the rain, not for awhile anyway. Guess I don't care where, as long as it's the sea, and you, you, you. Inward clangings and bouncings and I wonder how soon.

Glad you managed to give them the coffee and cocoa, our Greek friends I mean, to show them that we wish them well, and hope very strongly that they will get the government they want, though perhaps they live too close to poverty to think of governments. Still you'll soon tell me all about it.

What luck, being able to see and talk to the TUC delegation, just up your street, it was a wonderful idea. The socks, I hope they fitted. Not having a pattern for my working material, I had to juggle and felt a bit worried about the fitting. Yes, I do feel like you do at the moment, my darling, which is jolly good, in fact not bad, not bad at all!!!! You are coming home, and I am awake.

I Love You.
Bessie

~

7 February 1945

My Dearly Beloved,

How do you feel now, Ducky? I am gradually coming up for air, feel like turning cartwheels and standing on my head. So you are afraid, I wonder what about. I have a few apprehensions floating around, such as the actuality instead of letters. You know I say to myself, 'Bessie my girl, you're not so hot', but I think you may have a similar feeling. I say, how is your digestion? Mine's awful. I shall be reduced to taking Rennies or something, a wind remover. My tea at this moment is stuck somewhere in the middle of my chest. But despite apprehensions, it's not depressing me at all – I've got dancing feet, my apprehensions are literally giving me the giggles. Christopher is coming home, coming home, tra, la la la.

'Do not let us make any mistakes' now underlined. You dear old silly, do you really think you can guard against that? Or ensure the future? 'Plan our time' – I ask an anxious 'How?', because it all depends on you. I shall be with you, what's done with the time I don't care, as long as I get sufficient opportunities to cuddle you, and be alone with you. To feel what I have imagined. To know you.

A week somewhere together is a good beginning, a week somewhere together. Oh isn't it awful, so near and yet so far. Wilfred comes home on leave on Tuesday, that will help me through a week of it. I hope you don't have too long a wait in Italy, and please don't be ill. You have had such a bad time, and all this excitement, please be careful. Your experiences were a bit of a shock, I hadn't realised that there was any fighting, or that your captivity was quite so bad. The press for a change hadn't overdone the situation, it had given the impression of an exchange lasting for a few minutes and then surrender, and a prisoner who had been rescued before the end of the hostilities was quoted as saying that he had been well treated.

'I don't know what to say, and I can't think.' Yes, it does get you like that, it's just too much to say. The plea for me to write tons and tons and tons hit me hard. You weren't to know that you had flattened me out. We had both had a bad time, it takes time to recover, seems like a bad dream now doesn't it? The brightness on the horizon is beginning to glow vibrantly, thoughts of the future make me palpitate with expectancy. If I could only squash you to me, just squash you to me – umph. I adore you with my very bones, my hairs, my everything. Love me, go on loving me.

I wish we could have a weather forecast. Rain is something that can't be ignored, even by lovers, it's so wet and uncomfortable. Anyway we shall see. I can't help wishing that you won't get these letters, that you'll be on your way, that the time to wait is that short, because my impatience is getting pretty bad. Being able to write like we have has been a wonderful thing, but it has always remained only the beginning, the contact for our future and a beginning must change to something else.

What do you think of the war news? Don't like getting too optimistic, but wouldn't it be wonderful to come home to stay? Oh you must, must, must.

I bet Ridgeway Drive is a very joyful place, two sons coming home, crikey. I bet your mother felt slightly flattened out at first, but she'll be bouncing now.

I Love You.
Bessie

～

Interlude: Chris and Bessie meet at last. Their time together was a success, although the very fact of meeting would subtly change the nature of their correspondence in the future. Chris spent about three weeks in England, and the couple shared five days alone – in Bournemouth. We do not have precise details of how they occupied their time, but must piece together snippets of information from the letters that followed.

The Barker parents and sons reunited at home in February 1945: Herbert, Chris, Amy and Bert

7

Error of Judgement Regarding Salmon

28 March 1945

Dearest,

We arrived at Kings Cross at 1.30, got in the train, stretched out on empty seats, and more or less slept until 9.30, when we changed at York. We had another change at Edinburgh. I thought of you walking down to Charing Cross. We had tea, and shaved in hot water, and are in the Camp for tonight.

I hope you will not let the lack of news in the next few weeks make you worried. I shall soon be writing from Italy to you, trying to convey all you mean to me, all you are. I very much hope you will soon get some rest from the rockets, and that the Germans will collapse and assist my return to you, which will probably be not so long as we fear. Perhaps a year, possibly less than that.

I do not think we could have come any closer these last weeks, without making the parting unendurable. Regard, or try to regard, my visit as a link between the days of letters when we were finding each other, and these days when we know how great is our mutual dependence, how much we depend on each other for life itself. You know that I love you and will always love you. I am pledged to you. I am yours. You are mine. I want you.

I love you.
Chris

~

10 April 1945

My Dear One,

I do not feel in a very good state for writing at the moment, as the ship has been rocking a good deal, and I have succumbed once to the irresistible urge to be sick. However, Bert himself has been seedy and a great many other faces here have turned yellow above their Africa Stars, and I am in good company. We have now got ourselves onto a pretty good job aboard ship, each morning ten of us have to clean out the Ship's Hospital. It gets us out of other jobs, like Mess Orderly, Guards, sweeping the decks, so Bert and I get on happily with our three baths, the lavatory pedestals, and similar number of wash basins. I am not too keen on doing the Scabies bathroom, but never mind. Three weeks ago, when I was a temporary gentleman, the chap in Lyons' 'wash and brush up' washed out my wash basin, now I am doing the same.

Tonight there is a Sing Song for Other Ranks. One of our officers has asked me to do 50 words on it for the Ship's Newspaper they are starting. I told him I was out of sympathy with such things, but would let him have the item, though I would not go myself. I have just written the few words required and hope to hear the others shouting their heads off, so that I can mention a few tunes 'sung'. Very rarely does anyone start any educational or informative activity on ship. They assume that all we wish to do is laugh like healthy young hyenas. And 'they' are probably right.

You are putting your clock forward tonight, so you will be in advance of me for awhile. Reveille is 6 a.m. on ship, but we do not rise much before 7, and then I think of you still slumbering.

All the lads are buying hundreds of cigarettes, at 50 for 1s. 8d., and feeling happier the further away from home they get.

I hope you did not weep too much (if you did weep). And, if ever you do so again, let it be only at the hardness of our separation, never in despair of our future meeting and life together. I have become more than a little woebegone at our post-war hopes of a home, by ourselves. The figures lead me to think that it will be ten years before we get the chance to choose. I expect you will have to be discreet in what you say to your Dad, but it seems to me that we shall be forced to live at 27 after I return for a little while, in order to prospect for a place. When the war is over I know you will buy what you can to ensure we do not have many troubles in equipping our own home, and, if you can manage, to start house purchase (I know it is an extremely tricky business, but you could write to Estate Agents, and Simpson, Palmer and Winder, Southwark Bridge Road, SE1 would help you legally, and fairly.) Shall I write my Mother telling of our plans, and asking her to let you have what money you want? As you know, I have £350, and you nearly the same, so we could raise £700 for a first payment, if Simpson's counselled it.

Took my shirt and trousers off last night for the first time, a great treat, as one gets very hot and sticky sleeping in clothes below decks. The nervous ones are now all breathing freely again. Strangely, I have hardly thought of submarines during the voyage, although I had been fairly apprehensive whilst on land on leave. I think the feeling wickedly arose from the thought that, had we been hit, we might have got back to England as survivors' leave!

We got two bars of chocolate at Glasgow, and have also had four on board including Fry's Sandwich variety, which I expect you'd like. Sorry I can't share with you, as you did with me. I am waking up four or five times during the night, but very quickly going to sleep again. Several times I have thought I was still at home, and once when I woke like this I put my hand out as though to touch you. I shall always want you, always love you.

Chris

~

11 April 1945

I am now once again in Italy, and everything is going as expected. I shall be leaving here shortly, and shall not be very sorry, I fancy.

The dust is everywhere (much as the sand was in the Desert), and it makes us dirty and thirsty.

If I say or write a thousand times before we meet again, 'I love you', I want it always to come to you as a fresh, vigorous affirmation of faith, of deep feeling of my need of you, my desire for you. We are so much strengthened now by our meeting: I have seen you, your eyes when you looked at me – and I hope you've seen, and will remember, my eyes. I think I shall have to write to you rather differently from my 1944 items. I am now too much aware of you, too moved within me by the knowledge of you and the fact that now we are one. We now do know what we mean to each other. I think correspondence is going to be more difficult in the light of this, and I know (it is wonderful to be so sure) you will forgive me for my faults where they occur.

It is appalling to think of not seeing you for a year – if that be the period. 'Making the best of it' will be a hard job. I shall try to be humorous where I can be, but I shall not be surprised if you cannot laugh. And I keep on thinking of all the things I might have said to you, the things we should but didn't discuss. I think and think what a fool I was. But I suppose it was the character of the leave, all this recent upset and complete shock, that made me afraid, indecisive, careful, cautious, diplomatic, wasteful. What else was I? But yet it was wonderful, it was LIFE with a capital L, it was – YOU ARE – so much better than I have imagined. We needed such a meeting to make real our happy state, to be really certain we were indispensable to each other, to be really sure that our lives are joined for ever.

We are in the shadow of some mountains at the moment, and this makes it very hot, for the sun here is full and certain. (Didn't <u>we</u> have grand weather?) We have spent today at the Quartermasters, and are now 'Compleat Soldiers', a horrible melancholy. We each weigh a ton. It was grand to travel lightly, but those days are over. This is not a pleasant place, as they incline to treat you as a 'rookie'. I must finish this in 'Five Minutes', the man in charge has just said, so must conclude now. I am eager to get your letters. I expect they await me at my new unit. My thoughts are of you. Very much. I know that yours are around me; I feel the protection of your love. And I want you.

I love you.
Chris

~

14 April 1945

Dearest,

When I got your four Letter Cards yesterday after a day's travel in a truck on dusty Italian roads, it was not unexpected, but it was still the most wonderful thing that I can hope for. For goodness' sake don't picture me as a strong, silent man, patiently awaiting his turn to go home, happy meanwhile to do his bit. I am not strong, I am weak – as weak as you are. I resent our separation, our living apart. And I resent and violently object to it, inside me, very, very much more now that we are so certainly suited, so confirmedly assured by our brief meeting.

You say I exceeded your expectations. You must know that, high as they were, you exceeded mine. I am glad, too, that we now have these joint memories of being together. You say I am a wonderful lover. May I say it's wonderful to love you and be loved by you. May I say how thrilled and wonder-struck I was by your sweet reception, your lovely welcome. No, I want you to keep all my photographs, and I hope I shall be able to send you more.

I don't think you a 'silly gink'. I do know that you <u>are</u> intelligent. Don't say I am flattering you, or that I am deceiving myself, please. Wasn't it almost unbelievably wonderful to be in each other's company! I am sorry I was below par, and rather dazed throughout, and that you yourself had been going through a bad patch. The decision not to call up the over 30s disgusts everyone here. It makes it harder for us to be released.

Glad your vapour rub is now settled (myself, I think it went away of its own accord, irrespective of Iris's advice). I am mightily impressed by what I have seen of you, and I love you more and more, it seems, with every day that passes.

I love you.
Chris

≈

15 April 1945

Dear Bessie,

I am glad you have signed for your leave, and hope that when the time comes the weather will keep as fine as during my visit. I hope you manage to get good digs in Devon. There will be a great rush this summer, and a great harvest for the landlady.

I shouldn't worry any more about the war against Germany. It won't go on all the summer, as you fear.

I hope you manage your Spring Cleaning without any broken bones. I am sorry I am not there to assist. But, who knows, next Spring I may be parading with the Hoover for your inspection. I hope so.

I am glad that you solved the Problem of the Missing Grapefruit. Here we are lucky in an abundance of fruit and fresh vegetables. (For example, today we had potatoes, cauliflower and carrots, in addition to Yorkshire Pudding and mutton.) The food here is good all round, in fact. If I worried about nothing else I should be quite happy.

I hope you are well, and not too busy.
Love.
Chris

16 April 1945

My dear private and family matter,

I love you. I love you. I love you. I love you. I love you. I love you. I love you. – Don't just read and pass on. Please read this reiteration carefully and hear me saying it. Blow me, I <u>am</u> mournful at the thought of our distance. It seems so absurd, so wrong, so impossible that only a little while ago we were together and now we are apart. We were settled down to writing to each other, before, but now – what can I write? I can't help having a cheated feeling, and not much interest in anything else but you. Before, I loved you, my idea of you. But now, I have seen, heard, touched, smelt the living warmth and flesh of you. I was moved by you, and inside me still there's the new kind of knowing whirr which newly and more strongly unites us.

Guards and parades cause me to worry very greatly. If they occur (Guards) once every ten days, I shall spend five apprehensive days preparing and five days recovering. We had our first real parade today, up at 6, frantic preparations, and passed off OK as far as I was concerned. The inspecting officer checked each of us for some error we were supposed to have – collars undone, medals awry, belts too high or too low, and so on. But although I am terrorised and find it an ordeal, he was not ungentlemanly, and that was most welcome. We had about a half-hour's drill afterwards, not with our rifles, which we simply carried (and nearly broke our arms), and although I was always on the wrong foot, my misdemeanours went undetected, and my life of crime continues.

On Saturday, I saw *Thank Your Lucky Stars* (Eddie Cantor, E.E. Horton, Bette Davis), a lot of nonsense, badly projected. The religious influence in this country is sickeningly real and obvious; it is maddening to see the priests walking along the streets. Yesterday we went for a walk, down the road which leads to the nearest town. We said 'Bonner Sarah' (that is the pronunciation) to four women sitting on a wayside seat. They were chanting hymns, replied similarly, and then continued chanting as we walked on.

I think of you getting up, going to the station, getting to Charing Cross, walking back from Park Lane in the evening. I try hard to imagine the grandness of you, at long distance. I hope you are not feeling too bad, my darling, my love, my dearest. I'm not so good, myself.

I love you.
Chris

~

28 April 1945

My Dearest,

I returned to camp yesterday evening, after having had a very nice little run-round. Within a couple of hours, along came the mail, your arms were around me, and I was with you.

One subject in your letter cards I must comment on. The question of being 'afraid'. If you read my LC from Greece again you'll see in what connection I used it. I was afraid of marrying you, not because of my 'trouble' (which you rate low, and anyhow is your responsibility now), but because, at all times mortal, in war, man takes more risks than usual. I do not want to marry until I am sure that only natural causes (including your cooking!) can separate us. Lying on my stomach in the dark cold night, with the ELAS banging away at us, I realised with clarity that we have no automatic assurance of life together until both wars, German and Jap, are over. I do not want to leave a widow (perhaps with a child) behind to mourn me. It is bad to mourn at all, but it is (in my understanding) much worse to mourn as a wife than as a sweetheart.

Marriage provides certain conveniences, but I do not think they were large enough to make it worthwhile for a month. As you say, we are together, anyway. I wondered if I should marry you, and you should marry me, in order 'to be sure' of each other. But the more we were together I thought (I was right?) I saw you understanding that you could be sure of me, and that you knew I believe in you as absolutely essential to my future. Four of our Section chaps married this leave. I do not see that now they are any closer to their wives than I am to you. Marriage would have perhaps been a conventional act. But I rather ponder whether it isn't a greater achievement to love one another as we do without having any legal tie. I hope you really have no regrets about not being Mrs Barker just at present. I have spent about 25,000 miles on the sea this war, and been under fire for 30 hours without hurt.

I think I shall return OK, and I shall return to you, as fully and completely as if we were married.

I know that this separation is worse for you. I cannot convey by words the mounting need for you, the extra rottenness of being apart, the greater unbearability of separation, the growing love, the 'more and more and more' tumult that rages now that I have seen and touched and approved you in person. To think that we have touched! What luck I have had, to awaken to you at last, and to find you still ready. I hope you will find the time pass quickly – already it is nearly five weeks since we parted – I know that you will remember the way I have looked, and the enchantment we experienced together when our flesh touched. I think of you, and try to reach you, always.

I love you.
Chris

~

28/29 April 1945

Dearest,

You say I said enough while on leave. I am disgusted how little I said, about ourselves, and about my impressions of 'life abroad' and the Army. I am not very happy about my deficiencies as a sweetheart – I think I teased you too much. I should have been on my knees before you, confessing my utter dependence on you, imploring your interest though I may seem to have it, telling you always that without the hope of you, I should starve and thirst. I could have been so much more eloquent, yet my stutterings satisfied you. I am sorry we wasted those five nights at Bournemouth, it seems to be beside the point that there will be many many more.

I am sorry about the error of judgement regarding salmon. I'll catch a whale for you on my return journey.

I hope you are getting on alright with your spring-cleaning. Personally, I think far too much is made of this event. A properly run house would be ashamed to admit it needed a really good clean-up once a year. It is a suburban blight. But you enjoy yourself, don't mind me.

I have the same 'you have always been there' feeling, too. I seem to have grown up with you, and loved you since we first met. Certainly I have strong upon me the happy thought that you 'always will be there'. The future, once the war is over, lies entrancingly before us.

Have I said something wrong about sleeping bags? I am not wanting to have a solitary wedded life, of course I'm not. Re single beds, I was thinking earlier (you know how we write letters to each other with each passing moment, and how we forget the 'really good' things, when we come to pen and paper) that I would suggest to you that if your sheets on your present bed wear out in the next year, it would be a good idea to buy double to replace them, then the sheets would be OK for our own bed. Of course I want to spend all my time as physically close to you as possible, just as I am happy at our mental closeness. Really, didn't you think that toward the end of the leave we had settled into such a good understanding? I am sure you could fit into a sleeping bag, but it would be a tight squeeze – a grand tight squeeze I daresay!

I am glad you are going to my home. Mother and Rosie have mentioned you phoning, in their letters. I am very unhappy at my Dad's condition. My Mother is having a very bad time. My Dad is complexity itself. I hope he pulls through his difficulties, which I believe are more mental than physical, poor old boy.

No, I didn't notice a lot of complaint from you about your cold. We can't have two martyrs in the <u>family</u>, and as I also make a fuss of any ailment, am afraid you will have to be the tough one! I say, what a pity I didn't apply that vapour rub.

Don't think I have the slightest objection to 'Darling'. I think I cautioned against its use when third persons were present. Probably I was shy. So do, please, call me anything you like. I shall like it, too. Sorry the picture frame wasn't a success.

Last night I was on guard, and thought of you sleeping peacefully, while I patrolled the almond trees and listened to the barks of distant dogs, and the 'perlip, perlip' and 'whirrip whirroo' of the birds around here. A feeling was with me that distance doesn't matter.

In one of your letters you say your heart beats within me. That is good. I will look after your heart. Please always try to be happy because of future prospects, rather than sorrowful because of present separation.

I love you.
Chris

≈

2 May 1945

Dearest,

I had just addressed the front [of the envelope] when someone called out 'News Flash', we all rushed to the tent with the wireless, and heard the announcement that the German armies in Italy had surrendered unconditionally. Coming on the same day as the 7 a.m. announcement (which I heard) that Hitler was reported dead, it gave us a certain extra elation and hope that other Germans will also surrender rather than make it necessary for our chaps to get killed unnecessarily. We have again been warned that sobriety is expected of us when the great announcement is made. For us, I don't expect the change to mean anything except more spit, and more polish, more parades, more guards, more sickening routine and regulation.

[Continued 3 May 1945]

I am very glad that the rockets have finished. What is it like to be able to go unthinkingly to bed, and to know you will be undisturbed? I wish I had not been windy of the rockets, it 'stunted' my actions and chained me down.

Your comments about my greatness over my Greek experiences are very welcome, but they are by no means correct. I am not a great man nor have I ever behaved like one. I am a very little man, with his ear close to the ground.

I hope you <u>will</u> buy clothes. Don't wait for my approval – you have it in advance. You should beware of a clothing shortage and buy normally. It is also by no means certain that the items will remain at their present low prices. If the profiteers win, things will go 'up and up and up' alright. It is not 'saving for the future' to denude yourself or deplete a modest wardrobe. Carry on, and buy, and if you want to save, consider again the smoking habit. I thought of an idea. Suppose you smoke 20 a day now, carry on smoking 20 each day for a week, then smoke 19 each day. At the end of that week, reduce to 18 for the next seven days, and so on. It would take nearly six months to reduce to nothing, but it might be the way out, to slowly slide away from it. You say you wish you were thoughtful like me – well, I'm not thoughtful, only artful! I think we'll rub along together very well indeed. I feel fairly certain we both have sufficient intelligence not to try to make the other unhappy.

All this morning I have been helping to shift scenery in the dirty little theatre (Teatro Mercadante) of this town, in preparation for an Italian Variety Show, which I expect I will see tonight. Backstage was even dirtier than the front, though more interesting, hauling on ropes to bring scenes down, shifting pianos, and so on. Quite a change from the putting up (rather than use the slick word 'erecting') of tents and barbed wire, in which campaign I have gained several cuts and blood blisters on my hands. The weather here is rainy, and it is dismal to hear it pattering down on the tent roof, when you have just moved from a waterproof building. It is very cold in the morning, particularly as I only wear my rompers (overalls) during the working day. I think of you always. I love you always. I need you always.

I love you.
Chris

~

4 May 1945

My dear Bessie,

Thank you for No. 15, the one in which you referred to the engagement ring idea, received yesterday.

Today I have made a round trip of 60 miles to the nearest town to have my eyes (not my brains) tested, and now have two new pairs of Army spectacles to replace those lost in Greece. The whole business did not take more than 15 minutes.

I think I would like you to say, about the ring, that the money could be more wisely used and that we don't need to conventionally demonstrate our undertakings to the world. We do not need a symbol, and our love is strong. Perhaps you are thanking me for being 'thoughtful'? I don't know. A point I had in mind was that the Ivy-type of mind might be saying 'Ah, Chris has been home, but I see that Bessie is still on the shelf.' Or something cheap and silly like that. This para will, I suppose, displease you as much as the original one pleased you. Isn't it just too easy to put one's foot in it, in correspondence?

Thanks for the account of the Bromley visit. I am glad you feel a little more happy about it now. I know that my Mum will welcome your visits, and I hope you will be encouraged and make them regularly. It is well to bear in mind that families do not like being told they know not the mind of their sons, or I would ask you to tell my Mum that Bert has never said 'all women are bitches', in any final way, though he might have said it tentatively. My Mother's memory is very good, but you will have to beware of her telling you that I have said such a thing as well. I do not intend to discuss this with Bert, by the way. It is ridiculous to say 'all men are' this, or 'all women' that. But, please don't get all pro-woman, for I am not all pro-man. I've seen some of them; and in the quieter moments I have thought a lot (27,000 cases of VD in Italy last year among troops).

I understand that it is snowing in some parts of the UK now. Good luck to you.

I love you, and you respond. Thank goodness for that; thank you for goodness.
I love you.
Chris

∼

6 May 1945

Dear Bessie,

I suppose that everyone at home is feeling happy about the end of the Germans. It is a pity that the Japanese remain to be dealt with, and that so much more suffering has to be endured on that account. I imagine it will be many months before any large number of chaps start discarding khaki for colours of their own choice, but with no blackout, sand-bagged windows, or ARP,* things generally should be easier. I imagine that your Foreign Office task will cease, and that most of the wireless stations will close down.

Yesterday evening I met Bert and we saw a film, *Candlelight in Algeria*, John Hall, Carla Lehmann, Enid Stamp Taylor, an account of the events leading to the Allies landing in North Africa. It was tripe, but of the edible variety. Earlier in the week we saw an Italian variety show, 'Dots and Dinahs', which was competent and clean. I had a special interest in it, because I had spent the morning shifting the piano, and getting the scenes into position, and having a peep behind the scenes, backstage being even dirtier than the 'stalls'.

I heard a broadcast record by Bevin yesterday, in which he said there would be a short standstill period before chaps started demobilising. Some of our chaps with low numbers are not happy about that! We just listen in, and imagine things to suit our own cases. What is your brother's number? Is he stopping on to help the war effort?

---

* Air-raid precautions.

Love.
Chris

~

> 'The Socialist Party constitutes the most dark and formidable menace with which, now that German militarism has been ousted, British civilisation is now confronted.'
>
> – W.S. Churchill, March 1920

My dear,

I am still in a glum state and I believe that only the news that Japan has surrendered also would be sufficient to un-glum me. I am very thankful that the end of the war in Europe has come at last, and all the terrible things that war involves will now cease there. But I am very conscious that the people generally have suffered much, and I do not believe we are any nearer a decent state of society. On top of all my general mix-up of confused thought and regret is a more acute realisation that we are not together, and the chance of being so is remote. I know that it doesn't make you happy to have me fed-up (and I <u>am</u> that) but I do not feel like a song and a dance just at present. It's grim.

We put up a tent. We take it down. We are told there will in future be no trucks to the village (a quarter of an hour's walk). Today and tomorrow we <u>must</u> ride in a truck (because of possible trouble with celebrations, I suppose). We exhibit our kit daily so that all the dust can blow on it. We must take mepacrine* tablets daily. We must have our mosquito nets down by 18.00 hours daily. We must roll our tent walls up by 00.00. We must not perform our ablutions outside our tents. There are many items. Ordinarily you just grin, curse and bear it. At the moment, I am not very happy about such things.

I expect you are left pretty cold by the bomb-free atmosphere of London, although you will understand that it is grand for me to know that now you are safe, that 27 Woolacombe is not likely to fall down on you, that really and actually only natural causes can come along to cut you from me. Does that seem to you as selfish as it sounds to me? I'm sorry.

Thanks for the news of the *Express* Exhibition of the concentration camps. The photos we have had reproduced out here have been pretty horrible, and aroused bad feelings in some of the chaps. Main thing for me is that these horrors went on from 1933–Sept 2nd 1939, without apparent condemnation from our peace-at-any-price leaders. The hanging-up of Mussolini after his death (and all the talk of his mistress, as though we ourselves were so moral) are unpleasant.

We have again been reminded we mustn't get drunk. Chaps are getting 1½ bottles of beer this week. I was going to have mine just now, but remembered I had already promised it a bloke. It is horrible stuff (light ale) I'm told. This week, has gone up 3d. In the nearby town, cakes and tea were free today. There are to be certain 'planned modifications' for us. We shall get half-an-hour extra

---

* An anti-malarial tablet.

in bed (and start work at 8.30) and get 12.30–2.30 off for dinner, instead of 12.30–2, as formerly.

Sorry to be such a cheering influence, my girl, but you know how it is. I'll send you a page of jokes one day. We get tomorrow off, I'll try to force a smile then.

I love you.
Chris

∾

9 May 1945

My dear Bessie,

I will try hard to be merry and bright – though don't be deceived, I am not feeling so good.

I finished off my last letter in the canteen, surrounded by ale and vermouth imbibers. We had a sing-song, and I joined in a few of the songs. It was not easy to get 'order' for the King at 9 p.m., but I was near the wireless and heard all he said. What an ordeal for him it is every time, and how, of recent years, he has become adept at just avoiding a wrong word. I bet he is glad it is over. I thought there might have been greater mention of his Allies in the struggle, but otherwise it was a reasonable effort. If only everyone would recall that we are at peace in Europe only because of the death and mutilation of literally millions of our fellow countrymen (and women) and of our fellow world citizens. Yet, if 'private enterprise' had its way, the air raid shelters that are being dismantled in England would be sold at a handsome profit to Japan. They will need them alright.

The truck back to camp left at 10 p.m., and what a ride it was – short maybe – swaying all over the road, narrowly dodging pedestrians, carts, dogs, crazily turning corners. I was in the front and could see all sorts of thin‿s happening . . . so when the singing happy crowd stopped at a casa (house) for a 'final drink', I quietly and un-bravely dismounted and walked safely down the lane to the camp, while behind me about ten blokes banged on the front door and yelled 'Rosa!' to open up. Rosa must have been more discreet than avaricious, for I learned later they had banged in vain and come home drinkless. This morning officers and sergeants came round to our tents and served us with coffee and brandy (I gave my brandy to a Scotsman) in bed, as is the custom on Christmas Day, and today is being similarly celebrated. Tonight we are having a special dinner and this also will be served by the officers. I think I have told you I wonder and envy the chaps who can free-wheel alcoholically along.

Regarding spring cleaning: you ask what do I know about house cleaning? Why just <u>house</u> cleaning? I bet I have done more cleaning and sweeping in the Army than you have done in your life so far, although it might not have been done so carefully. Remember the first qualification of a soldier is his ability to be a domestic servant.

Do <u>you</u> have a specially good bath in the Spring, by the way, or do <u>you</u> get yourself as clean as you can every time you bathe? I wonder if next Spring we shall be doing the Cleaning together? I hope so. I hope we shall both be really living, really living together by then.

I LOVE YOU.
Chris

~

11 May 1945

Dearest,

This abolition of unit censorship is a bit of a godsend to us, because now I can write you as often as I feel like it, and say as much or as little as I like.

I have started today a job I am scheduled to be on for the next fortnight with three other chaps. 'Malarial and Hygiene'. The Hygiene part deals with flies and what not. The Malarial part takes us out in the fields looking for cesspools and stagnant water, which we have to make unsafe for mosquitoes.

I was pleasantly surprised to get the snapshots – the one with the puppies was perhaps the best. Something else to look upon when I am in the dumps, to revive my hopes of early meeting, and to centre my rather idolatrous thoughts upon.

I don't want you to have the miseries. I can tell you one way of dodging them. Don't write so much, so often. You wrote four letters in five days, lovely, wonderful, warm letters. But you can't really afford the time, and their writing upsets you. Couldn't you settle down to writing me twice a week? I really would prefer it if it helped you to have more settled moments. As you say, you really can't go on like this.

We may be together in the flesh much sooner than we think. Wish away and get a little happiness, don't pine away. I know that the only fact of real value to us is our togetherness. But will you just think of the <u>facts</u> that should make us hopeful and happy, compared with our position six months ago?

THEN – We were correspondents.
NOW – We are <u>confirmed lovers</u>.
THEN – Hadn't seen each other for years.
NOW – Saw each other recently.

There is no danger in Europe now. I am in the Signals, not a dangerous job. We can write plenty.

Love,
Chris

~

14 May 1945

My Darling,

Today, 22, another beautiful letter.

Today I have disinfected the urinals; replaced burnt-out latrine buckets; made and placed under the bowser taps, two drip cans; knocked down a big stone wall in a field; emptied Bert's truck of its load of sand; put out three toilet rolls.

At noon today came a flood of 'Gen' about impending movements, and I started getting ready to pack. Now the 'Gen' is still there, but I have not heard anything officially. I do not want to raise your hopes (or sadden you) unnecessarily, but you know the Army. Nothing happens for a long while, then everything all at once. It may be that the time has arrived for me to be fitted into the intricate military pattern designed to crush the Japanese, and that soon I shall be in England again for a short leave (28 days) preparatory to being sent to SEAC.* In my own mind, I feel that I will go. I do not dread it as I once did, foolishly. The change is due to the fact that I will see you again (and more, much more if it should be), that it is more time passed, and that in 18 months I shall get home finally.

I love you.
Chris

~

---

* South East Asia Command.

21 June 1945

Dear Bessie,

I decided to inflict pencil on you, and write this on the beach, with bare knees as a table, and the grand sun getting at me. I wish very much that you were here. In England I can't see us getting by ourselves on a beach very much. We must 'go abroad' one day, where the opportunities are so much more.

I don't think I quite understand the 'please don't harp on it' appeal in your letter, referring to your weight. Have I distressed you with some earlier comment? It would be a pity if I had. You are foolish to 'suffer' from women over your size. May I not hold the view that you could be worse off than taking cod liver oil? I said that what you fancied did you good, and if you don't fancy cod liver oil, for goodness' sake chuck the bottle away. I do think you need – all war-weary 'civvies' need – a stimulant. If you think Sanatogen was useful, you are silly to stop taking it just yet. Surely you don't think I am getting at you, when I express a view that you should look after yourself.

During our MO's lecture yesterday, one chap said, in order to stop VD, why didn't the Army honestly advocate masturbation. MO retorted that they might as well recommend buggery. I felt sorry for the bloke who had asked the question.

I shall be back at Altamura by the time you get this – thirty miles from the sea, not such a good thought as you and I on this beach.

I love you.
Chris

30 June 1945

Dear Bessie,

I enclose a photograph which I have just had taken on the beach at Bari, whereon I am now sitting. The chap with his hand on my behind is Ken Solly, probably the best Socialist in our Section, and quite a decent chap. He is only 22, comes from Reading. Has a reputation for being a 'binder' – a chronic grumbler, and he certainly can moan.

Frank Sinatra was in Bari yesterday, some of our chaps got in to see him but were not very much impressed. I think he is hardly likely to be popular with males; the chaps that saw him say that one of the songs was 'Ole Man River'.

I love you.
Chris

～

Chris on the beach at Bari, 1945

2 July 1945

My Dear Bessie,

It is my 'all day on' today, so I can only send a very short note. Apart from the fact that I have had little time off, I have had a number of other things to do, including seeing Bert off to his Rome leave, probably not to see him again until he is a civilian and I am returned on leave, in about a year's time. He'll be my Best Man! I think that he will be sent to Ancona (which is further North) on completion of his leave, and there wait about for a month until the time comes for him to embark. Saying 'Cheerio', exchanging messages, has taken a little while, and of course I have inherited some of his kit. I met him first on July 16th, 1943, at Tripoli, so we have nearly had two years together. It has been very good for me. It has kept in me a certain tenderness of manner which some chaps lose. Being part of a family, we have had that mysterious mutual binding power which is worth more than any money.

Today's mail was also fated to be a bumper one, so that I should get nicely full up with unanswered letters. Mum's letter again made some very pleasing references to you, and showed me that she was thinking of you as a daughter.

One of my washer-up colleagues is a very decent chap (he was one of those I mentioned originally) and I have just discovered that he used to tour the Yorkshire villages during the Spanish war, with projector and film *The Defence of Madrid*. He did it after his day's work, and I think he is a genuine old soul (he's about 36!).

Certainly he is not asleep or putting a halo round Churchill, like so many.

I love you.
Chris

~

3 July 1945

My dear Bessie,

I am sorry that your Labour Party efforts are such eye-worriers. I used to find that if my eyes ached the rest of me was not so good as well. I am glad you can rise above the poor organisation that probably exists. At least, you'll have the satisfaction of knowing you did more than vote at the 1945 Election. I got my papers yesterday – I will send them to you later on perhaps, although maybe you will have seen them at 161 [Ridgeway Drive]. I like the Liberals' address best of them all. Yes, I have heard of Alderman Reeves. James or Joseph, I believe. He is a Royal Arsenal Cooperative man I think. Probably not too bad a candidate. I'd like the chance to heckle a little – it's an art.

My darling, I think you'd look lovely in a jumper. I much enjoyed your drawings – the fact that you had done them was the important thing. I will not pretend to be an expert on brassieres, but I think I should say I shouldn't adopt one if I were you, unless you feel it's desirable of itself. Never mind about what you are supposed to do at 30. They'll probably tell me I should put my hair in curlers, next. When I come home I don't suppose your brassiere will last long – nor anything that impedes my meeting you, gets between us.

I shall be glad to read Shaw's 'Ibsen'. But I think it unwise for you to send it to me out here. If I can discover a copy somewhere, all well and good. All the Shaw one gets generally in Service Club Libraries is *Pygmalion* in Penguin edition.

Don't really resign yourself to twenty months' wait. That is the maximum, if the four years remains. If it is brought down to 3½, I shall be back in August 46; if to 3, then in February 46. And remember that the aim is 3, and that our letters to MPs and the War Office can keep them alive to the fact that we are really human beings and don't regard this separation as a long holiday provided by a kind country. Sometimes I feel quite hopeful about seeing you earlier than 14 months' time, and that we shall certainly be on our honeymoon in August or September of next year. The time will pass. Sometimes slowly, sometimes with a rush. But pass it will, then I shall come to you.

You commence your letter by saying you can't understand why I decry my lack of education and knowledge. Well, I am sorry about that. I feel I could be much more useful to society (whom I like to think I indirectly serve – while remembering I'd ditch it or anything for you) if I had received more than an elementary education, and had I spent my years 16–28 acquiring book knowledge instead of hacking and huckstering around in the Labour Party and 'Mets'.*

---

* The 'Mets' was the *Mets Journal*, a publication of the Union of Post Office Workers. Chris was a regular contributor and then editor.

I am glad that Iris and Lil have received [the almonds], also that you have one packet. Blow me, I posted two lovely bags on June 5. I hope you get them eventually, as the bags looked a smashing bit of work, apart from the contents. When eating them, do you put in hot water, and remove skin? It's better I think.

No, I don't think I am paying undue attention to childbirth, but when I think of a woman's body – it's yours I have in mind – and as the MO spoke of painless births (did I tell you he said larger heads of Scottish population is responsible for higher infant mortality rate?) and the agonies of the mother, it was natural for me to think of you, and your agonies, whether you eventually endure them or not. Perhaps I have your body too much on my mind.

Think of me when you put on your brassiere, think of me when you take it off – no, think of me always, and know that I am your man, a long, long way away, but ever-conscious of your beauty, your delight, your loveliness, always wanting you, always weaving the pattern of our lives together in imagination. I could wake you as you have never been wakened, love you as you have never been loved.

I love you.
Chris

≈

5 July 1945

Dear Bessie,

Today being Polling Day I wondered how you were employed, and if you were knocking on doors or carrying on work as usual. It is very hard to arrange the Army vote, and so we are having about four days for the job, spread over about a week. As I had received my papers, I marked and posted my voting paper today. I do not know how many chaps are voting from here. Many have not got a vote either through their own neglect (in which case they would appear to be satisfied with the Fascist conception) or mischance. There must be many, even at home (like Deb and Marjorie Webb), who are on holiday and will also lose their opportunity of 'striking a blow for freedom'.

Went along to see the Variety Show, which was a mixed Italian-English affair. I came away after two acts, one a blonde Italian female who sang a song in English, I thought obviously without knowing its meaning. And another, a quite good card conjuror. There was one mentionable joke, about Dirty Gertie of Bizerte, who lived in a street 'three smells along' somewhere.

Tonight there is a film in the village, *Irish Eyes Are Smiling*, and I am glad I am on all day, so prevented from attending.

S'all for now. Sorry.
I LOVE YOU.
Chris

~

6 July 1945

Dearest,

The newspapers you have sent have been most useful, and have been well read by myself and others. When the results are announced, will you try and send me a copy of them? *The Times* has the best, but I doubt if you can get that. Maybe all the papers will have them in full at this election.

I am eating well, though my bowels are not acting properly. It's a 300-yard walk to the latrines and I think this has something to do with it. One of our chaps actually can't go to the lavatory if anyone is watching (in the Army that's always) and goes out into the fields on his own, for that purpose.

I wonder, do you think I could send you back one or both pairs of the socks you knitted me? One pair has holes in them, the other's OK, but I think civilian use is better for them. I have a spare pair of Army socks, making four. What do you think? I don't like to wear them out, out here, I'd like to send them back for you to keep.

Ignore all the stuff you read about the Allies being out of Italy by November, December or any other time. Italy is a good strategic centre from which to send troops to Spain, Greece, Yugo, Syria, Palestine, Egypt, Tunisia. All reports I have seen say that garrison troops will remain. You can bet your front door knocker that I shall be classed as garrison troops.

I love you.
Chris

9 July 1945

Dear Bessie,

What I find myself pondering now is the smug way in which we both allowed ourselves to measure how much of ourselves we should pour out. Inside we were raging, tempestuous, tumultuous. Outside we were almost always so naicely self-contained. I should have crushed you to bits when I put my arms around you. I should have kissed you to pieces. I should have done everything. And yet, most all I produced was a sweet smile and a correct embrace. Is this the civilising influence at work? It might be the wisest thing at the time, but it seems madness now, when I can imagine you, see the shape of your breasts – yet vainly stretch my arms towards you. Yes, my darling, I was home for five weeks, and it did happen. Where ever I touched you I found beauty, acceptance, willingness, a claiming-ness. I wonder if you understand that 'claiming-ness'? I know that you want me and that we complete each other. I am happy that our minds are together.

I want you to carry on with your clothes as though I was at home, because I'm sure we shall not seriously differ about what you should wear, though I'd like you sometimes to heed my own choices for you. Could you send me the little pieces of cloth that might suit you, so that I could send you some cloth, if obtainable. I don't want you to cut up your frocks to supply the material for the pattern of course, but I daresay that even you hoard some little pieces of cloth?

I love you.
Chris

11 July 1945

My dear Bessie,

Regarding Deb, I will write her, in reply to the next letter I get from her (but not specially), that I have noticed her 'earlier observations about Bessie, and can only say she is my heart's desire and I have every reason to believe that I am hers'. Does that seem satisfactory to you? I shall wait your reply before I actually write to her on the point. Now, do not be too, too crushing with my old pal Deb if you start any conversation with her. Certainly you may say I told you of her enquiries – but do avoid the wonderful chance to slosh her for her inquisitiveness, or however you regard it. You may say what you like and I will support it, but be a good girl and don't be too eager to bash her. If you do, then of course, I am with you, but I hope you'll be content to be nicely and possessively quiet. You must concede her certain rights about me (although I don't say necessarily on this subject) and you won't really gain anything but a momentary satisfaction from sloshing her.

I am glad you think old Churchill hasn't necessarily been hailed very enthusiastically in all places. We shall soon see.

Always I must want to keep you fully and completely aware of the immensity of our being together. I don't want my views to be hidden by neglect or forgotten by default.

I LOVE YOU.
Chris

12 July 1945

My dear Bessie,

I am very sorry to hear, in No. 48, of the pain in your chest which continues although, according to X-Ray, it is 'nothing'. If the doctor only had said there was no need to worry, I should have been anxious and unhappy, but what about the X-Ray, was it done at a hospital or under proper control? If so, I think you must force yourself to believe it is something which will go when you cease thinking of it. I am under the impression that you cannot beat the X-Ray. If we do not accept its findings, we shall never feel sure about anything. So, be sure the X-Ray is OK – go again to a hospital if you feel you must – and then try hard to forget it. It is quite possible that the pain is a digestive one, I think, and very likely that your mode of living has ruined your digestion for the present. But what I feel is that your pain comes from wanting to hug me, which impulse probably overcomes you during your sleeping hours, and plants the pain there. It is perhaps a silly thought, but it's the one I have. I am so sorry you are troubled like this, and would so much like to be with you to allay your fears, to comfort you. I am disturbed that you should have held on to your 'secret' for so long. Please do tell me all you can as early as you can. Because nothing can be gained by non-revealing (I use that instead of 'concealing') and I would much prefer to worry or feel with you than be kept in ignorance. This is my right and your duty and obligation.

I am marrying you. Do keep me informed all the time about everything, so that I can always be sure I know just what is going on. It is a good motive not to want to worry me with your fears – but I would prefer the idea that you bring me your fears and cast them away by my knowledge of them. I think I told you once that I had a 'fear' that I had TB or something as terrible, through finding a little clot of blood in my mouth in the mornings. I went to a doctor in fear and trembling (and so bravely I thought) to be told it was excessive whistling and speaking that had caused the slight tearing of the tiny little flesh-parts in my throat.

I very much favour you having some sick leave, plenty of it as it seems even slightly desirable. I object to the thought of you working when you aren't really well. I resent the idea of you 'keeping going' just because you either feel there is a war on somewhere and ought to do your bit, or you are too conscientious to stay away. For goodness' sake, rest when you need it, relax when you feel like it, and give your nerves and body a chance. You have had a very bad time in the last five years. Start realising it's time you took it easier, and 'taking it easy' will be better for you than all the medicines in the world. Blow me, just think of my life of idleness (which is good for me up to a point – I've had a wonderfully idle time since I joined the Army) and your scurryings – sometimes you get frantic, don't you?

Sorry the brassiere did not fit. I should chuck the thing if I were you. No wonder you have no coupons! Oh, I wish I was a brassiere, touching you like that.

How do you pronounce DEVOTEE?

As I write this, you are probably pouring out tea for Mum. You dear girl.

I LOVE YOU.
Chris

≈

8

Do Mention Marriage

16 July 1945

Joshua Reynolds born, 1723. Chris Barker conscripted, 1942.

Lovely woman, Darling Bessie, My Dearest, Dearest One,

Today marks the third anniversary of my being joined to the Army. The three years seems to have gone with fair speed, although I feel at times that certain periods have gone rather more quickly than others. I have been abroad 2 yrs 5 months. I have been writing you hopefully (I think it was hopefully) for nearly two years, lovingly for nearly eighteen months. Both periods seem far longer. I saw you last nearly four months ago, it seems much longer than that. I was captured seven months ago. It seems very much less. My impression of time is jumbled and confused. My main aim now is to get back to you, as soon as I can. To many, being apart must be almost like losing everything. But we have our written words to assure us that nothing of our understanding is forgotten.

This morning, I started Morse training. Said I could do five words a minute, and I am doing six, running the words together, putting Ys for Cs and so on. I don't know how long it will last, but it is probably better than picking up stones in the camp and it gets me out of the wind and the dust, which in the daytime are not so good.

One good thing that has been installed here is a Laundry, where you can go to do your washing. Plenty of hot water, scrubbing boards and brushes, and (take your turn in the queue) an iron. I am afraid I don't use it, as it is ½ mile away from my tent, and I can wash my clothes very easily at the 'ablution benches' only fifty yards away. They soon dry in the sun and roaring wind, and I sleep on them at night to give them a crease.

I love you.
Chris

~

18 July 1945

Dr W.G. GRACE born, 1848

My Very Dearest, Loveliest One,

This morning I decided I would have a break. I reported sick, a beautifully long, drawn-out job. You report at 7.30, wait for a truck to take you away at 8 o'clock, its motor is not heard till 8.30, you arrive at the Sick Bay at 9, and then wait for your name to be called. It was 11 o'clock before I got in to see the doctor, and by that time I had completely read *King Cole* by W.R. Burnett, an American published book portraying the Election for Governor of Ohio. I shall go sick again on Saturday. It's just like leave!

Last night in the camp, we had a turn by a magician. Rather boring after an hour. He explained, Italian fashion, his earlier tricks. The big thing, the piece de resistance, was that lead was turned into molten metal, he poured it into a spoon, and put it in his mouth, then spitting out a solid, but still very hot, piece of metal. The lead was heated by blow lamp, it was too hot to be touched by the two 'witnesses' on the stage. I suppose he had some false plates of special heat-resisting metal in his mouth. But it was pretty good.

How would you like to live at Sanderstead, Croydon? Have you thought about moving out that way? As it is 'one of those things', may I warn you not to discuss this with anyone. Later on it will be obvious why; for the moment I want to know what you think of Sanderstead; no chance remarks to anyone at my home, please, my dear.

I wrote yesterday to the Tottenham Registrar, Mr Grimaldi, asking for details of how to get married quickly. I pointed out it was a general question, particularly now that short leave is likely to be more widespread.

Incidentally, this morning at Sick Quarters, in a German POW Camp, I saw more Germans than I had ever seen before; thousands. I have only seen them in ones and twos, in hospitals before we started having them working in the camp. Strange how we 'fight' without seeing our mortal enemies. They have no doubt seen as few English as we have Germans.

I have written 298 letters in all since April 10th: 98 to you, 59 to Mum, 141 to others. 98, the number of this, was the last you got from me last year, I believe. So we are well up on the numbers this year, though the sooner we can talk to each other rather than write, the better for us both. Oh, my darling Bessie.

I love you.
Chris

~

19 July 1945

My Very Dearest,

I read with regret of the extraction of your teeth. The racketeers. I think I should go ahead and have the whole lot out now. It will save you a lot of trouble later on. And you'll almost certainly find a dentist who will tell you you would be better off without them.

Will not proceed further with these comments – as they are the major items you mention. But, take my advice, and watch your engagements carefully. Try and get some time to yourself. Certainly don't start leaving your Dad's darning and your own washing for non-important things. You must learn to refuse. I shall be annoyed if you don't. It may be very wrong of me, but I shall be.

As for having your teeth out and do I still love you – I love you alright. I love you always. But your letter 52, comparatively long, gave me the impression of being rush-written, quickly and hardly with thought. I feel that you are riding for a nervous complaint, or something, and I am displeased. I'd very much like to get home and organise you, tell you what to do. I expect that is rather 'bossy', but that is the feeling I have at the moment. But, for goodness' sake, do try to take it steadier. And do love me more than anything.

I love you.
Chris

≈

20 July 1945

Dear Bessie,

I am sorry about your chest. You appear to have received expert attention, expert assurance. Myself, I should rub it with Vick, or Ellimans, anything, to try and produce a move. You say you have lost that 'tiredness and general run-down feeling'. I must congratulate you, but I must warn you, too. I think you are rushing around too much.

I am not a bit hard on 'The Tories'. They quite definitely are the biggest, the most expert, beautiful liars the political life of this country has ever seen. They lie every time they say they are National, they lie about what they propose to do, and what they have done.

I had better try and get a few words over to you on this Deb business, upon which you are 'sorry', 'No, I'm not even sorry', 'really angry', 'bloody trivial' and 'truly sorry'. I am glad you are so frank, and hope you will always show me in this way how your mind is working. I find your plea for 'more understanding' a bit awkward. Do you imagine me to be likely to intrigue with Deb against you? Or that I am likely to fall in love with her? Or to spend time on her instead of on you? Or to treat you in any inferior way because of her? What, otherwise, is this 'torture' you suffer from? You say you are no longer desirous of sloshing her. I have a woman friend who happens also to be a friend of yours, or so I had imagined. Do I ditch her, slap her down or what? You be bold enough to tell me how you think I should act, and I have no doubt I can be understanding enough to do as you want. There are no secrets between you and I (I hope). I am a worried man at the moment, but I hope not a foolish one.

Please believe. I love you.
Chris

~

21 July 1945

Dearest Chris,

You blooming old Darling, I could hug and hug and hug you, for somehow saying all the right things, and being your so beautiful self, do you wonder that I get so blue? Look what I am doing without.

Yes, I felt more excited about the Labour Win than VE Day. Reeves got in with a 10,000 majority. Labour gain from Conservative too. I do wish everybody would stop striking now and give the government a chance to get into action, dash it all, a 40 hour week at this stage is a bit precipitate.

No, no, no, you are not wrongly interfering in my affairs, I want you, want you to interfere, for they are our affairs, our affairs, even when I protest, I want you to go on interfering, because maybe I am not very used to it yet, but I want to get used to it, we are dependent on each other, we cannot have any private life apart, for two people loving each other so much there is no other way but complete and utter surrender of everything. I should feel desolate if you didn't want to interfere, if you didn't have bossing thoughts, it gives me happiness to know that you have, forgive me any perversity I may indulge in, I am rather ordinarily human. Yes, it is my duty to us, that I take things easier, and I am trying to do that, I have become a martyr to my engagements and am cutting them down.

I know you are right Chris because they have been fretting me. It's funny how when you are run down, you seem driven on to do more than you can, it's so difficult to stop rushing, even looks as though you've detected my state of nerves in my letters, never thought of it showing like that, but how I hated being told. Bless you dear for being what you are, for noticing, for being strong enough to tell me. You make me feel safe and sure in your keeping.

Re Deb, of course carry on as usual, I hadn't ever thought of you doing anything else. Didn't you know that trying to discuss rationally an irrational point is a feminine foible? Darling, you have made me feel coolly detached about Deb by saying 'who are all these other people, what are all these other things?' So don't worry anymore. I felt the same myself, we belong, the rest doesn't matter.

So sorry to have caused so much upset, but so glad to have you say all the things you have said, I adore you. Yes, I am yours, yours alone. We are hungry for each other, oh so very hungry, for everything you have to give me. Your hands, your arms, your lips, your body, the smell of you, to know again the exquisite magic of being so very close to you. When I imagine hard, I can feel your hand on the top inside of my thigh, why just there I don't know, but that spot is what I can recapture sometimes, just your hand there, so vividly your hand. Don't you think that odd, it's quite a feeling, and always the right leg. Did you rest it there most, or something?

I guess I haven't felt that 'calmness of spirit' since Greece, it came home to me then how easily I could lose you, just like that, and I haven't been able to erase it from my mind, it impressed me too deeply. I thought then, can this happen to us, it can, we were lucky.

Lick for me, rise for me, yearn for me, go on wanting me, always – need me, need me, need me, feel my pain, my misery, for we are one.

Your hand in my blouse, on the tip of my breast – sweet delight – wonderful man.

I Love You.
Bessie.

~

26 July 1945

My Dearest Bessie,

There was plenty of excitement here today. I came back from giving a lecture on the Cooperative Movement at about 12 o'clock, and got the news that there had been 20 Labour Gains in the first 61 seats declared. After, at each hour, we crowded around the wireless to get the latest figures, doubting yet hoping that 'the people' had given Mr Churchill the right to retirement, and the Labour Party instructions to proceed to secure a fair share of the world's goods for all who work. At the time of writing, 7 p.m., the Labour Party has a majority of 160 over all other parties and is bound to be called by the King to form his Government. It is a great surprise to me, and gratifying in the extreme. Not only because Labour now has the chance to repair some war damage, but because the Tories lied so viciously to retain office, with Beaverbrook the biggest story teller of them all.

I suppose now that everyone will expect the Millennium, miracles overnight, the immediate Heaven. Personally, I am advising chaps to take it easy and expect little or nothing. It will take years to modify the existing private interests, especially in face of their opposition.

All the chaps here voted Labour, and always have been Labour. That's the impression! A sort of Boat Race night.

I love you.
Chris

~

27 July 1945

My Darling, My Dearest,

Let me say another word about Deb.

If you had a regular man correspondent in the same relationship as I am to Deb, I should probably curse his luck, but how, in face of what you tell me of your love for me (which I absolutely believe) could I entertain any serious ideas? He would be your pal, not your lover. You say I threw in a lecture with my observations on Deb. I expect to be lecturing quite a bit, remembering questions and discussions can always follow a lecture. When I say I want you 'entirely', 'wholly', 'completely', I do mean it. Because I believe that you possess all that I want – an honesty of mind, an interlocking temperament, a superb body. Oh, I know and I am glad, that you are a living, breathing woman, but what can I do about Deb, other than what I have done, carried on as usual. I am at your feet, content to be there.

I want you to understand and be uplifted by the awareness of my body's urgent need of you, I want you to feel (not just while you are reading, but always) my primitive urgings, my great mental and physical desires around you, my unbounded affection, my complete devotion.

Oh, these miles are bad, I need you. I am hungry for you, hungry for your body, your body, your body. Hungry. Hungry. Hungry.

Will reply to the rest of your letter tomorrow.
I love you.
Chris

≈

28 July 1945

My Darling,

I have today won a draw for a 'Victoria League' parcel, and in a couple of months, all being well, you'll get one. They are 5s. each, and contain something like a pound of jam, a pound of sugar, a tin of fruit, or something like that. They are moderately worth winning in the draw. I believe they come from Victoria, Australia, as a kind of help to people in England.

I am glad you are not opposed to the idea of Sanderstead. It is very important that you don't breathe a word anywhere. I have hopes. Some hopes. (You know how in these times the securing of a place is dependent on about ten things going as you want them.) This is one of those cases. There is a chance. With Wilfred actively pursuing the matrimonial idea, you must be prepared for him to live at 27 with his bride. This is inevitable, and would effectively eliminate any hope we might have in that direction. I can quite believe that your Dad could get £2,000 for 27. But it would be folly to sell unless a better place had already been secured. I am sorry you can't be told more at present.

The housing situation is now very hopeful, long-term view, as Labour will not dally on this, if on any other issue. But even in the next five years sufficient houses cannot be built to overcome the shortage. We shall certainly be in a tight spot, unless we do 'strike lucky'.

The thought of being in a house, alone with you, with closing the front door and taking you to me as I wish, is a tremendous thought for me to have. It seems impossible, yet one day such an event will occur.

I didn't go into Bari today, as I took on the job of colouring the map of UK we had supplied to us, showing the constituencies. Almost all Southern England is blue, and almost all Northern Scotland. In the scattered areas, the Conservatives have still got their supporters. It is up to the Labour Party to show them, by 1950, that they are best served by the representatives of the working people.

I LOVE YOU.
Chris

~

30 July 1945

Dearest,

What a rotten hound I feel, what an unthinking thing for bringing all this reproach on you. I don't know what I can do about it. Nothing now. You chide me about Deb, and I feel displeased. I say so, and you ask forgiveness. And I now ask for yours. I really don't know why I must insist on being right, and of needing that you be quite above human feeling. I want you to think, if you can, how I can avoid doing this again. For, there can be no question that when I wrote I knew I would upset you, and I must have wanted to upset you, just to squeeze out of you some expression of regret. But had I just passed your Deb remarks by, you might have thought more that I was more interested in her than I am. What sort of method can we adopt, so that if we disagree upon something the other has said, we can say so, but not go into details. How can I mean a damn thing I say if I go out of my way to cause you distress by saying I am distressed. I love you and yet I hurt you. What an abject distasteful specimen I am. To the misery of our separation (which you do everything to lessen for me) I add half-insults and gratuitous doubts.

Please, please, don't tell me your life has been misery but for our five weeks. I am appalled at that statement, devastated by the anguish of that cry. Can you not modify it? Remember how you must have felt when you got that first sea-mail letter of mine in September 43, and of when you came home and read the second letter with hat cocked over your eye? And of the hopes I aroused in you, and you aroused in me. How magically we claimed each other and proudly granted everything we had. You only imagine that 'the rest is misery'.

My dear Bessie, I think I have told you twice already (I know I have done it once) that my fear about marriage related to the fact that I might get killed in a battle. There is not now very much likelihood of that, as I am fairly certainly not going to Burma. Therefore, only your agreement stands between me and my ambition – to have you for my wife. So, I do 'visualise it' for my next leave – when I get it! I visualise confessing personally to you that I have been a hound over this incident, of asking and receiving your pardon.

Saw Japanese Suicide Planes on British Movietone News yesterday. Deadly. Came out 5 minutes after Boyer and Fontaine's *Constant Nymph* had commenced, as it was very bad sound.

My darling, I am a hound, I am sorry. I love you.
Chris

2 August 1945

Dearest,

Yes, the election results are a bit of a shock. I hadn't noticed that Hampstead, of all places, had gone Labour. You are supposed to be cut off from the world in your Italian village, but you still remain better informed than most. I am a bit amazed at your ability to supply information on anybody I seem to mention. How is it done? I am really more than a bit amazed, generally speechless.

My indigestion is still awful. I don't think it's 'chewing', I fear it's nerves, though how it happens I don't know. It reminds me of when I first started work. I had been in for 3 civil service exams and matriculation, what with that and the upheaval of starting work I had 'orrible indigestion for goodness knows how long. I thought I had grown out of such things, but it doesn't seem like it, does it?

Perhaps the circumstances are excusable, but when I shall recover from this business I don't know, makes me get rather fed up with myself. I must phone your home tomorrow, for they will wonder what has happened to me. I don't like to admit to not feeling up to scratch, but guess I shall have to before long. Thank you, very very much, for the 'Victoria League' parcel, it sounds a spot of the right stuff. I shouldn't say anything about it to your Mum unless she should ask, I think it best.

My goodness, I am glad you abandoned the idea of not writing for a week because of our misunderstanding. I should have been in a fine state, makes me quiver to think of it, think of my poor old digestion.

I do wish I could be a bit more like you, you remember detail and always somehow comment on the right things. It makes me feel hopeless, you know. You satisfy me so much that I don't feel you get it back from me in full measure.

I won't breathe a word about Sanderstead, just keep my fingers crossed and hope.

To come back to the Labour Government. I do think they should make a good job of it, I do think they have more brains to work with than the Tories. When you compare the two, Labour show up rather well, don't you think?

I wonder how our leave is getting on. I do think your commanding officer is a bit thick, surely you should be entitled to some compensation for being POW. It wasn't exactly a picnic.

Goodnight Darling. I Love You.
Bessie

~

2 August 1945 [Second letter]

My Dear One,

Please do mention marriage to my Mum just as much as you want. I have already (some time ago) told her I shall be marrying you a few days after my next return home, and although she did not reply, I know this was because I had already conveyed this state to her previously. I wish I could write you quite frankly on this point; but I do want you to avoid giving Mum any kind of impression that she will be left alone because of the married lives of her several children.

Had a busy day today. Up early and spent the whole morning on the range, firing the rifle. I believe the total possible, in about 25 rounds, all different styles of shooting, was 100. The top man got 66, the bottom 12. I was next to bottom with 22.

You need not feel anxious about how the Labour Party will manage, I think. They certainly cannot do worse than the Conservatives, as you say. But I am sure they will do very much better. Most of the Labour members are experienced in the school of life and socially competent to deal with its problems. I think the Tories are in for a shock in about three years, when our initial conservative reforms give way to more sweeping ones. The only thing that can confuse us is the little jealousies of the Big Men, and I rather think that Attlee's ordinariness is a guarantee that some of them will be held in check.

There is some scheme of a week's leave; I believe it starts after this month's leave has been had by all the lads. That's where I come in. But it may be much later than this other. And I want to get to you now, as soon as possible. But I should be home by August 1946 (3 yrs 6 mth) on my Python,* as it is called. You say the *Express* is prophesying the end of the Japan war by the Autumn. They are,

---

*'Python' was slang for army leave due after a particular length of service, usually four years. A soldier's 'return' suggested a snake eating its own tail.

as you suppose, notoriously unreliable. According to them, King Edward VIII would not abdicate; there would have been 'no war this year or next year either' in 1939; and the Conservatives are in power in Parliament now.

Regarding letters, we'll leave it as it is. I am not reluctant to reduce your one source of contact with me. And certainly I don't want you to 'hate it, hate it' through any action of mine. But, I really would like you to write me rather less, because I believe you are doing too much. All your many letters only increase your 'tenseness', as well as more practically take up your time. I want you to take me in your stride. Every other day, at the most, twice a week at the least. Five times a fortnight is what you want to aim at. I think you will find the tension relieved a little by this. And – and shall I suppress conveying my physical thoughts? It doesn't do me good, really, I think. The thought of you stirs and pulls me too much for my physical quietness. Half my time I spend physically raging for you. The other half I spend between the blankets.

I think you are very brave about your teeth. I should say you'd got roughly ten times the guts that I have.

I want to be just what 'kind of a man' you want. I want to be everything to you, now and always. I didn't want to laugh at your 'I want to get married'. I wanted to put 'Me, too' by its side.

You are beautiful.
I love you.
Chris

∾

3 August 1945

My Darling,

You say you haven't thought seriously about leave or marriage because the fear of disappointment is too horrible to think about. Don't, then, worry about any such thing as disappointment. I know that I shall marry you. Can't you just make that break, and know, too?

You say that marriage to me is your one ambition. That is my position too. It is my one wish above anything else, it is my one desire. I want to bring you relief and myself be relieved. I want to come to you and love you, come into you and stop with you, warm you and keep you warm. I want to be everything to you. I want you always to have the same high, undeserved opinion of me as you have now. I want the increased communion of our minds, the greater understanding of each other. And I want for myself the dear flesh of you, I want the wonder of your body, the magic of your breasts, the happiness of being with you, near you. If you do not hear the plain deep cry, my vitals to yours, it is not because I do not thump and bump and shake and tremble at the sheer beauty you are to me, the wondrous loveliness of your body, the delight of your hands.

It has just come over me – the thought of us being married, together, naked, alone. How I want to traverse your flesh everywhere with my lips. How I want to place my hands, my lips, my everything, to the vital vibrant spot. To be lost completely in you, to be entirely, absolutely a part of you. I hope you are right about your ability to learn to obey, because I have probably the makings of a real Victorian in me, as I believe you once discerned. I shall be doing a lot of ordering about unless I use my brains. Query: will I, and can you take it?

Don't 'hold out on me'. Let me have you, every bit of you that I can. You are wonderful. I love you.

Chris

~

6 August 1945

Dearest,

This is a very brief note, as I am about to start for Rome. We stop in Bari for the night and then have a day on the train.

As I finished yesterday's letter, I discovered that Bert had come back to camp. He left here this morning on his first stage homewards. By the time you get this, he may be home, as he is almost certainly being flown. But do not tell Mum, she is nervous. Although on guard it was good to be able to see him go, smiling, homewards.

Sorry your digestion is still troublesome.

More as soon as possible.

I love you.

Chris

~

8 August 1945

My dear Bessie,

This is a brief and formal note to let you know that I am now in Rome. We arrived at 8.30, and are not free to leave until about 3 o'clock, by which time the CO will have given us a lecture, telling us how many VD cases, and so on. I have spent the last hour having a shower and handing in my dirty clothes. Last night, I made myself comfortable on the floor of the train compartment with another chap, while two chaps had the seats, and two the racks, both seats and racks consisting only of their wooden slats and not comfortable. I am rather tired from the journey, and my old bones ache a bit, rather naturally. Brigadiers do not travel this way. The Rest Camp is 7 miles from Rome, through which I have only just travelled by truck at the moment. It is a former hospital, a very large one.

There is a large Italian staff, and the girls are (rather expectedly) 'fresh'. Some of the chaps sickened me by calling out to many of them. The journey through the hills was laborious and punctuated by many stops, where poor little Italian children, bare-footed and clothed only in the merest of threads, happily caught the bully and bread with which we were abundantly supplied. Usually prostitutes work the trains, are hauled aboard at one station and set off many miles down the line. I don't know if it happened this time. The scenery is really wonderful. I hope we can see it ourselves, together, one day.

Let me end by saying I love you and that whatever I may see this week, it will be less valuable because I see it by myself.

I love you.

Chris

~

9 August 1945

My Darling,

It is already clear to me that all my efforts at description will fail to convey to you anything but a tenth of what the parts of Rome I see are like. The buildings are tremendous, and many. The statues are magnificent and everywhere. The shops are full of good (manufactured) things of life, and they range from the car to the cosmetic. I saw a pair of shoes at £22 10s.

The people are not so different as I had been led to expect. They are more friendly than in Bari, but this may be because they know more English. The clothes of the Romans, particularly the women, are quite easily superior in fashion and variety to those in London. I cannot say about quality – most of the material used by the young is what is naughtily described as diaphanous. The beauty of the Roman girls is a bye-word throughout Italy. Many of them are indeed splendid sights. They freely use beauty-aids, do not wear stockings, but colour their toes, easily seen through the fact that most wear sandals. I should think there are many prostitutes here; as we came out of the theatre last night, there were many beauties walking singly. Two people invited us to a 'Clean

Bedroom – Respectable' – but I rather feel that maybe their idea of respectability is based on Tiberius or some such humanitarian. Two women we saw 'giving the eye' rather disgusted us – one of them was soon to be a mother. Seeing these places under war-time conditions is a disadvantage.

The atomic bomb announcement* (which I don't understand) makes me wonder about the future. What a life!

Whatever may be the reasons, the end of the Far East war is surely to come sooner as a result of it. And (since we can only interpret such news in a personal way) for you and for me, that spells earlier happiness. The Japanese may sling it in, but more likely they will be blasted utterly and earlier than scheduled.

I love you.
Chris.

At the Vatican, August 1945 (Chris front row, third from left)

---

* A second atomic bomb was dropped on Nagasaki on this date, three days after the first destroyed Hiroshima.

10 August 1945

My Darling,

Sitting in the YMCA just now, I heard a news flash from the USA Soldiers' Station, that the Japanese had broadcast the acceptance of Allied surrender terms. It is already in the Rome papers, and just after the original announcement there came from below the cheers of the Romans. I hope it is true.

My first thought was of thankfulness that our chaps will not have to die in greater numbers to tame the Japanese. My second, and subsequent thoughts have been of how the news affects us. It must surely mean that I shall be released from the Army much sooner, that more leave will be allowed even to chaps who are in the Army. It spells happiness for us, rather earlier than we could have expected. So rejoice that we are nearer, rejoice that our wasted years really are ending, and that soon we shall be together, not only for a little while (fine though that is) but for always. I do hope that your constitution will be able to stand all the rising emotions it needs must support. If you are anything like me (and, gloriously, you are) you are bounding forward, surging onwards, though yet there is time we must wait.

I am enclosing a photograph taken in the Vatican Gardens today. On my right hand side there are three chaps I spend the days with: Barton, Tuckey and Thurgur. The tour this morning was of the Vatican Gardens and Museum and Sistine Chapel. The Museum contains the gifts of all the European sovereigns, the kind of Blackmail to the Eternal, which the RC Church has practised since its inception. I cannot convey the beauty of the tapestries, paintings, sculptures, mosaics, which the Museum contains.

His Holiness received me (and 400 others) in audience, spoke in Italian and English for four minutes – I caught one word, 'Blessings'. Brazilians, Americans, S. Africans, New Zealanders were amongst the crowd of the blessed. The Swiss Guards would do credit to a D'Oyly Carte show, the priests are an anaemic looking lot of stupids.

I love you.
Chris

~

20 August 1945

My Dear Bessie,

Well, today I got the letter card from Mum which I have been dreading. I expect you'll know all about it by now, as you might have been at Bromley the day Bert got home. I needn't bother with the details. Bert was friendly with a chap named Wicks when he first joined the Army. He wrote him irregularly whilst abroad, and his letter sent last December was acknowledged by his friend's wife. Her husband had been accidentally shot in Italy last July. Bert sent her some nuts, and letters became quite frequent. He had fallen in love with her, and she with him. He was very confident (as honest innocent people are) that Mum would find it easy to adjust herself of the new situation. I thought it possible but unlikely, and tried to tell him what I could of the disadvantages. (Mrs Wicks lives at Sanderstead, hence my suggestion of the name a month back.) He said that he would tell Mum the first day he arrived, then call on Mrs Wicks. I presume that he has done that. Probably Mrs Wicks was as happy as Mum was unhappy.

I am quite inadequately provided with genius to meet this situation. Personally, I find it easy to say that Bert is acting naturally and wisely and that Mum is too closely concerned as a principal to be anything but selfish and jealous.

You are in an awkward situation too. I should be very surprised to find you had different views from me, but I would be very grateful for them. Your awkward situation is that you have to try and stop neutral and be helpful to both parties, principally to Mum. Please have a shot. What a life.

I LOVE YOU.
Chris

~

29 August 1945

My Very Dearest One,

I hope the enclosed 'brochure' broke the news gently to you. The operative date for us is October 10th, by which time I should have done 2 yrs 8 mths abroad, and by which time, also, I hope that the 2 yrs 8 mths men will be proceeding on leave.

In a real sense I may, I think, regard myself as on the way to you. We'll discuss how it was done, or why, and whom it affects, later on – for the present, I am very happy to think that WE shall BE together in a measurable distance of time. Perhaps as little as two months, maybe as much as three or four. It means that I can put my arms around you, and call you my wife. It means that we can marry and sleep together. It means that your name will be Barker and you'll be a 'Mrs'. It means that I shall cast away your last doubt by a legal act, and that in a slightly different fashion we shall face the world together. It means each of us giving all to the other and holding nothing back in any way. It means new responsibilities and duties. It means settling down in faith and hope in each other. It means you'll be taking on a very hard case, and [section of letter torn off].

I must say I think you are lovely and tell you I want you and need you. That I want to rub myself against you, realise the full fleshly dearness of you, appreciate the grandeur of your beauty, the call of your body, acknowledge, honour, you.

I love you.
Chris

30 August 1945

Dearest Bessie,

This is a quick letter, rushed, crowded in.

I am glad you are getting olive oil in England.

This week in Bari I have been able to look in most of the footwear shops, and I can tell you that there is no chance at all of getting warm winter shoes. Everything is very skimpy, wood or cork, with a few little strips of stuff to keep the shoes on the feet.

I have sent you off three parcels of new season's nuts today (as a matter of interest I tell you they are 7s. each).

It occurs to me that Bert might make some suggestion to you that, should I arrive home at about the time he gets out of the Army, we might get married on the same day, or something like that. Please do not favour this course; I don't suppose the position will arise but it might do, hence the observation. I would very much like to get home about October 24th, and get married on October 26th, but I don't suppose anything so specially nice as that would happen.

I know nothing about rings. I suggest you do a very little bit of window gazing, with the idea of familiarising yourself with the kinds of rings there are, so that when we buy it, there will be only one dumb bell present, and that me.

Yes, my cold went OK, but yesterday after three very bad nights in which I slept little owing to the type of bed I slept on I found myself with stomach trouble, heartburn and one or two other bad things. Of course, that must be the day on which I was giving my specimen lecture, and when it came to it I was very tired and not very well, so that I was nervous, and very ordinary. Although I got certain commendations from the very radical Major who is in the command, he also said my voice became monotonous after a time (which was quite true, but I hope not, normally) and that I was too much of a propagandist (a fault I really am well aware of).

Your body, your breasts, your hairs, your moisture, they speak to me, they say to me: 'Come!' I must have you, have you, for I can only be happy through you.
I love you.
Chris

~

2 September 1945

My Dearest, Loveliest, Most Wonderful, Delightful One,

I received your letter of the 28th today, with more than a little relief, as another day without the joy your letters bring would have been rather bad.

What you need to look out for now is 2 parcels of roasted nuts, posted July, and four more fresh posted in the last few days. That will give you nearly a stone of almonds, but I shouldn't squander them too rapidly, as I am not at all sure if I can send anything like them from Egypt, should I get there . So, I think if I were you I should put them in a dry spot and eat them with a view to their eventual disappearance. (I have now spent £11 on nuts since my return here in April, by the way.)

'Moving' is in the air, and a fortnight is mentioned. So if you get few letters for a fair time (I mean only a little, I shall write daily while I can), it means I am packing up books, maps, pens, blackboards, and so on, for the sea voyage (sickening thought, I hoped I'd finished with water, water everywhere).

I am so sorry that I must go away again after my next leave. It will be hard. But the leave will make it worth it, and your new status be a mental help to you during my next, and perhaps last, absence. Bessie, my darling, my lovely, wonderful woman, it will be such sweet delight to be in a room with you again, to be able to put my hand up your skirt, to put my hands in your blouse, to grasp your breasts, to touch the tips of them. What grander sight than to contemplate your loveliness, to see your breasts, to look upon the vital spot? My darling, five months ago (see, five months have gone!) you were very good to me.

I will not say very much about the Bert business. But, I must be honest and think that Bert would have been wonderful had he 'given up' Daisy (Mrs Wicks) and there is plenty of justification, superficially, for much that Mum says. Logically, I am with Bert. Sympathetically, I am with Mum. You do well if you can behave neutrally, but I think you should.

My Darling, I need you more, really need you more, every day.
I love you.
Chris

~

My Wonderful Woman,

I posted letter 50 earlier today because I had to be sure that you would be getting the earliest possible answer to your letter saying you knew I was due for leave sometime.

I ought to explain how the leave is given. They take chaps in order of seniority of overseas service. When October 10 arrives, my claims have to be considered, and if I am the senior (2 yrs 8 months) I go. Actually, I have just spoken to a 2 yrs 9 months chap who has not yet gone. Whether I go in October or later depends on the number sent, but anyhow it is quite clear that it is only a matter of months before I am homeward bound – although blow me, it will be hard coming back. There's one good thing, though, no other separations we shall have are likely to be as long as our first. Six months is about as much as we shall have, I think. I very much hope so, too, for I have been away from you far too long already. My darling, you were lovely on leave, I was – I am – delighted with you. A good thing this time is that you won't have the worry of considering if I may change my mind upon sighting you.

To proceed to other points in your letter (though I don't want to, for all I am saying is 'She knows. She knows. She knows').

Glad you think Mum is a little better. Please see her as much as you can. It is important, more so than before. It'll tire you and try you, but please do this.

Regarding the 28 days, I feel that purely because of the need to demonstrate my kinship with Mum, we should try to spend most of our time (apart from that fourteen days when I get you ALL TO MYSELF) at 161 [the Barker family home], that is, sleeping there and visiting 27 (reverse procedure to that you suggested). It is not likely to be so convenient, but there are obvious reasons for it. Let me know your views, please.

I hope we can get somewhere fairly private – where going to bed early can be accomplished without askances.

I love you.
Chris

∾

9 September 1945

My Dearest,

We are stopping the night in the lofty tree-filled park which is the Transit Camp, Naples.

I am familiar with the road run to Naples, having done it several times before. This is a wonderful run and is reminiscent of some of the Scottish trips. As we ran through the villages there is the usual unceasing activity – almonds drying, being shelled, maize drying, tomatoes strung up outside the houses also drying; a girl walks along with half-a-dozen turkeys, a boy with a pig, adults bare-legged and -footed wait at the fountain for water then carry it away on their heads, three or four horses labour under a heavy cartload of stone, as we stop boys come along to ask for 'biscottys' as they call them (biscuits). My driver is in charge of the truck, and more or less in charge of me. I wouldn't take an order, but I can't give him one, so am more or less compelled to tacitly agree with his actions. He gave three people a lift as we passed through a village near our Camp, but later would not stop for anyone – Poles he hates, the coloured American he regards as a black illegitimate, ordinary Americans he won't help, and so on. He told me before we started that there was a good 'racket', picking up a load of grain in one village, and dropping it at one miles away (you might get as much as £2 10s. for such a service, he said. I bet it's to avoid tax or something).

Well, he stopped on the road and took aboard an elderly woman, shrivelled as are most old Italians, and a girl aged about 19. He had agreed to take them and their two bags of grain to a village about thirty miles away, in return for (he explained to the young Italian) 'a little love'. Well, this is a serious offence, no passengers are permitted. About five miles down the road he asked me (so casually) if I wanted to have the girl? I told him 'no thanks' and a few more miles along he stops and says we will have a 'brew up', so while I make tea, the old woman goes in one direction and he and the young girl disappear in the bushes in another. About ten minutes pass and he returns, to give me a detailed account of the copulation – not satisfactory to him. The girl returned, the old woman, and off we went again.

I LOVE YOU.
Chris

~

19 September 1945

My Darling,

It seems a long long time since I heard from you. I cannot understand your pathetic little 'No letters, no letters, none at all', as I have written daily and will always do so, though (as I have explained) it may be that my letters must be curtailed – against my will – on occasions.

Please don't tear up your letters to me – send them. Put a pencil through them if you like, to show the undecided state you are in. But please, please, please, send me what you think.

I am very glad that Mum paid 27 Woolacombe a visit again and I hope you can continue them. I know that she is extremely pleased that (as it seems to her) others are interested and 'want' her. I know how I should feel if you didn't 'want' me. That is how Mum has persuaded herself to be over Bert's legitimate if precipitate declarations. (The news in her letter to you that she has burned all our letters is a big disappointment to me. I had such a lot of anecdotes hidden in my letters home. All my Army antics. It's a cut at me.)

Am glad you received the knife and scissors. It is a ladies' knife, is it not? Glad you did not pay duty. Bert paid 8s. for two knives I sent him (one for him and one for Archie), a blooming twist.

And all the time I am thinking of you: your new photo in my pocket: the hairs on a piece of paper which says 'I love you': your preciousness, your real wisdom, your gentleness.

I love you.
Chris

~

22 September 1945

Dearest,

I do not feel very happy at the thought of your self-made misery, yet how can I administer a corrective without being much blunter than I wish? What I am continually sorry about is that you cannot spread inside you the idea that I love you and that NOTHING ELSE MATTERS. Regardless of what popular novelists may or may not say, I do not feel that I shall be equal to the task, or even willing to perform, spectacular exhibitions at regular intervals to persuade you that I love you. My wish (at 31) is to settle down in mutual confidence and trust, and share both our joys and sorrows, so that our joys may be doubled and our sorrows lessened in the process. I rather think that it must be my Mother who is the cause of your present 'struggles', and this is a particularly obvious case of where I am impelled to pursue a course by circumstance rather than choice.

If you think and think about something without reference to me, you are failing in your obligation to trust me and my desire to help you. I do not say we do not require education in the 'US' way of looking at things, but I do feel you are holding on much too tightly to your right to fret and worry on your own. What am I for, if not to help? PLEASE do not think I am 'hurt' 'by all this'. All I am doing is to try to help you out of your chronic independence of thought. My love for you is strong, and you must learn to use it. From now on, try and write me all about our leave, and say what you want rather than you suppose I can judge better. There are many things in which we must take equal part. How we spend the 28 days? If 'you and I' was all that need be considered, I should suggest going away for 28 days and spending every moment of every day saying 'you're lovely'. But, of course, that can't be done.

Mum. Your Dad. A few friends. Bert has asked me to see Mrs Wicks if possible, and so on. So what we have to decide is what we will do, not what we want to do.

It is not possible to disregard others. When we think of them we shouldn't let them upset us.

My Darling, My Dearest, let us try harder to understand each other and the meaning and application of our love.

I love you.

Chris

~

23 September 1945

My Darling,

I am inclining to the view that you really ought to give up the South Kens job when I have departed, and really take a rest, as complete as possible, so that you can have a physical and mental free-wheel for a time, and concentrate on our future life together, which is now a near thing.

About concentrating on 'our future life together', I mean that you could do some unhurried thinking, some cool reading and so on, about housekeeping. I am not suggesting it is wise to 'swot' how to make a bed, but I mean as regards getting things together, or preparing a list of the things we would need. Do you think we could get a little booklet in which we could insert items we want, to get the 'bricks and mortar' going? Although we may need to live in someone else's home, I think you would agree that we should acquire our own 'wherewithal' as early as practicable. I enclose an idea for you to think about. I suggest we prepare for a two-roomed establishment, with kitchen-scullery (I know it is not ambitious), draw up a list and cross out the item when it is acquired. I have inserted your possessions that I remember and my own, except that in my case I recognise that they are not quite what you want. I hope you agree with my wish to press ahead with the preparation of a list with a view to the acquisition of things as they become available and reasonable in price.

It would be pleasant, no doubt, to have bags of money and buy all that was required without trouble. But we must get down to this one day, and I think it not too soon, now. We can do a lot of these things by letter, and I hope we will. (For example, we could discuss what we think of buying some kinds of second-hand things, and so on.)

Unbelieving though you may sometimes be, contrarily though I may occasionally appear to act, you are my life, my all. I see the future with you, and there is none without you.

I LOVE YOU.
Chris

∾

24 September 1945

Dearest,

This is where we went today, a trip by car across Exmoor to the Doone Valley. It really was glorious, and the weather though chilly was good, lots of sunshine. How about starting up a cafe in Devon with cars for hire? My goodness I should think you'd make your fortune in a season. 6 in the car at £1 per head for an all round trip of about 70 miles. The people who shared the car were very nice and we all enjoyed it.

My cold is still hovering and I am swallowing aspirins for dear life. I had a bath tonight, hoping it would help to keep it at bay. Felt disappointed to find no mail, am wondering how you are getting on with your course, the place looks delightful. It had a wonderful write up in the Encyclopaedia. I wonder if one day we will be able to go abroad. I have a desire to go with you sometimes, some place. It's rotten not sharing these things now, isn't it? To be doing things together. We have a retired chap here of 80, who works in wood for a hobby, lovely stuff, also he haunts antique shops and collects things, ivory, old silver etc. He lives at this place, and works in a garage, Tonight he is entertaining us with records of Tauber.* I think he is retired Indian Civil Service. I felt inspired by his woodwork, want to do some myself, so satisfying.

I fell for a couple of books in an Ilfracombe shop. A new appreciation of Kipling by Hilton Brown – some of it is enraging me, odd how subjective our criticism is. Also one of Bertrand Russell's, *Conquest of Happiness*. Have only had a glance at that so far, but looks good, he is a wise old bird, one of the greatest minds of today, with real commonsense thrown in, an unusual combination for a scholar. Did you know he was more or less thrown out of one of our universities (Cambridge I believe, not too sure), but feel that is a recommendation. Excuse this rather

---

* Richard Tauber, Austrian tenor.

chatty epistle, but this is an evening of being surrounded by people. I hope tomorrow brings news of you, if only a note.

Goodnight Dear Heart. I Love You.
Bessie

~

9

What Is Truth?

25 September 1945

EVERY DAY IS ONE DAY NEARER.

My Own, Wonderful Woman,

Well, it is off my chest at last. I delivered my speech on 'The Press' this morning and am now safe to contemplate returning to the unit without any ordeal yet to come. It went down fairly well, though I floundered and fiddled and didn't get half of the lesson done. But the teacher said it was very good, and I can't do anything about it. The trouble is that our teacher has praised all who spoke so far, and is not very discriminating. I have been selected to represent our class at a quiz, tomorrow night, so I hope I shall know the answers, or at least be able to think up some decent repartee. Tonight there is a Debate on the Atom Bomb. I could have been principal speaker 'Deploring the discovery' – but decided not to do it, especially as I don't agree it should be deplored any more than some other things. I hope to speak for three minutes against the motion this afternoon.

Regarding your weight, I hope you didn't feel I brushed the question too brusquely aside. I hope my short chance to worship you as you deserve to be worshipped will correct some of your little troubles. But have you tried regularly taking cod liver oil or some such help?

I am pleased you got the first leg of the stocking. I know jolly well it is one thing you really do want anytime. But the cost and my fear of your disappointment at me being 'done' is the thing that has stopped me so far. I hope the second leg turned up OK, and depending on what you say about their quality, I will try to get some more if I pass through Rome on the return journey. I have another pair in my kitbag which I may decide to bring home with me – and put on your lovely legs with my own trembling, wanting hands.

My Darling, I hope we can get married within twenty-four hours of my arrival in London. I want you so much.
I love you.
Chris

∼

26 September 1945

My Dearest,

The Debate went off well, with the motion 'That this House deplores the discovery of atomic energy' being defeated 47–18. I made what I think would be described as an 'effective' speech in opposition.

One thing I believe I have not mentioned in any letter so far is that several times since I have been here, I have felt tremors, caused by earthquakes of minor importance, which are always occurring in this part. It is rather strange to be lying in bed, and find it shake a good deal, as though a tram had passed by outside, or a 20 stone man was doing a tap dance at its foot.

Do you ever wake up in the night and, finding me not with you, feel yourself robbed? I think you must do, because it often happens to me. I wake up and am momentarily surprised you are not by my side. Then I feel, 'Ooh-er, I have been robbed.'

INTERVAL. I am now able to tell you that I didn't disgrace myself in the Quiz, which is now over. Four questions were asked, 3 marks each. I got 7½ out of 12, my side scored 18½ altogether, so I was well up on the average. My team was second, the top team got only 24 (48 the max). My questions were: (1) Who said 'What is truth?' and did not wait for the answer? Correct answer: Pontius Pilate. (Mine: jokingly, GB SHAW – for which I got two marks, ingenuity.) (2) Who was 'Boz'? Correct answer: Dickens. My answer: 'The artist who illustrated Dickens' work' (1½ marks).

(3) Who took part of Mr Chips? My correct answer: Donat, 3 marks. (4) What nationality was Columbus? I said 'Portuguese' but he changed it to Scottish (we had a Scot adjudicating). He was Italian, I got 1 mark for cheek.

Now I must go on Guard, my darling, and in the night hours, think of you by yourself in bed. It will not be long before I am with you. I love you.

Chris

~

1 October 1945

My Dearest, My Wonderful One,

Isn't it wonderful to see the days flicking past, October 10th coming gradually nearer, and our hopeful stage coming closer and closer? Even if it should be some time after October 10th I can bear it, as I shall know then that, any moment, someone may sing out 'Chris boy, your LIAP's come through,'* and that it will not be more than ten days before once again I am with the wonderful reality of your kindliness, your beauty, your softness and your love.

---

* Towards the end of 1945, a new scheme was introduced named LIAP, short for Leave In Addition to Python. Under LIAP, any person who would have served overseas three years before being demobilised was to be given a short home leave.

I am sorry about the non-arrival of both the legs. I posted one on the 15th, another on the 18th. Perhaps the second has gone by ordinary letter post, or been detected, and may reach you with some duty to pay. I doubt if it will really disappear.

We finished off today's proceedings with Community Singing. 'Men of Harlech', 'Hearts of Oak', 'Lincolnshire Poacher', etc. (Hope you like the song book I sent you.) My class sang 'Loch Lomond' – and came first! Despite my grunting tones, which I confessed beforehand.

Have thought just this moment: how about giving a few nuts to your postman? He (she) labours well for us.

I love you.

Chris

~

9 October 1945

MY DEAREST ONE,

I need no longer say 'One Day Nearer'. By the time you get this it will be only a very few days before we are together, before we are communing, expressing, telling all.

I have to go for a medical examination at 2 o'clock tomorrow; and on Thursday the 11th, I leave here on the first stage of my journey home, across Europe by rail, over the Channel and land at Dover. It will take no less than 5 days, so I cannot be with you before the 16th, and I doubt if it will take any more than ten days, in which case I shall for certain be home by the 21st. BUT, the last party that left here waited at the Transit Camp for a week before departing, and this must be borne in mind.

Nevertheless, I think you should resign from the office forthwith by handing in a paper indicating your intention. So I shall come to 27 Woolacombe upon getting to London, although I may ring Iris to make sure you have managed to resign OK. Have a word with her to let her know I may be doing so.

You will be able to go to the Registry Office, procure the licence, and ask how much notice they require of the marriage. If I arrived on the 16th or 17th for example, could we tell them at 4 p.m. one day we wanted to marry at 10 a.m. the next? Get that clear. Could we go there at 9 a.m. and ask to be married at 10.30 a.m. same day? You know what we shall require my dear.

Of course, you should not write me further. Or, at least, if you do write, hand me the letters, not post them.

I shall write Bert also tonight, telling him that I am on the way, but that he need not inconvenience himself to attend the ceremony. I want as little fuss as possible and the more people the more fuss one is likely to get. I suppose I shall now be compelled to attend his wedding. And you!

If you are as pleased and thrilled as me, you are very pleased and very thrilled.

Dearest One, I love you.

Chris

≈

10 October 1945

My Darling,

This is not so good news. Our move from the unit has been postponed until the 16th – 5 days.

You can imagine my rage at hearing the news late this afternoon, after a day of rushing around handing in kit, having a medical and waiting for pay. Most of all I cursed the fact that I had raised in your heart the thought of a very early return. I do feel an ass for telling you as soon as I knew we were to go. Apparently some release men from Greece are to take our places. I hope you are not feeling as damned annoyed as I am. But I hope that, like myself, you will recover quickly.

There is no need to alter any of the arrangements, as it is only a holdup, not a cancellation, this being impossible. But, if you like to carry on at work until the last moment, just please yourself. I thought later that perhaps they wouldn't let you go until you had actually got married.

I could write a terrific lot more, but will leave it for tonight. The extra time here will be in some ways useful for me to do some odd jobs.

Soon I shall be with you. I am sorry for this little further delay. I love you.

Chris

~

11 October 1945

My Dearest,

One good thing about not having left today is that I can still get your mail.

MUM AT THE WEDDING. It seems that I have too easily accepted her declining the invitation to be present. In view of what you say I am writing again tonight asking if she will come as a necessary expression of goodwill to us, as you are rather unhappy at her decision. At least, I will write something like that. Maybe she would come to Blackheath if she cannot stand the ordeal of the ceremony, and make tea for us when we return. With her attitude so much savouring of 'losing' me, it is hard to expect her to come to the affair. Oh for Gretna!

It won't be long now. By the time you get this I should have started on the journey. I am sorry I can't be sure what date I shall arrive. Mark down the jeweller's, and have about £5 in cash handy to pay for ring and licence as I shall arrive without more than 5s. (Stockings, undies.) Don't have more than £5, as Mum will have plenty of my cash in hand.

I love you.
Chris

≈

13 October 1945

My Darling,

Well, for me, half the five days of postponement have now passed, and I am beginning to get a little nervous about further chances of delay! Really, in the blooming Army there's no knowing; but I don't think there will be a second delay from here. Of course, if there are rough seas running in the Channel, they will muck up the sailing schedules. But, really, I feel pretty optimistic and hope your own condition is not too 'jumpy'. Really and truly we are both in the Army, aren't we!

One thing we must try and avoid is discussion about 'going back' if it is going to make us unhappy. Already I am cursing the need for it, and crossing the usual bridges. We must certainly not look on the after-leave period, except to think that, as we are man and wife, we can now have our ROWS with the knowledge that we will not go astray as a result of them, as I think you have apprehensively wondered.

If convenient could you buy me a pair of rubber heels for a man's shoes that pattern, not the circular type? I believe that the nails are supplied with them. I could do with a pair on my shoes. Thanks. I hope you have your case part-packed. Warm clothes, scarf, the BR umbrella, your little clock; if you get a little bit prepared it will help a lot.

I want to visit my Dad's resting place* before I go home. Would you try and remember to remind me? I may forget in the whirl of events.

I have strangely little else I feel I can say.
I love you.
Chris

~

---

* Chris's father died on 5 June 1945. In a letter to Bessie on 15 June he wrote: 'Please do not speculate about my reception and treatment of the news. I have taken it, I regard it, as dispassionately as possible. It is the distance which counts, and the fact that tears in a tent are out of place. I am very concerned about my Mother. I am anxious to stop her remembering. I am desirous of comforting her all I can.'

10

Janet or Christopher

SIX WEEKS LATER

26 November 1945

Dearest,

CALAIS

Everything has gone all too smoothly so far. I arrived at Victoria
at 9.0, and at 9.30 the train drew out. At 12.15 I was one of
eight chaps in a room of the Royal Pavilion Hotel, Folkestone,
a very large building, now a transmit camp. I got a few hours'
sleep before Reveille at 5 a.m. At 5.30 I was eating breakfast, at
6 I was lining up in the cold dark morning to get a blanket. At 7
we moved off to the cross-Channel boat *Canterbury*. At 8 we left
the shore, and at 9.15, after a very quiet serene trip, we touched
France again. We are now in a transit camp in Calais (I have a
bottom bunk in a large Nissen Hut which holds 120 men) and
will be leaving by train at 7.15 tomorrow morning (Reveille 5.30).
There was a NAAFI buffet car on the train, and we could buy a bar

of chocolate and ten cigarettes in addition to tea, cakes, etc. Coffee awaited us at Folkestone if we wanted it. This morning about 6, we paid over 7½d. and received five cigarettes and another bar of chocolate. I have eaten both bars already. Scrumptious. Fry's TIFFIN and Rowntree's FUDGE. Like other things, it was good while it lasted.

I felt quite a hero to be able to get into the compartment without having blubbered. (For me it was either very good, or a commonsense appreciation of the fact that it is different this time, and that the next time we meet it will be for good.) You were outwardly FINE, however you may have wibble-wobbled inside.

I expect it will be some weeks before I am able to write connectedly. For the moment I am too close to your goodness, too humbled by your affection and too proud of my having been with you in all ways, to be settled in my thought. Above everything, I love you, I have had the chance to tell you, and I know that you are mine. My thoughts will always be around you, and I hope to be progressively successful in my letter writing, to avoid some of the jarring elements I have previously sometimes introduced.

I have just got another bar of choc, two boxes of matches and 50 cigarettes, free. And bought another 60 cigarettes for 2s. With 110 cigarettes in hand, I feel happy! I have seen *The Three Stooges* and Frank Sinatra in *Step Lively* at the Camp Cinema (free). It is a wet day here, sometimes the rain is very heavy.

Will you please again convey to Wilfred and Dad my thanks for their kindness. Forgive this scrawl.
I love you.

Your grateful husband,
Chris

~

30 November 1945

Dearest,

I am still at this Transit Camp near Milan, expecting to move off
to Naples tonight. It is very cold and misty, and the camp is very
crowded. I spent at least an hour and a half lining up in mammoth
queues for my meals yesterday. For the NAAFI I had to wait only
a quarter of an hour, but when I came out, there were nearly two
thousand queuing for the hope of cake and tea.

The cooks here are German prisoners and the servers
Italians. There must be a lot of 'flogging' going on. In the town,
which we saw by dark last night, several shops are selling Army
medal ribbon, official pattern, sixpence a piece; it is difficult to get
from Quartermasters. No wonder! The ride through Switzerland
was very good. Passed through Lausanne and ran for five miles
or so beside Lake Geneva, bordered by the millionaire's chalets.
It is a great sight to see the mountains high in the background.
Everything is almost perfectly clean, the chalets and other
buildings are freshly painted, railway stations are neat and tidy.
Many people waved Union Jacks and Tricolours out of windows,
others waved their hands. Whether this is a bit of pre-tourist

traffic beckoning, or genuine appreciation, I cannot say. But at least a dozen troops' trains pass through daily and have been doing so for over four months.

I saw some of those midget umbrellas last night, £2 15s. 0d., but had no money for the purchase. I would like to be stationed around here, but there is no likelihood.

Later. We are definitely leaving tonight. I hope it will be much warmer down South. It's perishing here.

I love you.
Chris

~

1 December 1945

My Darling,

RIMINI
The journey from Novara to this place has been a disgraceful business. I was lucky enough to be one of eight chaps in a compartment, quite full and no spare room. In each of the coaches, however, there were seven or eight chaps who had no seats, and had to wait huddled at the end, in front of the (frequently used) lavatory. The lads in this state in our coach were all RAF, and I was very sorry for them, they could stretch their legs only by standing up. They must have had a terrible night. Our compartment had

the usual two on the racks, two on the seats, two on the floor, and two had to go in the corridor and get as comfortable as possible. We shall repeat the performance tonight, and perhaps tomorrow night, if the train carries on at its present rate.

For breakfast this morning at a wayside halt we again had fried egg! The Germans at these halts have done very well, clean cooking and tables. The last halt was called 'The Gothic Grill', a strange compliment to them.

The train is going now, and my news is little. I am still at the game of guessing 'what we were doing this time last week'. I think of you. I love you.

Chris

～

2 December 1945

We are now in Southern Italy, about twenty miles from Naples. The sun is shining, it is beautifully warm after the cold of the last week, and around us is – scatterings of orange peel. Oranges can be bought for about 1½d. each, or, more usually, changed for cigarettes. In great demand by the peasants is bread, etc., an indication of their very real need. You can imagine with what glee we exchange our Army pattern Sausage Roll for a luscious orange.

I lost my toothbrush at Calais, and left my hat in one of the feeding centres en route. Will be pleased to get in a town and secure some replacement. A sad occurrence befell one of our chaps: he put his kitbag on the Bari pile at the start, instead of the Naples lot. He had put all his kit, except his eating utensils, in it, and had his birthday cake (icing and all!) for December 9th in it. Whether and when he will get it is very uncertain.

8 p.m. I am now in a Transit Camp in Napoli – the same one I was in when there was a terrific storm, on my way to Perugia; formerly a park. As usual we are nobody's baby. We are ten to a tent underneath the trees. I successfully discovered and lugged to the tent an iron bedstead, in which I shall repose tonight. A chap has given me a hat, so my pate is now covered. I have bought a toothbrush, so my teeth now feel lovely and clean.

I have just had two cups of coffee and two sugary doughnut rings in the NAAFI – and appreciated them. True, I consumed them standing, but they were good. I shall have to get you on making doughnut rings. Did I tell you I thought you were a jolly good cook and that I thoroughly enjoyed every munching moment? I love you. I daresay I would do if you were silly and useless – but it is such a consolation and satisfaction to know you are not. My beautiful, capable woman.

I love you.
Chris

≈

In Naples, December 1945

8 December 1945

My Darling,

Once again we have been disappointed, and we are still here. How long it will last, blowed if I know. It is cold and unpleasant and Bari, a little further South, sounds good to me. I haven't had a real night's sleep since I came here – in fact since I left 27.

I went into Naples this afternoon and had intended going to *For Whom The Bell Tolls* this evening. But, as has been happening a lot lately, the electric light failed all over the town, and the cinema was in darkness. So we came back to camp and consumed yet more of the cakes that inevitably cannot be resisted, yet are so sickeningly indicative of our Army-ness. We came back in the rear of a tram which was full to capacity – which in Italy means full to capacity. One of the Italians dropped a cigarette on the floor, tried to bend down and look for it, an almost impossible task. When he got a chance, he had a look for it but couldn't find it, so accused a neighbour of pinching it! Started fighting but had to stop as he wanted to get off.

I am sorry about this scrap of a letter. I am in a somewhat 'suspended' state at the moment, and can only hope I shall recover something of my zest when I am with my unit, instead of messing around in this cold hole. I hope you are feeling OK but I am pretty sure you are feeling as sick as I am, though fortunately your bed is warmer! But the time is passing. The great consoling thought. Excuse this scrap.

I love you.
Chris

10 December 1945

My Darling Bessie,

I see from the papers that it has been very cold at home.

I observe that Charlton did well on Saturday. I suppose that Wilf is just about to start work by the time you get this letter. The demob figures seem very encouraging, no slackening and everything in hand. I feel fairly hopeful about getting out in time to have a good-weather holiday with you somewhere. I was glad to see that 100,000 chaps were called up in the last four months and 140,000 are to be called up in the first half of '46. I think the wrong chaps are being called up, though. We are getting boys of 18-and-a-half who have only been in the Army a few months. There is no doubt that the Army will mould them the wrong way. If they called them up at 25–30, it would be better. Blow me, that is as clear as coalite! I think that the influence of the Army has been mostly for the good on me – but there are thousands of chaps now aged 24–5, who have grown up in the Army and have little conception of civilian standards, or individual responsibility.

We are hoping really to get somewhere tomorrow, as we went along to the Orderly Room and again reminded them that we were here and wanted to AVANTI, and we have been told to see them again tomorrow at 8.30. We are all in a state with our socks, etc., but determined not to change anything till we get a possibility of a change.

Mail is our main desire. It is over a fortnight since we left England. I am feeling better now than I did then, because

I well understand that every day is counting towards my release.

We have to collect our 7 free issue cigarettes each morning between 7–8. If we don't go, we lose them. I haven't lost any, but you can imagine how many cigarettes are 'made' by the chap whose job it is to give them out. Three chaps in my tent never go for them, and at 9s. for 20 to the Italians, the Quartermaster must be making a fortune. How are your efforts at reduction, pal? Am afraid the 'ciglets' were not a great success, but who knows what may come of such an idea? I think I'll start up a Company, 'Halve Your Smoking', and put that invention forward!

I love you.
Chris

~

14 December 1945

My Dear Wife,

This morning at 10 o'clock saw us all with our kit, outside the departure hut, ready to move off.

We proceeded to a place called PORTICI, 6 miles from the centre of Naples, along the 'autostrada' (the fine road which connects the city with Pompeii). The Unit Headquarters are situated in a building near there, and I am (hooray) sleeping in the building tonight.

The RSM [regimental sergeant major] has asked me since the first querying if I have had experience of acquittance rolls (pay sheets) and I have told him 'yes' (I have – at Whetstone where I did Pay Clerk), whether I was used to money, and I said 'yes', and if I had ever been Post Corporal, to which I said I was in the PO. He says he will try to get me a job as Assistant to the Group 28 Post Corporal, who also is Pay Clerk for the soldiers and Italian civil labour. If I do get the job I think I shall be fairly happy for the present, as the food here is very good indeed, and that is a large consideration in the Army (for tea today, our first meal, we had tomato soup, and a salad – well served – of a nice slice of corned beef, cheese, and cold peas and beetroot. There was a piece of cake, as well as usual jam, etc. The bread was very thin, a great change, and the plates are supplied by the Army and don't need to be washed by the men). Our job for the next few days is to clean out a house in the village which is being turned into an Officers' Mess, and to shift furniture and so on.

As this unit maintains the big aerodromes at Bari, Foggia, Naples (Pomigliano this one is called) and Rome, I cannot see the unit breaking up for a long while, and probably my Army days will be concluded around these parts. Naples is horrible, the wretches who inhabit it are worse. Out here it is not so bad, because there is some foliage (the trees in the orange orchards have their bright yellow gifts sparkling upon them now) and (unlike Bari and Foggia) the landscape is not wholly, monotonously flat.

I changed my socks – after 19 days! They are black as anything, but I hope to get them washed sometime. So now I feel quite spruce – though I am still wearing Wilfred's shirt. If you care to lecture me, carry on. I will get young Solly to answer it – he is still in the same socks the 'erb!

Three or four children have just looked in here, to pick up half-eaten cakes left on plates. All are thinly-clad. One has no shoes or socks on. Poor little soul. In this weather, and wet underfoot, it must be very bad.

I love you.
Chris

~

17 December 1945

My Darling Bessie,

A year ago this morning we were attempting to assess the damage done by the first night's attack on the Hotel Cecil. The smoke of battle was in the air. This morning there was another smoke in the air. Acrid; sulphuric – from Vesuvius, which was puffing it out very liberally at breakfast-time, but has ceased at present. There is always plenty of notice of any eruptions, so don't get alarmed.

At the Transit Camp I glanced at a copy of *Married Love* by Marie Stopes (which was being read from a most unscientific angle by some Infantry lads with us). It might help our ignorance. There is a table in it showing the ups and downs of desire in a woman. If you think it would be useful, you might like to get it.

[Incomplete]

19 December 1945

My Darling,

This afternoon I went to the Bulk Issue NAAFI, to assist in drawing our Christmas rations. A fortnight's rations were drawn, about eight pints of beer, five bars of chocolate, two hundred cigarettes, per man. We had a couple of thousand bottles of beer, several dozens of gin, whisky, sherry, and port (for officers and sergeants), 18,000 cigarettes, and various oddments like oranges, mincemeat, tinned turkey (a precaution against having our live turkeys purloined?). Our three ton truck was well stacked on the return journey. I always find myself meekly wondering when I get to these wholesale places, 'How is it all done?' Great feats of organisation are accomplished in the supply of necessities to armies.

Here I am, in the YMCA at Portici, with two Indian soldiers drinking tea and eating cakes at the next table. When they go back to civilian life, the whites will shun them, cordon them off, deny them intercourse. How will the Indian take it? The soldiers like the average English soldier because we treat them decently. He must ponder our way of life and that of our wealthy prototypes.

What do you think of ole' Mosley[*] and crew? There's a lot in the paper about banning them. I don't agree, myself. I think that all the 18B clients[†] should have been tried for their projected

---

[*] Oswald Mosley, leader of the British Union of Fascists.
[†] The legal Regulation 18B came into force early in the war to detain those deemed hostile and dangerous to the defence of the realm.

treasons, and in the event of guilt being proved, at least had their estates sequestrated. If nothing has been done up to the present, I can't see why we should prohibit peacetime part-time lunatics.

I hope, hope, hope for news of you tomorrow.
I love you.
Chris

~

20 December 1945

My Darling,

I shall go berserk unless I get some mail shortly; today was another blank day, although one of the ex-4 AFS [Auxiliary Fire Service] chaps did get 14 letters.

Blow me, this not having any mail is a blooming bind. Suppose you had not heard from me for 25 days. What a lark – you'd think I had deserted you, wouldn't you? I very much hope I shall hear from you before Christmas. I reckon I will swoon when I see my own name on a letter. I know that some Air Mail must be held up going your way, as some of our releases are not getting away by air, due to the bad flying weather. We have had a bit of rain lately. I don't care if it snows.

Sorry for the oil stain on the first page of this. It comes from a YMCA cake I have just consumed.

Lovely Bessie, I love you.
Chris

~

21 December 1945

My Darling Bessie,

I fear that you are due to hear more weepings and wailings and gnashings of teeth from this direction. But the fact remains, no mail, no mail, no mail. Not a word from you for a month all but a day. What a joy it is to be out, here, in the blooming Army!

Our turkeys met their deaths today. Not a gobble did I hear as I went for my tea today. All that remained of them was red bareness hanging by a hook. The Italians killed them. Laid their necks on the grounds and chopped their heads off.

This afternoon I went for a bath to a place called Annunziata, about half an hour's ride away. A BATH! The first all-over wetting I have had since you (my gracious, wonderful wife) scrubbed my back. The Army pays over 9d. each per man. It was jolly fine and I feel beautifully clean.

I understand, by the way, that soldiers with a year to do in Italy can have their wives out here, as the Colonel is doing. So that if I had a year to do, it might have been worth considering (though what a hole this is!). The wives get Army rations and so on, and I believe the Army finds them billets, too. Your remarks on this may be interesting, so please let's have them.

I hope for mail tomorrow. I must hear from you, to tell me you are alright, to hear about the 'smashing' dinner you've just cooked . . .

The time is passing; I hope now only for our next meeting, our always-togetherness.
I love you.
Chris

~

22 December 1945

My Dearest, Loveliest, Wonderful-est One,

Today was THE DAY – sixteen letters (marvellous, kind, warm, human, real, sweet, delicious, joyful, you-ey letters) arrived, one direct to 6 AFS, thirteen forwarded on to me from 4 AFS since my leave, and two old ones (good nevertheless) sent while you were still a spinster and I a single man. I also had another 20 letters – what a difference reading yours, delighting in the real beauty, the warm sympathy, the grandness of your nature – and all these others. I'll send you some of the more interesting ones later on.

I am in a terrific whirl at the moment, because such a confrontation of your wonderful expressiveness has to be allowed to sink in. Not all the paper in Italy is sufficient for the quantity I want to write you. Although I got your letters at 10 a.m., I had to rush around until 1.30 p.m. before I could start reading. After reading I had a busy afternoon on redirecting mail. So I have only read you once. Tomorrow afternoon I will read you more and more and more.

Janet – Christopher? struggles, asserts, demands first mention. Probably at this date you already know; I can still only speculate. I shall reserve my comments until you write me again. I want to be everything to you. I love you and I need you, I love you for what you have said about this possible event. You are everything to me and the world is a wonderful place because you are in it.

The Christmas present for Mum: whatever you did, OK by me. I thought we had said we'd let it slide. I have only had occasional stabs of sorrow at the thought of her self-made miseries. Please do what you think is best, and don't fear at any time that I shall wish anything different. Another thing, if, say, Mother or anyone ever refers to something about me that you didn't know, say if you wish that 'Oh yes, he told me', or something like that. What I intend to convey to you is your complete right to do as you will, and my complete faith in you.

Yes, I have ached like you. It was wonderful being so close to you for so long. It was breathtakingly joyous. Being away from you is grim, being in the Army away from you is grimmer. But we have plenty of grounds for hope, plenty of reason to suppose that we shall meet again before next winter. I hope I can write you less critically and sound as near to you as I feel and know I am.

I appreciate the way you write of our bed, our room, our bottom drawer. My darling. I am so pleased you are happy about me. In my first leave I was too self-contained, this time it was grand to brim over.

Please do continue with your domestic details if you can. I am most interested in your dinners, your appetite and all that you do. You may bore yourself with a recital of your house-cleaning, but you won't bore me, because I imagine you brandishing a duster and wielding a Hoover – and imagining you is the most happy occupation I can have till I meet you.

Your 'ums' spoke plenty, don't worry about that.

I am sorry to hear about the FLU, but suppose you had to have it. Hope it wasn't too bad – don't go out of doors when you're not well if you can help it, there's a good girl – and that you are OK now.

Yes, it is a job with the whistling. It is an unconscious barometer. I stop short when I think of your horror, but I am by no means cured.

I love you.
Chris

~

23 December 1945

My Darling,

One of your letters today told of your visit to the doctor. I am disappointed as you are that he could not say definitely. You would think he would say why you had missed. Your symptoms are interesting but not conclusive. I suppose you will have to grin and (literally) bear it, although perhaps you could see another doctor if you felt like it. We are both so know-nothing on this that I am not happy about the doctor's statement about it not being broken not mattering. I should think it would be less easy for an exit (an entrance to the world). But I suppose he knows best. Am glad the hospital seems to present no difficulties. I think we should say nothing until you are certain. I have no doubt you think that, too. I hope that everything goes as you want. If it doesn't, well, we have plenty of time. As things appear, it seems I should be home within the eight months, with any luck. If it does transpire that we are to be parents, you can be sure that I am sorry that only you can possibly endure the pain. You can be sure that this addition is OURS, a physical sign of our mental togetherness. I should like to write for the rest of the evening, and try to say all that I can to encourage you in the event of it being true, or in the event of it failing. But I cannot, I must push on to another subject.

Sanderstead: Business deals with relations are notoriously awkward, and usually more savage than normal deals. I think £1,000 a great deal to ask. Could we enquire the original price (was it £550?) and say we will pay only 50% more (i.e. £775 if it was £550)? Would it be worthwhile getting a Valuer (Simpson, Palmer and Winder, 1 Southwark Bdge Road, SE1 would help) and stand by his opinion?

Payment: I believe we have a little over £1,000 at the moment. (I have £315 in NSC [National Savings Certificates].) Addition like Income Tax rebates, and Army Gratuities, should raise another £100. I believe you are saving about £1 10s. 0d. a week. If it reaches that stage, get the cash by crossed warrant, NSC and POSB, and send me a form to sign for the £315. Simpson, Palmer, will probably act for us both reasonably. Legal costs will be about £15, I believe.

I feel like a millionaire buying a mansion as well as like a little boy buying his weekly sweets.

Look after the stamps I am sending you. They are really very nice and when I get home I will put them in books.

Just room to say – what a woman you are!
I love you.
Chris

~

'Tis Christmas Eve 1945

My Darling, Wonderful One,

You may be interested and amused to know that the yellow mepacrine tablets we take as anti-malarial precaution are considered to render a man sterile. Reason: about twenty married men of 30 Wing came from the February leave, and none had any children as a result. This time (mepacrines not having been taken) three are 'certs' (they say – blowed if I know how they can tell) and two are (as it is put) 'sweating'. It is actually three, but of course I have said nothing.

Yes, I should get out as regularly as you can, for fresh air and exercise. A walk for twenty minutes daily is all that you need in poor weather. Try and keep indoors when it is rainy or very windy.

You seem to have made some reduction in your cigarettes. I hope you keep it up, but I shouldn't distress yourself.

While not opposed to four children, I suggest you see how No. 1 treats you, before we adopt it as a policy! It is a great test of endurance for you when the time comes. I shall have no 'say' in this. It is up to you and it would be unfair for me to suggest we have anything contrary to your wishes.

Please don't 'flop' if it isn't, my darling. We have tons of time ahead, and you must usefully occupy yourself in some way else.

Which pullover did you wash, the khaki, or the smashing light brown from Meakers?

I would like to consume one of your 'meat puddings by guesswork'. I could perhaps send you a good spaghetti recipe, but that's about all.

I love you.
Chris

~

Christmas Day 1945

My Wonderful Wife,

I will continue replying to your letters.

I do like short pants with buttons, please. Were not the matches handy? Please send the *Statesman* weekly if you can, ordinary paper with a piece of string to keep it together. Address in margin of paper, and only ½d. stamp. I like hearts better than liver, although I am quite content with liver for a change. A good deal depends on how liver is cooked, I think, more than other meats. Glad you had another go at the batter pudding, and it was approved. I am a very lucky man.

Does the 'peculiar sick feeling' affect one so early? What I wonder is, what about the chance of it forming in the passage, as it suggested in that book. Have you had time to look at the book at all?

Again, the house. The more I think on our chance to get it, the more thrilled I am with our luck. 'Get it if you can', I feel like urging you continually. It's a front door of our own, it's a place, it's our castle! It appeals to me a lot. It means security, independence and a place to think of. It means making a start.

The travelling is a bind, but it is NOTHING compared with the joy of having a place, especially one that you like. And if we had a child, a good open-aired spot would be most useful.

I can understand your concern over how I shall find Civvy Street, and I must say I am disturbed at reports of chaps who have just left the Army, being so dissatisfied with it. I think it must be true that civilians (late Army) miss the travelling. I think (as I write the page is wet all over with orange juice, as we have just been out, picked a dozen oranges from a tree, and started to throw them at each other, splashing all over the walls) all men want to climb mountains. The Army gives them that rare chance. If you find me wanting to climb mountains, I know you will be able to lead me to a nearby eminence. I think that, if the conditions were there, I could leave the Army and carry on in the 'Mets' Branch as though I had not seen the Pyramids, swum the Suez and had Vesuvius as my neighbour. But my old life has gone and I have no regrets. I expect that Army life is like an illness, which you notice when you have it and forget when you are cured. But I really believe I am a better man as a result of my Army life – the minor rackets in which I have engaged are transient, unmarking.

I have been amazed, disgusted and sometimes frightened by the Italian manifestation of joy at the Christmas festivity. The silly lot let off fireworks – I suppose this is the first time for five or six years. They started the 23rd, and we had them again last night. Continuous. And very, very loud. They put our English (even pre-war) fireworks completely in the shade – and I'd sooner be in the shade. The people are mad. It has been one terrific bang after another.

We drank 'The Loyal Toast', plus 'The Cooks', today. Before I drank my little drop of Vermouth, I said 'MY WIFE'.

I love you.
Chris

PS I have just had a word with a chap who lives only a couple of stations nearer London Bridge than Sanderstead. He says the fare is only perhaps 2s. return and not the 3s. I had imagined. Which would be a big help to us. The mile and a half walk to the station, or longer, would be nothing to a man with my energy.

~

29 December 1945

My Darling,

Vesuvius was not visible today when I looked out of the window on waking. Often the top is obscured by clouds, but today none of it could be seen. And it is very near. Thrillingly near, I think. We are as near to it as Ben Nevis is to Fort William. I am not going to say I shall climb it when the good weather comes, because I am hoping for plenty of scene-shifting during the next six months. But should I be here when the evenings are light, I shall certainly try to go up it a little. A truck takes one to a hotel used by tourists in peacetime in about twenty minutes. This is halfway up, and in a couple of hours one can stand on the edge of the crater (now quite large because of the 1944 eruption), and take a quick look down it, where it is red and hot. Sometimes great billowings of smoke are visible, other times just little frisky cigarette wisps. Really, I look forward to contemplating its hugeness.

At any rate it has saved me harping on the house, which I am rather barmy about at the moment. Perhaps it could be a better house, nearer a station, and so on. But it is a house, and it means we shall have a real home of our own. An invaluable asset in these days. Before the war, it perhaps was not so much to get excited about. But I do feel, now, it is a big thing. I shall be very pleased to hear you are the owner, and (as you once said in a letter) that you are mentally putting up the curtains.

I wonder how much a baby costs (in money; there are many tears!) in the early years? I should think the Income Tax would be reduced to practically nothing. 'If', we shall have to write to the Board of Trade to find out what coupons are available, and so on. You are going to have a busy time in front of you, 'if'. And it won't be only for eight months, either!

I love you.

Chris

~

11

Serving Hatch

3 January 1946

My Darling Wonderful One,

I will be at your side next Christmas, my darling. I am sorry we have had to spend this one apart. I was sympathetic about your four-hour struggle with the duck.

Be careful, when scanning the 'demob news' in the papers, NOT to get your hopes anchored to a date, or to have much faith in a prophecy. I <u>hope</u> to be out in June. I <u>may</u> be out rather later, perhaps several months later. So don't get a fixation on June, just take a little interest in it.

I am doing far less whistling though I still cannot bottle myself up entirely. Also I have said 'female dog' several times of late, and instantly regretted it.

I told you the Christmas pudding would turn out well. I am sorry to hear that you have a cold again. Try and eat plenty of vegetables and what fruit you can. I don't suppose you have started to take Cod Liver Oil and Malt yet, but I should get a big bottle if I were you. I am very concerned about your pain and your danger. It seems great whatever anyone may say. But it has to be, and I hope I can get stoical about it. (Those USA films of anxious fathers in posh maternity homes will have nothing on me! – Oh my darling, lovely one.) It is very desirable that I get home when you most need to have me, and I hope I can do it. But it is going to be a narrow squeeze.

The people who say 'Australia for the Jews' are merely side-tracking. Libya and Madagascar are also amongst the lands mentioned. I don't know the answer to the Palestine question, but I know that mentioning other places isn't the answer. Anyway, surely some questions have no answer?

I don't really think that 'bringing up baby' will be so very bad. All sorts of people do it, some moderately well. It will stop us 'gallivanting about', but I have no doubt there's a lot in the successful marriage depending on children idea. Of course, it also depends on the married couple! I am certain that we will be OK, though you'll have to tell me when, what, why and how to do the various fatherly tasks.

I love you.
Chris

~

7 January 1946

Wonderful One,

Congratulations on your acceleration, initiative, independence, resourcefulness, and absolute perfection. I wish I could have carried you over the threshold of OUR HOUSE. May you always be happy there, and may I be joining you soon.

I love you.
Chris

~

7 January 1946 [Second letter]

My Darling, Wonderful Wife,

I couldn't help but admire your infinite resource and initiative, and all the ability and capacity you have displayed.

£1,000 does seem a lot. As a matter of fact it is a lot. But I never thought I would start off married life in a house of our own, did you? We have been fortunate in acquiring the cash, and I think that the place will suit us fine until Janet – Christopher perhaps starts going to school. You have no idea how pleased I am you describe it as a 'nice little house'.

'How am I doing?' you ask. How can I say? There aren't enough words of praise, only my hug, my look, could tell you how proud I am of you, thrilled by your efficiency and competence.

I love you.
Chris

~

8 January 1946

My Wonderful Wife,

When the chance occurs, I would like you to tell me about the house. Two rooms and kitchenette downstairs, three rooms (?) and bathroom upstairs? I suppose the lavatory and bathroom (is it at all tiled?) are together? Have you got your eye on the nursery-room? Is it a very small house? How do the rooms (particularly kitchenette) compare with 27? Is there an air of cheapness about it, as there used to be about some of the £600 houses they built at Welling before the war? (I don't think there can be or you would not have said 'nice little house'.) Is there any Ascot, Geyser,* or anything? Why not write to Hoovers and ask them to put us on their waiting list? What is the garden like – as big as 27? Is it horribly weedy, does it have vegetables? (I advise employing a man to do the digging, if they can be obtained, like Aunt Elsie did.)

Don't do any gardening yourself, will you? You have so much to do, you know. Remember to rest occasionally, whatever you are

---

* A gas water boiler.

doing. I am as disturbed about your food as much as anything, and you must tell me what you propose to do about it, please. Can I send anything to help. How about soap? I could send a good bit if you wanted it. At the moment I have four bars of Sunlight soap weekly. Would you like them? You are bound to become friendly with some of the neighbours. There is no reason why real friendship should not develop, but do not forget all the tales about neighbours.

Haven't I heard there's trouble getting prams? If you do any painting, don't breathe it in, you won't get lead poisoning or Painter's Colic, but it may upset your digestion more.

I wish I could have seen you put the key in the door, my darling, my dearest one.
I love you.
Chris

~

9 January 1946

My Wonderful One,

It is semi-detached isn't it, on the 27-161 model. I think Bert said once there was room for a garage, but none there – I suppose like 27. I think I'd like to get a hut out in the garden or something. I don't know why. I want to acquire a set of carpentry and household tools, as I said on leave. Saw, plane, chisel, as well as the old hammer (an instrument used for bashing one's own nails and fingers).

I favour a serving hatch between the kitchenette and the dining room, for one thing! I bet you won't have that. Ten children will take some feeding though, won't they! Does the house need painting on the outside, as well as receiving your slight attention in some of the rooms? One good thing about not having a great deal of furniture is that you will be able to plan things better. In most homes, there's far too much and it's bunged in as few rooms as possible. You'll probably find it desirable to put a piece of furniture in each room, so that it is furnished. I was thinking about the floors – you know the polishing idea. If the wood was not altogether suitable, could you put a veneer of three ply down? It would only be needed round the edges of the room, I suppose, where the carpet touched it.

When you get a bit settled in I will get you to enrol me in the Croydon Labour Party, and (if you will) to join yourself. It is a penny or so a week.

I wonder if there is a privet hedge, whether the gate swings alright, and what the path is made of. In my imagination, I am already coming there for the first time (fancy finding your way to your own home) AND YOU ARE MEETING ME.

I love you.
Chris

10 January 1946

My Darling,

What colour is the house painted, my darling? Keep your eye open for a ladder in case I have to climb one to see what is stopping up the chimney! I say, are we bringing Janet – Christopher up to believe in Santa Claus? What a task that bringing-up is going to be – principally for you, I am afraid, my darling, my heroine. Have all the rooms got fireplaces in them? (In Italy there are very few fireplaces in houses. They don't need them. In winter they just have a brazier in the middle of the room.) We must get electric fires in all the rooms – and bags and bags of switches everywhere!

Is East Croydon nearer London or further from it? My idea of a back garden is either all grass (they call it LAWN in those parts) or a good lot of space for such vegetables as lettuce, celery, radish, rhubarb. The grass would be for Janet – Christopher. I am busting with the news about Janet – C, but shan't tell anyone here.

I love you.
Chris

~

11 January 1946

My Wonderful, Wonderful Wife,

I hope you went to your old friend's wedding, but that you didn't feast too much.

I am quite the same as you about family, friends and old associations. I don't want them now. I have no urge towards them, I am disinterested. I am only interested in you, and you take all my thoughts and all my time and I am very pleased about it. This relationship is wonderful; I am entirely, completely and absolutely satisfied in and with you. We have to drag along with some acquaintances, but it is no good pretending they have any real claim.

My Darling, I could cry for you sometimes, too, because in my way I could do with some soothing too – and you are the only one to do it.

Will you try to feed Janet – C. yourself if you can, or will it be a 'Glaxo' baby, please? But then, I don't suppose you know till you've seen the Clinic. Of course you won't be a blind and stupid parent – but you'll be vocal to me about 'young Janet' or 'young Christopher's' alleged shortcomings as well as their evident excellences. And I shall encourage it. Of course we'll discuss our children – <u>and</u> their friends. Our children will have all the freedom that <u>we</u> think is good for them. I believe that a parent has a useful purpose, and I am not going to be a neutral and I won't let you be. <u>Our</u> parental powers, though, will be 20th century, mutually-agreed between us, and wisely wielded. I hope.

We should be silly to keep our children in ignorance because we also want them to have 'freedom'. Our children will respect us as people, not as mere parents. I hope.

[Incomplete]

~

13 January 1946

My Darling Bessie,

Do you prefer a hospital to a nursing home, Bessie my darling? I hope you do.

How are you going on about your 'artificial dentures' (to give them their modern and almost unrecognisable name). Hadn't you better get them as soon as you can, in order to get used to them while you are fairly normal? I believe it is true that child bearing is bad for teeth, the calcium being required for the baby, so I am afraid your teething troubles will just about be starting.

A bright idea: going to Sanderstead gives me another MP I can legitimately write to! I have not yet heard from Joseph Reeves, but Harold Macmillan has written twice, so I think I'll vote Conservative next time . . .

All the oranges and lemons in the grounds of my billet (the Via Vitello, near Via Salute stazione, if you are ever this way!) have been picked by the owner, so now, for a sly suck, I am dependent on the orchard where our cookhouse is at present. Of course, we get oranges for rations. I eat all I can get, most chaps just ignore them.

I am always thinking of you, wondering what you are doing and knowing that you look lovely doing it.

I love you.
Chris.

~

19 January 1946

My Darling, Wonderful Wife,

Have just decided we must get a magic lantern for Janet – C. A little previous, but there you are, we are projecting ourselves six months ahead all the time, until we are together; it is only a little step to think of Janet – C. as a bouncing reality.

The VD Film Show was a flop as far as I was concerned. Three films, two hours the lot. *Sex Hygiene*, *Pick Up*, and *DE733*, story of a submariner-chaser that didn't chase because its crew were in hospital or sick through VD contracted at the last port. The films were all American, and the tempo was very different from our own. They might have made an appeal to US troops, but not to ours, I think. There were plenty of close-ups of the male sex organ that might have caused some of the chaps to pause, but judging by the remarks everyone makes as they come out, I would say it was nearly useless.

I love you.
Chris

~

21 January 1946

My Darling,

Today has been clear and crisp and sunny – but mail-less. Probably the weather over France has stopped the planes, I hope there'll be something tomorrow.

And now I have 'a statement to make' which may surprise you and probably please you – I have sold my last cigarette, done my last deal, on the Black Market. The decision is quite likely an important one in my little life, but perhaps not so much against the pitiful background of the world today. A lot of little things have caused this reversal. Perhaps my first real thought was caused by your letter acknowledging the money from Bert, that 'I do not like this for you.' Lately, I have seen a cartoon (I believe by George Whitelaw of *The Daily Herald*) showing Mars, God of War, looking down on a world with 'Atom Bomb', 'Java', 'Persia', 'Black Market' shown on it, and underneath there was a caption 'Carry On, My Children'. Although I have previously said to myself 'Cigarettes are luxuries. That's alright, it's the food that is criminal', I clearly see now that the people who buy cigarettes are those who sell the food and other things, and the prices are related. I have said before 'If I don't do it, my mates will.' That is certainly true, but it does not constitute a moral justification, only a plausible excuse.

In a way, I am proud of being 'different' from other chaps. And when I 'flog' things I simply descend to their level. Earlier, I have said 'The money is very handy.' That is true, but no argument. If I disagree with Black Markets, or profits anywhere, I cannot morally justify fostering them here. I think I have made, in money and kind, about £65 by selling cigarettes, etc. In the next five months I could add another £60, easily. And it is the fantastic ease of putting down 50 cigarettes and picking up £1 5s. in exchange that has at last shaken me into correct appreciation. I cannot undo the evil that I have done, but it is incumbent upon me now to stop doing it, so that I may hold on to my righteousness; so that you may continue to think I am a good man; so that Janet – C. may be proud of me and not be ashamed. Don't think that I am going religious. I shall still do many things that are wrong, like putting 'FIGS' on the outside of the parcel, finding things as soon as they are 'lost', telling usual lies to get out of trouble.

Please tell me your troubles and let me know how things are.
I love you.
Chris

~

22 January 1946

My Darling,

Three smashing letters came tripping in today.

I was very glad to get the maps of the house and it certainly gave me a good feeling to get them. It looks smashing. I can't judge the size, but that <u>you</u> say 'nice little' means a lot to me. On the exterior, I have always liked the 'pointed' effect with bricks; I am not too keen (only a photo glance) at the wooden fence outside. I'd prefer bushes. We can discuss this <u>when</u> I have seen them. Also what do you think about 'Woodbridge'? I don't like house names, and that one is singularly uninspiring. I am in favour of whipping it off. You'll probably agree, but may wish to wait until I get home to do the deed.

I like your garden ideas, and 'scratching' is all you had better do, me gal. If it wants digging, try and get a man in. It will be grand eating our own lettuce. The apple trees we could discuss. They take a minimum of five years (I believe) to fruit, and something else may be better. I dunno.

Pinks, primroses, beiges; if you want them, I've no doubt you will get them. Anything in this line that appeals to you will have a strong appeal to me. I can understand your excitement. You transmit it to me very acutely and expressively, and you transform my future into magic joy and pleasure.

I can help you consider our electric fire needs. Perhaps a couple would do and we could change them around as we needed them. We could then get a couple of good ones instead of perhaps four not-so-goods.

I hope you can get on the 'phone, for a help to banish loneliness. It may be a job, and if it is you must see what a bit of neighbourly cooperation can do. I don't know that we could afford it permanently, but it is a great help when you need to talk to someone.

I love you.
Chris

~

26 January 1946

My Wonderful Expectant Mother,

Today came mail (18 and 19) and THE NEWS that – as you joyfully declare – you are PREGNANT, and everything all very official and Town-Hall-ified. What do I say, my Darling? (Of course, I had to tell my mail driver – who is in the same position.) What do I do? Do I congratulate, commiserate, or commemorate? Think it better just to say <u>I love you</u>, and that your husband is proud of you, not only for those characteristics which are grandly yours, but because you are a successful <u>woman</u>. What a wonderfully interesting time we are going to have in the future. Non-Stop Variety, indeed.

I am very glad the doctor didn't think you were small; and you must get the hymen attended to as soon as you can. I wonder if you could put in for the Purley hospital now, even though you are not actually in residence. I don't have to tell you to follow the instructions on the bottles, and to be sure to get the extra milk, eggs, meat. (If it weren't for having the baby, it would be smashing, wouldn't it!) The sixty extra coupons seem a good many, but I suppose they will soon go. I hope you don't have trouble getting a cot. You seem to have been very lucky so far with baby wool (is it all white?), and the 18 ounces was certainly a grand capture.

The demob figures are OK, up to standard. I <u>do</u> hope I shall be with you when you'll need me most. But it is a hope, a chance, rather than a probability.

I love you.
Chris

~

27 January 1946

My Darling Bessie,

I have just returned from a walk this afternoon along the harbour and sea wall of Portici. Very nice and healthy. Plenty of activity amongst the fishing ships, taking on ice and boxes into which to put the ship's catch, when caught. I have a feeling I'd like to have a couple of days at sea with them, but I am afraid the Army wouldn't like it.

I agree with your remarks on Attlee. I like the idea of a middle class young man going down to the East End and feeling he should help the people there. I saw an interview Churchill gave to an American reporter, in which he was asked to describe Attlee, and said he was 'a sheep in sheep's clothing' which got loud laughter from the audience. He certainly seems an 'ordinary guy' likely to endear himself to us ordinary guys. One can understand the Americans, however, feeling that he is a poor substitute for the glamorous Churchill, as we feel Truman is no successor to Roosevelt.

No, my darling, of course I am not fed up with your baby talk. Please carry on, thinking on paper, I am very anxious to know all you are doing and thinking. You never bore me, you always, ALWAYS, always delight me, my very own wonderful expectant one! I must see if I can get a book about bringing up a child, for although there are obviously good general reasons for thinking I shall do the job, with you, as well as anyone else, I am very keen that we shall do it a great deal better. Suppose it was TWINS! It might be better, I don't suppose it is anywhere near double your expense. Bear this in mind when you are knitting, oh fruitful one, you never know! What a pity that I cannot knit, I could do the pants and you the vests.

I love you.
Chris

2 February 1946

My Darling Wife,

I hope that by the time you get this, you will have been at 55[*] a few days and be fairly settled in, and very comfortable in your mind. I hope that, if you get the time, you will let me have a full account of the move, whether your Dad or Wilf came with you, whether you were allowed the privilege of a ride in the van, how that old well-packed wardrobe stood up to the journey, if anything was lost, and so on. It is not important but I'd like to feel the atmosphere. Then, later on, perhaps you'd send me a little description (and a plan!) of your bedroom at least (sorry my darling, <u>our</u> bedroom) and maybe the room where you'll knit and eat and write to your loving husband (that's me!). I'd like to be able to picture you in the right position.

Have we got French windows or the ordinary pattern, dear? And what about an Air Raid shelter? I have thought rather unhappily about the stairs. I don't suppose you will be able to get carpet, are you having to clatter up them on the bare boards whenever you need to go upstairs? Are you sleeping upstairs? I shall be interested (very, very interested) to hear all about your doings, and I hope you will be expansive about them.

The break-up of the unit is proceeding and I should get a move before long. Strange how men behave. I have just heard that

---

[*] Their new home at 55 Ellesmere Drive, Sanderstead, near Croydon in south London.

312

on the February leave one of our men did not go home till 8 p.m., as he suspected his wife. When he arrived home, she had a one-year-old in her arms. He patched it up, but my informant has now heard, rather enigmatically, that 'George Jenkin's wife has done it on him again'. 'George', by the way, was one of the worst chaps I've known for being unfaithful.

I like all that you say about our need in the future to avoid becoming suburban married 'types'. I think we have between us a good deal of commonsense, and that we really will succeed in retaining all the good parts of our earlier approaches to life. I am, therefore, very pleased you support my view on overtime, because there's no doubt to my mind that most people are much too keen to get money, forgetting that its pursuit interferes with the joy of life.

So you reckon it was the first time when 'it happened', do you? I don't remember the day, does the doctor ask, or do you have to tell him approximately?

Eat as well as you can, sleep as much as you can, keep as warm as you can.
I love you.
Chris

~

9 February 1946

Well, My Darling Bessie,

Today was my DAY OFF, and off I went to Naples. I'm too pleased with myself, because tomorrow I shall take to the APO [Army Post Office] – a carpet! It cost 2,100 lira (£2 7s. 0d.), is a little smaller than a hearthrug, and will just do you for putting your beautiful feet upon when you get out of bed in the morning. Your beautiful feet – ah, my beautiful darling, wonder-one, I wish I could put my lips to them <u>now</u>. I love them, and every bit of you. You will be in a state of suspense until you get the carpet (registered) but I am quite sure you'll be delighted with my purchase.

I thought while I had a chance, I would have my photograph taken (only 1s. 6d. for the two, now) and it is enclosed. Sorry I am no John Barrymore, my sweet. But at least you can have a good laugh at my tunic, how well it fits me, and you can admire(?) my medal display. I don't wear medals, this was the first time today, as the Ities are inclined to think you are a Rookie if you walk around 'nude'.

Met a very woebegone Italian in Naples this morning. He had just come back to Italy from Shrewsbury, where he thought things were grand. Please write me plenty about the carpets, etc., when they arrive.

I love you.
Chris

~

10 February 1946

My Darling Wonderful Wife,

Sunday afternoon. The shining sun. The very blue Bay of Naples scene before me. You in the same world – but miles and miles away.

I can't tell you how pleased I am with my carpet purchase. If I had had the money I should have bought two, but I happened to see it after my other purchases. I have already made up my mind to spend your £3 Postal Orders (when they arrive and unless you earmarked them for something else) on a carpet.

Could you try and discover the kind of electric current we are on? I believe the voltage varies, and of course there is AC and DC. An enquiry at the showrooms is probably the best way. I was attracted (are you, please?) to an electric coffee pot, 15s. 6d., I saw in Naples. (But it was 150 watt, or something.)

Do you know where the Postman comes from who delivers at OUR HOUSE? I suspect Croydon.

I beg to report that I have just looked through your letters to note your colour scheme ideas which I hadn't previously absorbed, as perhaps I should have done. Pink and primrose bedrooms. Rust and beige dining rooms. Don't like blue, rather tired of green. I am sorry that the carpet has a lot of green in it, but anyway I am now warned against a light blue one they had.

I am in a shocking mess: there is such an Eldorado on the old doorstep, I have little money, bags of ambition and no YOU to help. My eyes popped out of my head at the sight of <u>carpets!</u>

I love you.
Chris

11 February 1946

My Darling Beautiful Wonderful and Lovely Wife,

Today came No. 30, to tell of your arrival, and that you are now the mistress of 55 Ellesmere Drive, in Sanderstead, County of Surrey. My very sincere congratulations on all that you have done, leading up to this historic (for us) occupation. You really have achieved something; you are such a refreshing contrast in action to the wibbly-wobbly faint-hearts who wave to opportunity as it passes. Do not trouble to deny your capacity. Do not claim to be the Greatest Wibbly Wobbler of them all. Your protestations of what you call 'female weakness' laugh at you. My darling wife, how proud I am of you!

I got Bert to address the envelope with my 'note of welcome', because I had to get him to post it to be sure of arriving in time, and I fancied that my writing on an envelope which had been posted in England would wantonly cause you to think I was there.

I enjoyed your 'no stove, no current, no fuel' and 'then they started to turn up'. I hope the coal turned up OK, and that you haven't used up the whole three months' ration (say) in three days. I am glad you met a wonder-workman (I bet he got at least five shillings!), a good man. The electrician seems to have also been helpful. What a thing it is to be an attractive young woman!

I love you.
Chris

Their first home: 55 Ellesmere Drive

15 February 1946

Dearest One,

Today I broke into your three pounds and paid £1 4s. 6d. each for two carpets (brown and mainly red, I thought OK for your pink bedroom idea). I shall await your comments before buying anything further in the carpet line. For £7 10s. I could have purchased a set of three (1 large, 2 small) carpets, pink, of very good quality. This morning (as a result of scrounging in the drawers at the Sergeants' Mess last night) I sent you an electric light switch, bedside pattern. Hope you can utilise it, thought they might be unobtainable in UK.

I shouldn't worry too much about the knitting. I believe one of these South African firms specialises in the provision of all required for a brand new baby. Much can be got out there that isn't easily got in UK.

I love you.
Chris

~

20 February 1946

My Darling Wife,

I was pleased to read you had someone coming to lay the lino (was it any good?), as I had imagined you wrestling, cobra-like, with it and having a job with it. A pity about the wireless connection, I hope you can get the rooms swopped, or some other arrangement, without too much trouble. It is certainly awkward as it is. Also, I don't like knitting etc. in bed too much as it is usually easy to catch a cold that way.

I am very pleased you received the full 12 tins of tomatoes. I hope to send you more as I get money. I should think you could eat three tins a week very easily. I wonder why the kitchen tiling has to come down, hope you can get it done soon.

Thank you for what you say about never thinking me vulgar. I want you so much (and also I want so much of you, if you understand that) at times, there are so many things I want to do.

I am very pleased you mentioned your bias against Make Do And Mend Lectures. I'll do what I can to avoid over-painting that particular picture, though now you must keep a careful watch that I don't suggest that leisured ease and unending comfort are your lot!

I read that 70–80,000 of the 300,000 wanting telephones are in the London Area. Although still a luxury, I certainly think it would be potentially very useful to you and that is why I suggested you try to get one. How about writing to SE Area Manager (if it _is_ SE) and quoting your condition as a reason for priority?

I love you.
Chris

~

2 March 1946

My Dearest,

Today I have acquired a pail (enamel), but have not had a lot of time to attend to it. I have only been able to clean it up a little, but have packed it pretty well and it should arrive OK. It is not cracked (at present) and I think you will approve its addition to your 'cleaning materials', when you get it. I have also sent you one

3 lb tin of marmalade (Palestine, but described on the outside as Italian) and one kilo of peas (they appear very small; cost 2s. 3d.). I have also sent your Dad about 300 cigarettes which I hope (very much!) he gets safely.

I am glad the carpet arrived at last, and that you think it jolly good. What I would like you to tell me is could you get one like it in England, and if so, how much?

I note you have done a lot of paint washing, stair washing, etc. I cannot say you are doing too much, but I rely on your good sense not to be scared of allowing even yourself to think 'I ought to do more, but I won't'.

A good idea to chop the bedspread up. You are a genius! Can I send a bedspread from here? Really, I am dying to do so, but I want instructions re colour and quality. There are grand ones available at a little more than a £1, but specially fine ones at around £2.

I deplore the sliding episode on the Italian rug. I can assure you that unless I feel safe when I tread around at 55, polishing will cease forthwith.

I hope you find a dentist alright. Most desirable that you get these jobs done while you are feeling fairly normal, isn't it?

I do not want you to write more than you have done of things of the flesh. Generally I too have avoided thinking along those lines. It has not been so difficult as before – I don't know why – but occasionally I get my fits of wanting YOU, the whole of YOU, the everything of YOU, and your letter must have arrived at the same time as one of my fits. Please don't use any words that don't come from your heart. Please carry on as you have so well done up to the present. It will only make it worse if you feel you have to write like that. We so much, so fully, understand what we are missing in mutual support. For me, it is completely, revealingly, warmingly, devastatingly lovely and wonderful to be loved by you. I know you feel all that I feel about YOU. I cannot really say I long to do anything. I just want to be with you. And if I cannot, then I am happy only when I am writing to you and reading your lovely writing, or when I am posting parcels which will feed you or please you.

I hope the crawfish suits you. The salmon was 2s. 8d., a tin, and I should like you to tell me if it was any good, when you open a tin. Glad you are laying in stores for a siege.

My darling, I love you.
Chris

~

12

In My Arms

3 March 1946

Dear Bessie,

Today has been very bad. It has rained heavily and the wind has blown violently. It stopped for a little while as we were leaving Naples, and it was lovely to see daffodils on sale from stalls, and, as we came along the Autostrada, the white and pink of the almond blossoms, a grand sight. When we came back (there was no air mail) we had orders to move down into the last billet remaining to the unit, and so we had to bring everything on board the truck in a hurry and come here.

And NOW, another chap and I have our beds in a passage 14 feet long by 3 feet wide. (As I write I have my back to one wall and my feet on the opposite one.) You can imagine how it is perhaps. I dunno. You are a civilian, after all, and the ways of the Army are (thank goodness) hardly civilised. When we got here, no one had any plans for us. In the Sergeants' and Officers' quarters there are many spare rooms. Here, in this position of a Fascist millionaire's villa, there is nothing but this passage. When we first set eyes on it, it was filled with about two hundred half-pint beer bottles. I cleared those out, moved a lot of old bric-a-brac, and then discovered that a dog had used the place as a lavatory.

And now our anxiety is whether we are on guard tonight. The RSM was going to tell us dinner time, but they have the usual civvy-dressed ATS* girls as guests of sergeants, etc., and he hasn't shown up; 'Blow the men' is the almost invariable motto of our superiors. The other night, a Capt. Lockett here brought a woman into the billet at 11 o'clock and she hadn't gone by 7 a.m., when the guard went away. It is all done so brazenly. How can chaps like that (and there are many amongst the Other Ranks as well) want to get home? I was amused by one of our cooks (he looks a harmless paternal type). He used to have a woman sleep with him nightly at the old billet. Last night she slept with him here. He said: 'If the Colonel can have his wife here, I can have mine'! If a man got caught, he would get about 3–6 months.

I am afraid this is not a very personal letter. But I am very disturbed and upside-down and balancing on the edge of a ha'penny. When I get somewhere settled, I hope I shall be able to write better.

I love you.
Chris

The weather may change, my billets may change, but there never is or will be anything variable about my affection for you. You are

* Auxiliary Territorial Service.

everything to me, everything, and I can never have enough of you. I don't know how ever I should have felt had you not found yourself willing to accept me.

~

6 March 1946

My Dear Bessie,

The hours of work here [at the Army Post Office, redirecting letters] are very easy, 8.30–12.15 one day, and 2–4.45 the next. We look after the mail of our own unit, but also help with that for other units who have not got representatives. It is quite a rest cure; there is a break for tea in both morning and afternoon. The food is much less and far inferior to the type I have been getting. But I shall not starve, and that is the main thing.

I have been thinking: what do you think your chances are of convincing your doctor that I am necessary to your health within a short time? If you could plead successfully, I feel that I might get a compassionate posting to UK; and I'd like you to consider whether you could act the distraught wife before the doctor. Your age, the war, the Greek business, might help the case. If it came off, I should have no bad conscience. Hundreds are getting out with far less reason. And having done three years abroad, I do not feel I am shirking anything.

Yes, we will have wallpaper one day. It can be bought out here, too. I'll try to enquire prices.

I love you.
Chris

~

9 March 1946

My Darling Bessie,

I feel like a weary traveller who plods on knowing that if he stops for a rest he will find it hard to get going again. That is a strange thing to feel, I know. But I am so fed up with this writing business, it is such a hopeless method of expressing anything at all. I think I am beginning to understand something of the mentality of people who write once a month. I am really very cynical, disgusted and bitter about what is happening to the Army in this demobilisation racket. I have the most immoderate and passion-full thoughts, and writing to you regularly at least keeps me on the rails and forces my expressions into civilised jargon.

I am 'down', very far down about this. I despise those running this demob affair, I despise myself because I am cowed by the circumstances. I hate the people around me, so much of an Army pattern. I hate horrible lavatories which smell and get blocked up and no one cares. I hate being in a room with five other men, none of whom want the window open at night. I hate myself for being 'touchy', being susceptible. For me, my darling, I am afraid, these are not 'struggling days', I have ceased struggling. I have succumbed. There is no need to refer to this in reply. I shall have been pushed by the pendulum, before your letter arrives, into an easy acceptance of another five months in the Army, another five months without you.

I am sorry about the peaches. What did they look like? Mildew or black, or what?

Was very interested to read about the trouble you are now having in doing your corset belt up. If only I was with you to help, to watch and take an interested hand in things.

I have written this in about half-a-dozen places and in a dozen pieces. Sorry, but will try to do better tomorrow. Forgive my anti-Army observations. I feel better now! Already!

I love you.
Chris

~

10 March 1946

My Darling Bessie,

Glad you enjoyed *Brief Encounter*. I expect the tear-shedding was good for you. It's all this bottling-up which is half of everyone's troubles nowadays.

Regarding curtaining, I want you to do a little thinking and let me have a list of the things still required, as I suggested in my miserable letter yesterday.

Re. decorating, I expect it will be years before we can have wallpaper for all rooms. The Paper Control is still strict. Shall I do the cream-distempering the first or the second week of my leave?

If nightgowns, or anything, were surplus to your needs, I would not mind you selling them, you know. No need to get cluttered up with things you don't want. But I feel that you will be leaving our warm bed more than once, to do a bit of child-pacifying, and that you'll need two nightgowns.

Your mention of 'thickening up, losing my waist, beginning to bulge', about which I commented earlier, made me wish, so much, that I could be with you, to eye you, to estimate with you, to consider how things are going with you. Perhaps to suggest that you walk a slower walk, and do not run for buses.

I appreciate that you have to go out to post letters. Is it very far? It's a good idea to keep in as much as possible. You must have done a lot of knitting to produce a cardigan.

I love you.
Chris

~

17 March 1946

Dearest One,

I am really delighted that the folding stool arrived OK, and not a little surprised. Painted a pastel shade, it will be an asset. I was glad to get the news that the lemons and the sardines had also arrived.

I am sure that there will not be any war for years yet. One very good reason why there will not be 'war with Russia any moment' is that USA has the atomic bomb and would use it quickly if Russia attacked her or us, and it is unlikely that Russia's researches have yet borne fruit, atomically speaking. Even were the Powers of equal strength (and wars only occur when the two sides are about equal yet feel they have an advantage over the other), I do not see there is anything to fight for yet. Russia will do nothing, militarily, to stop our wicked Capitalist machinations, and we are in no state to stop USSR's unique methods of colonisation.

Please, I am not horribly tired of packing things. Thank the Lord I can do something to help you, something to show I always have you in my thoughts. And when I send you camp beds, electric fittings, folding chairs, I am no less than a Dicky Bird gathering twigs for the nest. A good feeling, my darling Mrs D.B.

I love you.
Chris

∽

19 March 1946

My Darling,

On Sunday, Doug Taylor [old friend from Post Office days] and I went to the Museo-Aquario, not greatly different in appearance from most other aquariums that I have been to, glass panels and the twirling, circling occupants, unconscious of your interest. We went to the octopus exhibit and there was none to be seen. 'Aspet!' ('Wait') called the keeper, and goes behind the scenes and prods the water to chase out the poor octopus. Then we came to the anenome (if that is how it's spelt), which were floating gaily around. 'Aspet!', and back behind he goes again, to prod away and give us a remarkable exhibition of the anenome withdrawing into its tube or shell, away from the danger it discerns. The prodder was disgusted with his one cigarette reward, but that was all we gave him.

I have just been out, and accidentally met a chap called Scott (late 30 Wing) whom I imagined to be up in Udine, Northern Italy. He explains that he has been sent to Naples on leave (although not officially as this is not a leave area) to be with his fiancée, an Italian girl of 18, whom he first met 7 weeks ago. He has set in motion the machinery to marry her. You will get the complete picture of him when I conclude with the information that his young lady in Scotland (to whom he is engaged) expects him home in a fortnight.

I love you.
Chris

26 March 1946

My Dearest,

I have been thinking very seriously whether I should tell you the next bit of news. But I have had to come to the decision that you must be told. But, before you read on, I do want you to keep a very tight hold on yourself, particularly on your optimistic faculty.

Well, Deb wrote me yesterday, and enclosed a leaflet issued by the Mets Branch. It says that the PO have now agreed 'to . . . ask for the release of a considerable number of men from the Forces under Class B'. I should not be surprised if the Ministry of Labour agreed to the PO request. I don't know what procedure is adopted, but if this, if that, and if the other, you can see what might happen. I was thrilled and hopeful yesterday, and I can't say I have quite sagged back yet. For one thing, it is a step forward for the PO to ask for Counter Clerks, and indicates that there is the chance, there is a straw to clutch. But, my darling, I don't want you to get clutching it too hard. Nothing may happen for a month – and then – who knows? Or nothing may happen for six months!

I am sorry about your 'bee-on-a-date' state, I'm sure you are facing up well to the combined efforts of Janet – C. and the separation from me. I wish to goodness I could tend your toenails! I'm afraid I should kiss your toes whenever I got the chance, for I too want so much to be with you.

Darling Bessie, I hope the weather will keep on improving, and this period of separation will be made less unbearable for you.

Know always that you are in my mind, that you are everything to me.

I love you.
Chris

~

My Darling,

I don't think we need too much to fear the extent to which Janet – C. will modify our actions, and in any case there is no chance at all that our child will come between us. At the moment Janet – C. is waiting off-stage; I don't know what I shall think when he/she makes her bow, but I feel like telling any infant of ours that neither of us are going to be martyrs to anything. I am very sure, my darling, that our feelings for each other will continue as now, we shall love each other more and more and more – but I am sure we shall be lovers first, not just now, but always.

Well, I am sorry about the red carpet. When I first saw it, I thought 'This would be good for the kitchen', but the more I thought, the better I valued it. But you have spoken: 'The moth'. Wouldn't it do for cutting up? Of course, I am not 'hurt' by the prospect of it going in the kitchen.

Yes, Brighton was very wonderful, and although sometimes it seems so very long ago, there are times when I know it was only yesterday, and that tomorrow we shall be together again, just the same. Oh, it was such a grand period of no restraint, no repression; of the flow and interflow of our inner selves. It was wonderful to be able to express ourselves, with mind and with the flesh. We had loved each other for so long, it was such a relief to be able to say so. I enjoyed every moment I was with you, and I know I will always do so. Your lovely voice; your intelligence; the breathtaking beauty of your lovely body – oh! It was not because I was tired that I slept better when with you than I have done since I joined the Army. It was because you are my home.

I hope I shall be able to do some of the wood in the shed; did you enquire about the gas poker, chico, or don't you fancy it?

I love you.
Chris

~

1 April 1946

My Darling,

I am sorry that you have to go through a depressing recital of other people's matrimonial troubles when you go to the Clinic. I think people must want a job when they retail their husband's defects to more or less strangers, even though they are fellow expectants. What you have heard confirms my earlier observations that the war has been a very acceptable break from monotony for some husbands and wives. It is true that husbands will have changed – the mere process of growing does that – but I think some of the change will be imagined by the wife, who has probably invested her husband's shadow with all sorts of virtues that he never really had.

I have just read *Sex Problems of the Returning Soldier* by Kenneth Howard, with a foreword by Rev Leslie Weatherhead. It is very good and sound, so far as I can judge. Amongst the points made is that of the welcome break that Army life is in some marriages; it says that married couples must develop the 'us' to be successful, and that then children may well follow. It says that jealousy is very understandable, as the other partner desires passionately to completely possess the other.

On my own little problem, it says that there is a saying '99% of men have practised masturbation at some time, and the other 1% are liars.' It is not harmful unless done several times a day over long periods. The married man away from home may wake to discover he has unconsciously been doing so. The return to a natural life will eliminate the problem. He says that impotence (which he defines as inability to secure and maintain erection) is not unusual either, at first, in marriage or upon return, but is usually overcome with normality. If not, medical advice should be taken. The underlying purpose of the book is to show that the other partner to a marriage must study carefully the needs and 'likes' of the other. That, if one enters a trade, one studies for it, and that to successfully live happily with another person for 40 or 50 years, one must study similarly. I don't think I can manage to send it to you, but it is worth reading.

Our case is rather different from those who have been used to married life before the war. We do start, as you say, practically from scratch. I feel that between us we have gone a long way towards the 'US', and that our intelligence will enable us to meet the challenges fairly well. I wanted also to say that a lot of chaps leave the Army as 'Army types', they are loud-voiced, unthoughtful, and exhibitionist. I am little touched by my short stay in the Army and feel that I have lost hardly any of the civilian graces, and that within a short time of kicking off my Battle Dress I will be ready for

[Incomplete]

~

5 April 1946

I went to a Variety Show the night before last. There was a tough guy who put horseshoes (examined by soldiers on the stage) in his mouth, between his teeth, and with his hands broke them in half! (Brute.) A magician who produced doves from nowhere and made them disappear into nothing (also a Brute). The name of the show was 'The Get-Atoms', but it wasn't that almost indecent title that attracted me. It was the guest artiste, whom I had never seen in person, and thought I would like to – and there I was, second row of the stalls, about four yards along from – Gracie Fields. She was dressed in a dark blue lace gown, very well made up. She sang bags of songs, medleys, 'Christopher Robin', 'Ave Maria', 'Sally', 'My Hero', and I thought was very good. She had her own pianist, a great player; was presented with a bouquet. I thought of her after the show gliding back over the sea to Capri, so near. I am glad I went. The rest of the 'artistes' were quite poor, and the comedians were low. Perhaps one joke will appeal to you. A lady had a ride on a camel in the zoo, but it threw her off, and bolted with lightning speed down the road. The keeper asked what she had done to it, and she replied 'Only tickled its belly.' 'Well,' said the keeper, 'you'd better tickle mine, because I've got to get the blooming thing back.'

I can get boxes of Kleenex tissues here, by the way. Would you like any?

I love you.
Chris

I suggest something like this:

THE REGIONAL DIRECTOR, LPR, GPO, EC1

Sir,

Class 'B' Releases – CC and Ts

55 Ellesmere Drive, Sanderstead, Surrey.

I have heard from a friend in the Post Office that the Min. of Labour has agreed that certain Counter Clerks with three months to serve shall be released from the Forces under Class 'B'.

I am anxious that my husband's claim to such a release shall not be overlooked, and would be glad if you would note the following details in respect of him.

Army Rank, etc.:
Unit: ITALY.
Former District:
Date of Enlistment:
Date of Embarkation:
A/S Group No.: 14232134 SIGMN. BARKER H.C. 11 L. of C. Signals (attached 15 BAPO CMF), Eastern.

His release would be most helpful at home, as I am expecting a baby in July. With thanks,

Yours truly,
B.I. Barker

~

9 April 1946

My Dearest,

We must put aside a little money for some 'must-haves' in the household equipment line. Perhaps a couple of chairs, an odd table, glassware, curtains, lino, it might be anything like that but probably wouldn't be all of them. I suggest £20 as the amount to mentally set aside for that.

Then there's Janet – C. I haven't really much idea of the kind of expenses likely to be incurred under this heading. I imagine clothes will not call for much expense the first year (which is what we are thinking of), but that they'll about bankrupt us the next few. But I expect the cot to cost £5 and the pram to cost similarly, £5. Certainly not much more or less. And I think we must add £20 for a rubber sheet to the cot, for clothing, etc, making £30 in all. So,

Janet – C. £30
Clothes £35
Furniture etc. £20
Rates, bills, etc. £15
Making a total of £100

I had letters yesterday from Deb, Mum, Rosie, amongst others. Deb wonders if the atom bomb has caused the fine weather? Mum's – well, the same as ever. She actually said about Bert, 'He got rid of me', which is just about the limit, I thought.

In an American mag I believe I sent you, I thought another limit had been reached: they were advertising electrically heated blankets, 'just switch on a few minutes before bedtime'. A model announced for the spring was one which allowed the wife to heat her side a different temperature from the husband's! Blow me!

I love you.
Chris

∼

21 April 1946

Darling, Most Wonderful, Dear and Beautiful One,

The Class B has come through and soon we will be together. I have spent many hours trying to think up a better opening than that, but how could I improve on such a beautiful, wonderful blurt? The first thing to tell you is: please stop writing. (Better sit down, if you are not already seated, and just think how grand it will be not to write, write, write for the rest of time.)

It being Easter, I shall be a little delayed in getting away, but I do feel there is quite a chance of me getting home in the week commencing May 5th. There is the usual Army uncertainty. It seems a long while to wait, but I shall be able to write you daily and tell you where I am.

I think I shall go by rail, stopping at Milan a few days. When I get to England I believe I have to go to Thirsk, and then to Guildford. It all takes time. Please do not alter your habits until you get a telegram from me (which I will send from Dover) telling you I am in England. Then it will only be a few days before we are together, before I am happy. Oh, I cannot write what I feel!

Please take it steady. The first point to clearly understand is that you have no need to stop going out until my telegram arrives. Then, well, you can stay in, but do go out for half an hour or so if necessary. This is where you demonstrate your good sense: for the second point is that I don't want you to sweat yourself out getting things ship-shape, putting up the curtains, and so on.

There will be tons and tons more of 'what to do's coming from me before I finally come up the path.

Our plans have been subject to much alteration ever since we loved – and dared to have plans. This alteration is very wonderful, and I am grateful for it. We shall be together now for always, and these next months, which might have been so wretched apart, will be wonderful together. How can I stop my quaking when I consider that so soon I will be breathing the same air as you, that I will be smelling you, seeing you, hearing you, loving you. Darling, my dearest one, our long, long apartness is about to end. Thank you for the courage you have shown, the pluck with which you have borne your little fate. It will not be long before we are in each other's arms; before we are having a cup of cocoa and going to bed together. With what gladness and gratitude and pride of ownership will I watch you UNDRESS; with what delight and relief will I welcome you to the warming sheets, with what ecstasy will I take you to me.

Do try hard not to be too excited. But isn't it GORGEOUS that your vigil at home will last three months only, and that we have not only the home, but that we will be in it TOGETHER, and at this time. Soon, soon, soon, my lips will offer my love and gratitude to you, and my hands their allowance.

Dearest, Loveliest Woman, I am yours. I love you.
Chris

~

21 April 1946

Well, my Darling,

I hope you are by now taking well the really tremendous news that we are to be reunited, that soon you will not be getting any more letters, but be getting me instead. The idea that I really am coming home will take a little getting used to, but by the time I do arrive, you will have accomplished that mental leap forward, and be ready.

In a very true sense we shall be starting to live. It is really wonderful to allow one's thoughts to go to London Bridge station, to Sanderstead, to the bus; to you, and life with you. Please let me be your lover first and everything else second. And it is for always.

I would like to mention a few odd points, to keep in line with things prosaic: I have asked Doug to go ahead with the three mirrors. He insists on paying for the bathroom one. So the other two will cost us £3 4s. I shall be collecting them, isn't life grand?

Mum asks me if you would like a pastry board. She would be glad for you to have hers. We'll discuss this.

Tra la la.

I sent a box home today containing some odds and ends: I put on it 'PERSONAL EFFECTS OF RELEASED SOLDIER'.

I love you.
Chris

∽

22 April 1946

Dearest One,

I don't know how I shall react to civilian life; it is four years since I left it and it may shake me. I know you will help the process of getting used to it, by telling me what has to be done. Then, even before the Army took me in, I was deficient in many things. I have a lot to learn in all sorts of ways, and I hope you are going to see that I learn them. I can well understand that things I do at present, you would prefer that I didn't. Please do tell me what they are, as they arrive, or as I do them. I want to be the perfect husband, and I know jolly well I have precious few qualifications at present! It's up to you to do some grafting.

I should be able to immediately help, as maybe the stair cloth will come shortly, and I can help put it down. I suppose we will need stair rods, but they may not be obtainable.

I shall be able to do anything at all heavy so very easily. We should have very few worries, and money will not really be one of them, though it is a pity we haven't a few hundred pounds more. I hope your 'bulge' will not impede our hugging.

Later. I don't and can't know at what hour I shall get home, please don't be at the station, or waiting at the bus stop, or anything like that. Sometimes after arriving in England chaps take a week to get home, others only two days. Just go about normally till you get my telegram, and after that, well, you can go out for a little shopping but not to Croydon, I suggest.

A better man than me would probably arrange to arrive in 'civvies', but I shall arrive in the garb which seems most convenient. I will get the uniform off a few minutes after arrival, and put on my corduroys and whatever else is handy. I shall also probably have a bath, just to test OURS out!

Won't it be wonderful to sit at the same table and watch the other eating?

I LOVE YOU.
Chris

∾

23 April 1946

DEAREST,

Thank you for the SOON-TO-BE-SEEN room layout. The answer to your query 'Are you living in it?' is – I SOON WILL BE! The reply to your suggestion that we go to bed upon my return is: 'LET'S!' But, really, it will be so much better than before. In October, I had you warm and grateful in my arms for such a little while, and then we had to go and sit with your Dad in the sitting room.

Pouffes – I've got an idea – if they let me keep my kitbag, couldn't you make a pouffe out of it. Colour it, and pad it?

How are you getting on without writing to me? You will save a good few hours between now and my return – spend it knitting, my darling. And don't crochet a whacking big 'WELCOME HOME' sign, there's a good girl. I know I'm welcome!

I WANT YOU. I LOVE YOU.
Chris

∾

25 April 1946

Darling I Am Soon To Meet,

Well, I have made the first move, and am now writing from Lammie Transit Camp, a few miles from Naples. So far I have only been here an hour, got my meal ticket, a tent number, and have secured a bed. I am with eight others, all Class 'B', most builders. My original estimate of 'home sometime week beginning May 5th' still seems good, but it looks as though it will be towards the end of the week.

I don't want to have breakfast any morning, dear. I want us to stop in bed till ten o'clock as we did at 27, and then have a slice of bread and jam. I want to be in bed with you, not only in sleepy understanding and greeting of the night, but in happy realisation of hailing the new day. Oh, to kiss your dear dear lips again, to speak and be spoken unto. My dearest, I love you with all my heart and mind. My strength is yours, for all of it derives from you, rests with you.

I love you.
Chris

~

27 April 1946

My Dear Wife,

I have just heard a rumour, pretty authentic, that Derby beat our team after extra time. Hard luck. How pleased my Dad would have been at the result. There will be many sad hearts in London tonight, and I expect a lot of money changed hands.

Did you see the Grand National on the films? I thought it was a real scandal, like a blood sport, to expect those horses to do so much. Only six finished the course, and at least one had to be shot.

28.4.46 Sunday today, and all being well we shall get away from here tomorrow. So this is our last Sunday in Italy. There is a faint chance I may actually be landing in England next Sunday, which would suit me very well. I shall be happier when I get away from Naples, and actually get on my way to you.

What do you think of the idea of advertising my boots, shirts, battle dress at reasonable prices, and for the equivalent number of coupons? Would we get any takers? If so, I am all for it, as it would very conveniently dispose of them.

I shall only send short notes from now, I think. I am tired today and want the hours to rush till tomorrow night when we leave Naples. Then, every mile will bring me nearer to you, to home, to life. Dearest, this is a strain, this waiting, isn't it? By the time I get to you, I shall be really washed out.

My Wife, I love you.
Chris

~

29 April 1946

Dear One,

And now it is Monday.

It is 8.30 and the list of those who are leaving today goes up at 10.30, so I have two hours to fret away before knowing the best or the worst. No one knows beforehand, and our computations are based on hope rather than knowledge.

I have just been to the office to enquire about pay (and unsuccessfully), and heard that 42 of the 53 'B' Releases here are leaving tonight. I am almost certain to be in this lot, so thank goodness I shall at last be travelling in the direction I want to go. Tonight and tomorrow night I shall be sleeping on the floor of the railway truck, dirty, uncomfortable – and HAPPY. I have a lot to go through before I see you again, my dear, but providing I keep moving, I shan't mind. It's hanging around which is terrible. Like you now, having to hang around, doing nothing special.

The list is up, and I am on it. Hurrah! Away at last. I shall soon be having my final shower before leaving here, a late shave so that I need not shave on the journey. I shall be getting a little bag with my rations in it, and putting my kitbag out to be collected. And then an early tea, to wait two hours at the station before the train goes. I know the routine well. I have imagined myself doing this for a long time.

I am on my way; to our life together, to the place you bring, the coolness you mean; to the security of your bosom and the warmth of YOU.

I LOVE YOU.

Chris

~

1 May 1946

My Darling, I am yours.

I am starting this note in what for some is the Eternal City – after having taken eleven hours to get here. I have just had my breakfast, egg and bacon, a slight wash, and am ready for the next stop half a dozen hours later. 150 miles in 11 hours is hardly speeding, but why worry, every mile is one mile nearer my darling wife, my lovely Bessie.

We are hoping not to spend too long at Milan, as from May 2nd troop trains do not go through Switzerland, but use Austria instead. This may mean we shall be hurried through Milan, or maybe we shall be sent on to Bologna and thence to Austria. In any case, I really think that within a week I should be home (that is, on the Wednesday).

Unless there are fogs in the Channel or some blooming thing, I shall be with you in seven days, I think. That still seems a long, long way off, but, my dear and lovely one, it will soon pass. When you get this, with any luck, I shall be arriving in Calais (if that is where they send us).

I'll get into whatever clothes you put out, and be transformed quickly. I hope you have a nice lot of jobs wanting doing – that is something I badly want to do – any jobs you might otherwise have had to do yourself. Tomorrow – MILAN!

And now it is tomorrow. I am at Milan, and scribbling quickly to possibly catch the day's post before I go to breakfast. It is only 7 a.m., so anything may happen today.

Darling, Darling, I love you.
Chris

~

4 May 1946

DOVER

My Very Own Dear One,

My boat arrived here at about three o'clock today. We leave here at 8 o'clock in the morning for our Depot. I expect to arrive at Thirsk at 8 p.m. Sunday. If they get speeding on Monday (that is 'today' for you, my dear dear reader), perhaps I may be home for Tuesday. I don't know. We can only hope for the best.

Although tomorrow night I shall be 200 miles away, tonight, my dear one, I shall be only fifty from you, and at last on the same 'lump' of land. That really is progress! I feel sad and anguished that I didn't get to you today, but the Army doesn't consider people.

Everyone here looks fresh and healthy, and well-fed. There is a good deal of bomb and (presumably) shell damage, and little seems to have been done to mend it.

Darling, I love you so much. Perhaps you've got my telegram by now and know I am near you. Darling, tonight we will be able to go to sleep knowing each other's location more than we have done for months. I shall like that.

Lovely, warm woman, I am not very far away.

Dearest, I love you.

Chris

~

5 May 1946, Posted 7 May

Dearest,

I have now arrived at Thirsk, waiting an hour at the station in a bitterly cold wind.

I am very sorry I raised your hopes with my 'possibly Tuesday' – now it seems 'possibly Thursday'. I fret at the delay, as you must do. But I am afraid we must both be as good as possible. PLEASE don't try meeting me at the station, or anything like that, I might be on any train or may come a different way. I shall come as soon as I can.

The food we have eaten in England so far has been plentiful – cheese, sausages, margarine, bread, and also wholesomely cooked. There is hot and cold water in the taps here, and after going to the lavatory one pulls a plug. Home comforts!

Will continue this tomorrow, when I sincerely hope I shall have much more to say of my date of arrival. Am going to bed now. My darling, soon, soon, soon, I shall be going to bed with you.

I hope these last letters of mine are not getting on your nerves. I know they have many defects. But somehow, I do want to keep on writing, saying something, to keep in contact. If I knew earlier what I know now, I could have asked you to write me here. Oh why must there be this final maddening delay?

WIFE, WOMAN, BESSIE, I love you.
Chris

6 May 1946, Posted 7 May

My Darling, Wonderful Wife,

It should be Wednesday morning when you get this. WITHIN
TWENTY FOUR HOURS YOU WILL BE IN MY ARMS. I have
heard definitely today that I shall be out of the Army Wednesday
night, so, my dearest, that will be your last night of alone-ness,
and today your last day without me to make demands on you, in
person. LOVELY, ISN'T IT?

Put the alarm clock on for 6.30 when you go to bed
tonight (Wednesday), as I shall be along as early as that. WE
SHALL BREAKFAST TOGETHER TOMORROW (Thursday)
MORNING (I hope you sleep well tonight!).

I shall send you a telegram today (Wednesday) telling you
'THURSDAY BREAKFAST', and when night comes, I shall be
on my way TO YOU, TO YOU, TO YOU, my Darling, Dear and
Precious One.

When you get up, try and put a drop of hot water on, so that
I can have the bath, please. Then a little breakfast (how about
sausages and tomatoes, or toast and tomatoes), and I will WASH
UP FOR YOU! Prepare for the deluge . . .

My telegram will come from York, but I have to return to
Thirsk afterwards. We go there only for our civilian clothes, then
must retrace our steps after release! Army madness.

DARLING, DEAR ONE, WE REALLY ARE NEAR
NOW. WITHIN TWENTY OR SO HOURS, WE SHALL BE
TOGETHER, HAVE EACH OTHER.

I probably will make this the last letter. The post for 'Lunnon' goes from here at 3.30 in the afternoon.

DEAR,
DEAR,
DEAREST
Bessie,
I love you.
Chris

~

7 May 1946

My Darling,

Well, everything is going well now, and I have all the definite information needed. I shall be home for breakfast on Thursday morning.

Let us only have a light breakfast (for me), as I shall have been travelling and my stomach will be a little upset I dare say. Then, too, let us have only a light lunch that takes little time to prepare, and postpone the 'real meal' until the evening. Shall we? Then there will be no rushing about and we can take things as easily as we like. I don't suppose you will want to start showing me Croydon until Friday. I hope not, as I do, do want to have you to myself entirely for a little while. I suppose we shall be bound to plan a little bit, but I would like to have a nice three weeks' glide, a drift along, if we could manage it.

Darling, tonight I spend my last night in the Army. Tomorrow I spend the night in the train. As you go to sleep Wednesday night, think of me speeding along the rails towards you, sleeping this final separate sleep. And remember that when you awaken in the morning, it will be to hear my voice and see me.

Dearest, Darling, Only One, thank you for all that you have been to me through these years, and be sure we shall overcome with our love any difficulties there may be later on. I can never be as good as you deserve, but I really will try very hard, and I know you will help. We shall be partners, collaborators, man and woman, husband and wife, lovers.

I love you. I want you. I need you. ALWAYS.
YOUR Chris

~

Afterword

by Bernard Barker

I was born thirteen weeks after my father stepped through the door at Ellesmere Drive and was named after my mother's iconoclastic hero, George Bernard Shaw. My brother Peter followed in 1949. We became characters in a post-war story and for almost sixty years were unaware of the letters, romance and drama that had brought us to life.

This changed on a visit to my recently widowed father in 2004. He held out a small blue box and asked: 'Shall I throw these away, or will you take them?' They were his war letters. He said no one should read them until he and my mother were both dead. Following his instructions, I waited to open the box until 2008.

I pulled out the tightly folded bundles and found 500 individual letters written in a clear, faultless hand on thin blue airmail paper or on NAAFI headed notepaper. I read the half million words over a period of several weeks and immersed myself in a wartime world of love, longing and frustration.

I was in the desert with my dad as he recorded the death of pigs and rats; I was with my mother in London braving bombs and rockets. Through their words they were animated again in my mind – energetic, passionate, clear-sighted, wise and loveable.

I decided to create an archive and to include the war letters with the other papers I collected from my Dad's house when it was sold. Katy Edge, an administrator at the University of Leicester, agreed to type the correspondence.

I sorted and edited the documents and prepared a detailed inventory. We arranged to deposit the results in the Mass Observation special collections at the University of Sussex.

Bessie in the garden at 27 Woolacombe Road with her two sons
Bernard (standing) and Peter

My parents' letters describe dangerous adventures as well as lonely tedium, and express the love that grew from their experience of war. I began to ask whether the lives that followed, domestic and child-centred, were an anti-climax, marked by a retreat from passion and the sparkling language that made it.

Dad did not think so. In 1946, with the army behind him, he was delighted with his new wife and son and revelled in his house and garden. He was pleased to be back on the post office counter.

Mother was less settled; after the death of her mother during the war she felt responsible for her brother and father. She was dismayed by their unconvincing attempts at housekeeping at her family home in Blackheath, London SE3. Dad seems to have understood her feelings. So the new family moved in with the old, with Mother to look after us all.

Grandfather sold the Blackheath property to our parents in 1947. When Peter was born, he decided the house was too crowded for comfort and left to join his sister in Surrey. Mother and Dad lived at 27 Woolacombe Road for the rest of their time together.

Mother's brother Wilfred remained, to become an inhibiting presence in his sister's marriage. But Uncle Wilfred's shy, gentle and indulgent nature provided a marked contrast with Dad's energy and austere taste. As a toddler I became the centre of loving attention, with four adults available to talk, read stories and play games.

I have family seaside photographs from the late 1940s, with Mother holding Peter in her arms, and me at her side. My father's lack of Post Office seniority meant that our holidays were taken in early spring, from March onwards, and our photos tell a story of shivering, windswept beaches on the north Kent coast.

Mother was the constant presence in our young lives, cooking all the meals and greeting us home from school. When we were ill with chicken pox, measles or mumps, she would push two armchairs together in the lounge so that we were not alone upstairs.

She believed in the fundamental importance of education and its role in the development of individuals and their society. She taught us to read (a slow and frustrating process in my case) and had us recite the tables while our teeth were brushed and our knees washed. Later she used *First Aid in English* and mock IQ test papers to improve our verbal reasoning scores for the eleven-plus.

Mother's grammar school education made her useful with homework, especially when we were at secondary school, but tensions would rise as I struggled with algebra and French.

An insomniac herself, she put us to bed very early. We would bounce on the bed, unable to sleep in the evening light and would peep between the bedroom curtains to see the parents working in the garden and our uncle nursing his newly purchased moped, an NSU Quickly.

Mother was passionate and occasionally combative. At times she saw herself as oppressed by the men in her family, including her sons, and promised to argue with us, however successful and well-educated we might become.

She read eagerly all her life, especially philosophy, history and detective fiction. Mother admired writers who did justice to the courage and ability of women, and was devoted to Bernard Shaw, Bertrand Russell and Rudyard Kipling.

Bessie and Chris on Blackheath in the early 1950s

Dad was a tireless figure, always busy with household tasks. He was slightly built, never exceeding ten stones, but seemed mightily strong to us, a vigorous, sweat-encrusted engine turning clay soil in the garden. He had a voracious appetite for weeds, dug potatoes and followed instructions on the location and care of Mother's precious plants.

Eggs were rationed, so he kept chickens in the back garden and had to cope with escaping birds, broody hens, coccidiosis and a huge volume of droppings. He found the cure for feather-pecking: 'It was Stockholm Tar, a very sticky, smelly substance which I applied liberally to the feathers, realising too late that it should have been applied only to the wounds.'

He would tackle the washing-up urgently, rushing us to the rhubarb and evaporated milk before the plates were clear. But Dad enjoyed food, especially the particular favourites he liked to prepare, including the burned pancakes that he called flapjacks, and tinned salmon with grated carrots.

Compared with Uncle Wilfred, who built us wooden battleships and gave us cricket bats, bricks and soldiers, Dad did not seem well equipped for child's play. Once he came home early from work to declare 'I'm all yours' but none of us knew what to do next.

Later he said his thinking had been strongly influenced by Mrs Sydney Frankenburg in *Common Sense in the Nursery*. She advised against over-stimulating your children. So our parents gave us books (Arthur Ransome, Robert Louis Stevenson, H.G. Wells) and left the toys, games and sports to our benevolent uncle.

Dad was enthusiastic about his work on the counter and was a keen supporter of the Union of Post Office Workers (UPW). He served at various branch offices, including Shoreditch, and was in charge of 493 Cambridge Heath Road before becoming an overseer in the Western District.

Dad attended fewer union meetings than before the war but wrote over 250 articles for the *Post* between 1954 and 1967. His 'Counter Chronicles' provided a humane and witty perspective on the life of the Post Office clerk.

I can see our dad at his Olympia typewriter in an upstairs bedroom, tap-tapping in search of the right word or phrase. In 'Promotion Prospects' (1957) he reflected on his own career: 'There are three stages of Post Office man. He joins; he is promoted; he retires. Certain incidents occur before or after these events, but all that matters is concerned with his arrival, his ascension, and his departure.'

Our parents' close partnership could be a problem for us when we wanted to negotiate over TV viewing, homework, pocket money or bedtime. They were indivisible. Even when irritated frowns appeared, they never argued. You could not win.

Mother's passions became more evident when we were both at school. She was engrossed by the garden and grew a tremendous variety of plants. She would lift the head of a hellebore and exclaim 'Look, look at that!' as visitors stared at its intricate beauty. At the age of 40 she embarked on a career as an artist.

She began with watercolour and oil copies of painters like Rubens and Pissarro. She travelled to Paris and fell in love with Cézanne, Monet, Matisse and Picasso. She visited London galleries, attended adult education classes and scouted Charing Cross Road for books with illustrations of her favourite paintings.

She gathered flowers from the garden and strove to capture their beauty in a particular light and painted her own Cubist bullfight in the style of Picasso. She knitted a stair carpet (80,000 knots, eight yards long, two feet wide) that became a character in one of Dad's articles: 'It has become steadily heavier, more bloated, comfortable-looking. Now it spends all its time rolled up on the divan and is persuaded away for its feed with difficulty, pampered monster of my wife's creation that it is.'

Mother and Dad were both active in the local Labour Party and joined the Campaign for Nuclear Disarmament (CND) when it seemed that humanity was preparing to blow the planet into dust and ashes. They took part in the Aldermaston marches and remained active in the peace movement all their lives.

In his early seventies, Dad appeared at the Greenham Common Women's Peace Camp with his war medals on his chest, not fully understanding that the protest against cruise missiles was for ladies only. Mother's CND badge, fastened to her knitted hat, was in her bedside drawer when she died.

But Dad was more consciously political than Mother. He was an avid newspaper reader and understood the radical causes of his time through the pages of the *Daily Herald*, the *News Chronicle*, the *Manchester Guardian* and the *New Statesman*.

He threatened not to attend if his sons were baptised, and he insisted that despite success in the eleven-plus examination, we should go to a new comprehensive (Eltham Green) rather than a local grammar school.

This was a controversial decision. Friends argued that our parents were sacrificing us for their principles. Instead Peter and I flourished in an atmosphere of educational experiment where everything seemed possible. We both progressed to study history at Gonville & Caius College, Cambridge.

As we grew up, we became aware that our parents were unusual, even remarkable. Their energy and almost eccentric disregard for convention posed a formidable challenge – as well as an amazing stimulus – for their friends, their children, their children's friends and eventually their grandchildren. As visitors entered the house they would be greeted with ceaseless questions that drew them into urgent debate about politics, religion, philosophy and the meaning of life.

After promotion, Dad became a keen traveller. Family holidays migrated from the north Kent coast to France, Italy, Yugoslavia and Switzerland. His pre-booked restaurants, trains and hotels were meticulously organised, but on one occasion we arrived at Victoria to find no sign of the agent who was supposed to deliver the tickets. Dad took charge of the party and talked our way from London to Ljubljana on the strength of his reservation for dinner in the restaurant car of the Simplon-Orient Express. At every border wheel-tapping and ticket check we trembled, but Dad's fluent English seemed to outfox the continental inspectors who were unsure what to do with him or us.

On the summit of the Jungfrau, however, it was his turn to be confused when the water failed to boil on his pocket stove. Was there something wrong with the fuel tablet? He didn't understand about altitude.

Mother's art became even more important as we departed for university. She bought a kiln and fired glass on copper. She staged an exhibition of her enamels at Christ Church tower near St Paul's Cathedral in 1969 and sold many of them.

Her tutor remembers her at the pottery studio, 'pushing, struggling to develop her understanding of clay and its possibilities'. She used the techniques of the coil pot to produce original, large-scale sculptures and sensuous exotic vases. He admired her passionately held ideas, love of debate and strong sense of social justice. Like my father, she could grasp the essential point, often in a single, prescient sentence. Confronted by the Cultural Revolution, Mother remarked: 'Just wait until Miss Red China wants her lipstick.'

Chris and Bessie at an exhibition of Bessie's art, 1969

After Cambridge, I married Ann, a biologist from York University, and embarked on a career as a teacher, school leader and academic. Our children, Chris and Irena, were born in the 1970s.

Irena inherited her grandfather's love of language and has become a journalist, with her desk in Holborn not far from his last posting as assistant superintendent in charge of London Chief Office in King Edward Street. Dad lived to see her marry Nick, from Mauritius, but not to meet his great grandchildren, Conrad and Marcel.

Peter worked for the Probation Service for thirty years and married Penny (a civil servant) in 1981. He was a Family Court Adviser for a further seven years. In retirement he founded a child contact centre and initiated a campaign to ask that centres should be placed on a statutory basis. He acquired stepchildren, Sara who became a teaching assistant, and Simon who is a recruitment consultant in Perth, Western Australia. His granddaughter Rachel is a medical researcher.

Dad retired in 1974. At first it was a nuisance for my mother to have him home with his 46-year Post Office career behind him. But gradually they developed a new life together. Dad was intensely proud of his wife as the house filled with paintings, tapestry and sculpture, and the lawn was reduced to make space for a great variety of species.

They were vigorous members of the Post Office Art Club, joined the Royal Horticultural Society, attended the Chelsea Flower Show and toured gardens in search of ever more unusual plants. They loved the new National Theatre, especially when Bernard Shaw's plays were performed.

They bought a ground-floor flat in Folkestone to share with brother Wilfred and divided their time between London and Kent. Despite his rude good health, Dad announced that he needed to be near a hospital. After a final trip to Paris with friends, foreign travel was abandoned. Aged seventy, Dad became a vegetarian and hoped to convert his meat-eating friends and family.

He was interviewed in 1986 for the controversial television series *The Hidden War*, about the conflict in Greece after the Germans withdrew. Dad copied some of his war letters for the producer.

When Mother's memory began to fail, Dad took over all household responsibilities. For fifteen years or more he cared for her, maintaining the house and a wide circle of friends, old and new.

His fifty-year old Olympia typewriter kept him in touch with Post Office veterans, fellow survivors of captivity with the Greek communist partisans (with whom he sympathised), his grandchildren and his nephews and nieces, to whom he was devoted.

In hospital with pneumonia, Dad regarded himself as a prisoner and maintained a jail log, ticking off the days to his release. After a cerebral haemorrhage a few years later, he was equally determined to escape, begging me to smuggle him out.

He taught himself to talk, walk and write again but in the end recognised that coping with Mother was beyond him. With the help of relatives, friends and carers, he visited her in the nursing home every day, always taking with him pieces of carefully wrapped chocolate and apple.

If no friend could take him that day, he would go by bus, limping on and off the platform and hobbling down the street. At first he told me that he was not like the vacant and the demented people he met there. Eventually he worried that he was descending towards them.

Bessie died, aged ninety, in 2004; Chris followed, aged ninety-three, in 2007.

As Benedict Cumberbatch and Louise Brealey read their words at the Hay Festival in May 2014, my parents come alive again. They entrance a new audience with their tenderness, intensity and unassuming ordinariness. I worry that I have exposed their love when privacy was important to them but I am also pleased that their writing has won so many new friends. The unwanted attention and celebrity would have embarrassed them. They were both great debunkers. But now, I believe their life and love belong to the ages.

Epilogue

by Irena Barker

Thoroughly utilitarian beings that they were, I would never have imagined my grandparents to be romantic sorts. They were never much into giving each other gifts, expressing their feelings or being anything less than rigid and British.

Certainly in the case of my granddad, there was a strong flavour of puritanical discipline in everything he did. The way he attacked the washing up before the last mouthful was swallowed. The way he forced down dry, tasteless food, chewing mercilessly with his false teeth – because it was 'only fuel'.

His toilet paper of choice, attached to the wall in a special ceramic dispenser, was of the old-fashioned and uncomfortable 'tracing paper' sort. Granny probably had the romantic edge, with her youthful smoking habit and love of painting. Her choice of softer, more luxurious paper hung snugly alongside granddad's on a roll. Indeed, this toilet paper scenario and the many other hilarious eccentricities of my grandparents form some of my strongest and longest-lasting memories.

For me, Granddad was defined by the food he served: his firm belief that salad and good quantities of roughage were the key to a long and healthy life was forever represented in his meals, which he prepared with vigour and enthusiasm.

Until only a couple of years before his death, he was ferociously grating carrots on a rusty old grater and filling the house with the stink of grease as he rustled up fried potatoes in a pan, the handle held together with masking tape. He served a unique beetroot soup that tasted of dust and nothing else. Slices of beetroot and festoons of lettuce and watercress made it onto every life-giving platter. I always thought, as an atheist, he feared death, and he seemed to be a pioneer of superfoods way before his time. I can't look at a beetroot now without thinking of him – every mouthful feels like a homage.

But he also succumbed to treats – dates, brazils and halva – and he always sent us on our way with a carrier bag with a twisted nugget of these goodies at the bottom. I remember driving through the Blackwall Tunnel on the way home from visits, trying to make out the contents in the dim light.

Granny preferred chocolate. When she went into a nursing home, Granddad would visit every day, meting out small pieces of Dairy Milk each time, so she did not consume too much at once. As he cared for her in later years I remember the tiny squares of toast and marmite he made her in the mornings. The apples he cut into tiny pieces that would be easier to chew. The endless cups of weak, sweet coffee he would serve. Maybe it kept her from falling asleep in her chair too much.

Despite the puritanical approach, both grandparents were as warm and giving as one could hope. Granny would assault us with alarming hugs and kisses when we turned up on visits.

When my brother and I were very young, Granddad set us up a workshop in his shed, where we could bash away at bits of wood, metal and leather on every visit. It was a highlight of life at the time. 'The shed', with the strips of leather on rolls, pots of nails and screws and its mysterious musty smell, had an almost magical allure.

Later on, Granddad took to sending us many letters and numerous newspaper cuttings (mostly chopped from the *Guardian*, the institution that educated him).

When I went to live in France for a year, alone, he sent me every episode of Posy Simmonds' *Gemma Bovery* cartoon strip. I still have them curled up in a carrier bag in the wardrobe. He had faith in the postal service to inspire and revive a lonely soul.

When I was in my early twenties, I lodged with Granny and Granddad when I worked in London. I felt guilty every night that an old man in his eighties who was recovering from a major stroke was cooking my tea.

When I came back late in the evening on the train, he would risk being attacked, meeting me in the darkness of Kidbrooke station. He would hobble home with me on his arm (or was it him on my arm?).

There are too many memories, really. Everything about them made an impact on me, from Granny's devotion to wearing trousers to Granddad's funny bald head and itchy, tweedy hat.

It is a true delight to discover, through their letters, that there was even more to them than any of us could have imagined.

At Greenwich Park in July 2003, the last trip Bessie made from her care home. The couple are both 89, and have been married for almost 58 years.

Editor's Note

Editing these letters has been a wholly pleasurable task. I cannot express enough my gratitude to Bernard Barker for depositing his father's papers at Mass Observation and to the Barker family for entrusting me with their promotion and editing. (Bernard curated the papers with dedicated assistance from Katy Edge; the copyright is owned jointly by Chris's and Bessie's younger son Peter Barker and their granddaughter Irena Barker.) The fact that Bernard and Irena's epilogues complete the picture in astute and vivid detail is surely a genetic inheritance.

The entire collection of Chris Barker's papers is available to view, by appointment, at Mass Observation's home at The Keep near Brighton. Please visit www.massobs.org.uk for more information.

More photos of the letters and the Barkers in later life may be found at www.simongarfield.com.

TO THE LETTER

A CURIOUS HISTORY OF CORRESPONDENCE

Simon Garfield

Every letter contains a story, and here are some of the greatest. From Oscar
Wilde's unconventional method of using the mail to cycling enthusiast Reginald
Bray's quest to post himself, Simon Garfield uncovers a host of stories that
capture the enchantment of this irreplaceable art (with a supporting cast
including Pliny the Younger, Ted Hughes, Virginia Woolf, Napoleon Bonaparte,
Lewis Carroll, Jane Austen, David Foster Wallace and the Little Red-Haired
Girl). There is also a brief history of the letter-writing guide, with instructions on
when and when not to send fish as a wedding gift. And as these accounts unfold,
so does the tale of a compelling wartime correspondence that shows how the
simplest of letters can change the course of a life.

'A shining success' *Sunday Times*

'Excellent, amusing and moving' *Financial Times*

'Wonderfully elegant' *Observer*

£9.99

ISBN 978 0 85786 861 9

Also available as an ebook

eBook ISBN 978 0 85786 860 2

www.canongate.tv